Talking North

Talking North

The Journey of Australia's First Asian Language

Edited by Paul S. Thomas

Talking North: The Journey of Australia's First Asian Language
© Copyright 2019
Copyright of this collection in its entirety is held by the editor, Paul S. Thomas.
Copyright of the individual chapters is held by the respective author/s.
All rights reserved. Apart from any uses permitted by Australia's Copyright Act 1968, no part of this book may be reproduced by any process without prior written permission from the copyright owners. Inquiries should be directed to the publisher.

Every effort has been made to obtain copyright permission to reproduce the images in this publication. The editor would be pleased to hear from copyright holders to rectify any errors or omissions. Inquiries should be directed to the publisher.

Monash University Publishing
Matheson Library Annexe
40 Exhibition Walk
Monash University
Clayton, Victoria 3800, Australia
www.publishing.monash.edu

Monash University Publishing brings to the world publications which advance the best traditions of humane and enlightened thought.

Monash University Publishing titles pass through a rigorous process of independent peer review.

ISBN: 9781925835182 (paperback)
ISBN: 9781925835199 (pdf)
ISBN: 9781925835205 (epub)

www.publishing.monash.edu/books/tn-9781925835182.html

Series: Education

Design: Les Thomas

Cover image: Malay Town, Cairns, Queensland 1942 by Donald Friend.
Image kindly provided by Deutscher and Hackett art auction house, South Yarra, Victoria.

A catalogue record for this book is available from the National Library of Australia.

Printed in Australia by Griffin Press an Accredited ISO AS/NZS 14001:2004 Environmental Management System printer.

The paper this book is printed on is certified against the Forest Stewardship Council ® Standards. Griffin Press holds FSC chain of custody certification SGS-COC-005088. FSC promotes environmentally responsible, socially beneficial and economically viable management of the world's forests.

CONTENTS

Acknowledgments..vii

Introduction ix

Section I: Studies in Language and Culture.............. 1

Chapter 1   The Political Dimensions of Language Policies: The Case for Indonesian Language in Australian Higher Education
Firdaus..3

Chapter 2   Early Explorations of the Malay Language in Australia
Paul S. Thomas 31

Chapter 3   Translation as Persuasion: The Menzies Government's Sponsorship of Indonesian Studies during the Cold War
Paul S. Thomas 71

Chapter 4   Roller-coaster: The University of Melbourne Experience
Charles A. Coppel..97

Chapter 5   Goyang Lidah! Recipes for Teaching Indonesian
Julia Read and David Reeve......................................134

Chapter 6   Exporting Culture and the Indonesian World View
Hendrarto Darudoyo 169

Chapter 7   Facing the Twenty-First Century: Indonesian in Australian Universities
David T. Hill...200

Section II: Reflections 225

1. New Horizons: Getting to Know the Neighbours 227
    Jan Lingard

2. Indonesian at Sydney University in the Early 1960s
    Stuart Robson..230

3. The '60s, the Student and Pak Emanuels: An Indonesian Adventure
    Ron Witton 234

4. Webs and Rainbows: Accomplished Language Teaching and Pelangi Magazine Bridging Indonesia with Australia
   Lesley Harbon..................................244

5. Indonesian Literature and the Australian University: A Personal Journey
   Keith Foulcher..................................254

6. Teaching Indonesian Language through Drama
   Barbara Hatley..................................264

7. Reflections on Writing and Teaching Indonesian Grammar
   Dwi Noverini Djenar..................................271

8. On Teaching the Teachers of Indonesian: Looking Back over 20 Years
   Lindy Norris..................................279

ACKNOWLEDGMENTS

This book has been a long term project reliant on the good will and knowledge of many members of the Indonesian and Malay communities in Australia. On behalf of the contributors, I would like to thank them and pay respect to the pioneers of the Indonesian/Malay language in Australia whether they be accidental migrants, professional language teachers, cultural adventurers or parents who have endeavoured to pass their knowledge on to a new generation. I would also like to dedicate this volume to Pak Zainu'ddin, Australia's first Indonesian lecturer and teacher in the post-war period, and Pak Hendrarto Darudoyo, who contributed a key chapter to the book, both of whom have now passed away.

For their patience and support, I thank my colleagues at Monash University: Harry Aveling, Jemma Purdey, Julian Millie, Rita Wilson, Hashim Abdulhamid and Yacinta Kurniasih. I would also like to thank my colleagues at other institutions: Novi Djenar, Barbara Hatley, David Reeve, Haslina Haroon, Nani Osman-Thomas and Dom Santoro.

I offer my special thanks to Brett Hough, who proofread the manuscript and whose efforts often went well beyond the normal duties of proofreading. Finally, I would like to thank all the contributors who have had to show great patience over the very long gestation period required to bring this volume to print.

INTRODUCTION

What makes one nation curious about another? Sufficiently curious that the study of the other's culture and language becomes a natural commitment or something that could be described as a national project? This question lies behind much of the writing in this book as it explores the history and changing fortunes of the Indonesian/Malay language[1] in Australia. While there is a particular focus on formal education programs, individual effort and chance encounters with the language are also examined in the context of Australia's evolving historical ties with the nations Australia has come to recognise as its near neighbours. These relationships have grown in importance since the end of the Second World War, but Australians typically continue to view the region as 'difficult'. This is exemplified by the Australian-Indonesian relationship, the primary focus of this volume.

The Deficit of Communication

Pushing the need to overcome this ambivalent view is the rapid increase in mobility between the two nations over the last two decades. There are now over one million Australians who visit Indonesia each year and this figure continues to grow.[2] Australians and Indonesians are increasingly likely to meet across a broad range of fields, creating a clear necessity for improved communication if a relationship of more substance and promise is to be realised. However, exactly how this can be achieved remains unclear?

While much has been written on the Australian-Indonesian relationship, this book builds its view of the two countries' interactions on the activity of language learning, perhaps the most fundamental of cultural activities in any effort of cross cultural communication. As with all human relationships, Australia and Indonesia are heavily dependent on language to communicate ideas, hone perceptions of one another, and ultimately work cooperatively in pursuit of their respective national interests. This is not a difficult notion to grasp, however, amongst the many challenges in the relationship, it is poor

---

1 The Malay language in Indonesia was first proclaimed as 'bahasa Indonesia' in the Youth Pledge of 1928 but in Australia the term Malay was commonly used for all forms of the language until the 1950s.

2 Australian visitors to Indonesia between 2015-2016 climbed to 1,203,500 representing a percentage change of 416% over 10 years. Australian Bureau of Statistics, http://www.abs.gov.au/ausstats/abs@.nsf/products/961B6B53B87C130ACA2574030010BD05.

communication that is seen as one of the primary weaknesses. It has become symbolic of a deficit of cultural knowledge between the two countries and, therefore, a critical impediment to ensuring mutual understanding.

This has been expressed both in public debates and in more measured government documents. For example, after a sudden disruption to the live cattle trade from Australia in 2013, Jakarta Post's then Editor-in-Chief Meidyatama Suryodiningrat[3] commented:

> It is, I think, an example once again of an issue in which communication between the two countries, despite being so close together, has been very poor. Because as neighbours we are always going to have issues, but the way we communicate I think is really the problem. (Sales, 2013)

This echoed earlier admissions by the Australian Government in its own report on Australia's relationship with Indonesia:

> Australia and Indonesia have vastly different backgrounds and cultures. Such differences promise potential for rich exchanges. They can also lead to poor communication, misunderstanding and mistrust. Better mutual understanding is in the interests of both countries. (Joint Standing Committee on Foreign Affairs, Defence and Trade, 2004, p. 142)

These comments underscore the perception that communication difficulties are ongoing and arise, in part, because of the clash between cultural distance and geographical proximity. That is to say, Australia and Indonesia are too close to ignore one another but their cultural differences can sometimes feel overwhelming both at an individual level and at a national level. It is not surprising, therefore, that an oft-mentioned solution to this communication problem has been the recommendation that Australians and Indonesians learn each other's language and culture. However, the pragmatic motivation behind the language programs presents a problem. It can be conjectured that the utilitarian goals which have pushed the support for Indonesian/Malay programs in Australia through the decades have yet to produce the cultural curiosity in its neighbour necessary to sustain robust language programs across Australia's schools and universities. Australia has already experienced the loss of its Indonesian-Malay programs once in the 1930s, and again after the Second World War (see Chapter 2, this volume). The subsequent introduction of the contemporary university programs dating from the mid-1950s

---

3   In 2016 Meidyatama Suryodiningrat became the chief director of the Indonesian Government's news agency *Antara*.

was expected to result in a continued presence for the language in Australia's education system, but these programs have expanded and contracted irregularly, often resulting in an erosion of continuity and expertise. As Firdaus, Coppel and Hill make clear in their contributions, the fortunes of Indonesian language learning rise and fall depending largely on of political patronage, the bureaucracy constructed by educational bodies and the perceptions of Indonesia by the general public.

Utilitarian motives can be a critical spur for the introduction of new national language programs, but pragmatically inspired government initiatives need to make the transition to more comprehensive, grass roots forms of engagement. This can only arise through a mix of evolving cultural interest and opportunities for direct communication. A broadly engaged community of learners is more likely to sustain language and culture programs capable of making a difference in the relationships between nations.

Geography and Reorientation

A reorientation of Australia regarding its place in Asia has been experimented with in public discourse since the early 20th century. As will be discussed in this volume, even the basic geographic nomenclature of 'Near North' rather than 'Far East', 'neighbours' rather than 'foreigners' or 'natives', 'our region' rather than a generic 'Asia' have required reiteration and evolution for some decades before they have gained some traction amongst Australians at large. While this geographical reorientation has been an important development in Australia, Sobocinska (2014, p. 3) warns of the more ambiguous understandings of words such as 'neighbour' in international relationships:

> In the language of diplomacy, placing emphasis on geographical proximity can subtly imply a lack of a more meaningful relationship. Referring to Indonesia or Thailand - not to mention fairly distant nations such as India and China - as 'neighbours' suggest that there is little that brings Australia and Asia together, apart from the accident of geography. But there is no escaping geography, so a 'neighbour' is also among the most important of all international relationships.

The title of this book, *Talking North*, connects with Australia's extended deliberations on the country's geographical reorientation by reviewing the role of language as a primary catalyst in progressing a cultural reorientation. It also echoes Goldsworthy and Edward's (2001) title for their edited volumes on the history of Australia's relations with Asia *Facing North*, referring to a physical action leading to diplomatic and political engagement.

In this volume, the contributors review the advances made and the obstacles encountered in the process of Australia 'talking its way North'. They consider the influence of language study in creating a relationship that builds trust and cooperation. The learning and promotion of a neighbour's language represents more than a simple signpost pointing north. It is a project involving long term commitments by both the individuals who devote themselves to the task and the government and institutional bodies that support those individuals' learning.

The Shift away from Monolingualism

Talking North is also about a move away from monolingualism, a key contributing factor to cultural isolationism. While the English language has no official status in Australia's constitution, English has been the dominant medium in Australia's engagement with the rest of the world for most of its history. Australians have preferred to engage with the world mostly through Anglophone nations whether it be in literature, fine arts, theatre or in the popular culture of television, film, sport and music. This is in spite of the many migrant and Indigenous languages present in the country and the proximity of countries such as Indonesia. Even the cultural influence of non-Anglophone nations such as Korea or Spain may be filtered through Australia's traditional cultural allies of the United States and the United Kingdom. At times Australia struggles to find its own way of engaging with the world's cultures and therefore risks cultural isolation from cultures which are increasingly relevant to it.

This is also reflective of long standing concerns about monolingualism and political isolationism that have impacted Australia in the past:

> Monolingualism is related to a political isolationism as both product and cause. Australia's failure to adequately prepare for World War II, and the confused approach to world affairs in the post-war period can be related to both isolationism and monolingualism (Bostok, 1973, p. 43).

Political and cultural engagement with Indonesia can be considered a test case in Australia's independent engagement with the region. With Indonesia having little cultural impact on the United States or the United Kingdom, Australia needs to set its own cultural cues in the relationship. Australia's geographical borders are naturally defined by its immediate neighbours of New Zealand, the Pacific Island nations, Papua New Guinea, East Timor and Indonesia, but direct cultural relationships with these nations will provide the intellectual parameters capable of defining a unique nation.

As with most of its neighbouring nations, Australians in general remain unfamiliar with Indonesia. Indonesia still lacks a presence in Australian popular culture significant enough to balance the hard news stories in the Australian media. Even where there is contact it does not necessarily result in cultural exchange. Tourism, for example, sees large numbers of Australians holidaying in Indonesia, however, being in holiday mode many tend to be culturally numb in terms of tourists' receptiveness to Indonesian culture. The priority of many tourists is on shopping, seeking out a good Italian restaurant, a comfortable hotel room and a sandy beach. In fact even with a range of connections there is no guarantee of greater familiarity as noted by Fitriani[4] (2012, p. 12):

> Although there are many points of contact [between Australia and Indonesia] – through tourist visits, education, mixed marriages as well as mutual interests in terrorism, smuggling and so forth – in general, the people of both countries are not overly involved in the type of social and cultural interaction which would provide space for a relationship of mutual familiarity and understanding.

In the case of Australia, this leaves journalism and formal education settings as the primary prisms through which Australians view Indonesia. Consequently, motivation for language learning is narrowed to the pragmatics of trade, defence and diplomacy. While there are regular attempts to broadly engage with Indonesia such as through arts festivals that routinely program Indonesian performers, global cultural trends emanating from Australia's traditional cultural allies tend to be more alluring. It can only be hoped that as Australia matures culturally, it will more readily draw on its own regional interests. The journey to a more familiar relationship with its neighbours will be sustained by curiosity and imagination.

The Indonesian/Malay language arrived in Australia along with other languages from the eastern archipelago with Indonesian fishers and traders sometime in the mid-18th century. Its presence, therefore, predates European settlement and the arrival of the English language. Malay words travelled into Indigenous languages and some Aboriginal men and women, namely from the Yolngu peoples of Arnhem Land, learnt the new languages through

---

4   Head of the International Relations Department in the Faculty of Social and Political Science at the University of Indonesia. Translation Paul S. Thomas.

interactions with the visitors and journeys to the Indonesian homeland. The relationship between the two peoples was not always harmonious, interests still needed to be protected, transgressions were made, but nevertheless an inquisitiveness was sparked, as evidenced in the art, belief systems, material culture and language of Indigenous Australians. Australians today studying the languages of Indonesia have the choice of following in their footsteps.

Structure of this Book

Talking North is divided into two sections. The first consists of seven chapters which provide an analysis of the history and status of the Indonesian/Malay language in Australia. The second section consists of a collection of personal accounts of the teaching and learning of the language by prominent Indonesianists in the field of education, representing valuable primary sources for both this history and any future works on the subject.

Section I

In Chapter 1, Firdaus outlines the educational infrastructure emanating from both government and educational professionals which develops around a modern language program. She comments on the inevitability of politics being intertwined with the fate of language programs by virtue of the fact that both language and education policy is determined by the various levels of government.

While this is generally the case for matters related to education, it is doubly so in respect to the provision of language programs because there is little pressure from parents and students for the provision of foreign language programs in general, let alone Indonesian language programs. This can be contrasted with issues related to English literacy which have strong lobbyists from a broad spectrum of stakeholders. It is unfortunate that the relationship between English literacy and the study of foreign languages is not well understood. In essence, consistency in policy, political leadership and strong lobbyists are unquestionable ingredients for future progress towards sustainable programs in Indonesia.

In Chapter 2, Thomas explores the little known early history of the Indonesian/Malay language in Australia. The history of the language is reviewed beginning with the 18th century when Indigenous Australians commenced the informal learning of Malay and other languages from Makassar after contact with the trepangers and traders of Eastern Indonesia. The chapter then progresses to the early 19th century colonial appointments of Malay interpreters to the ill-fated European settlements on the north coast.

The early twentieth century is discussed in the context of the first proposals for the formal teaching of Malay emanating from the Australian chambers of commerce. Their motivating force was the search for alternative trading partners brought on first by the Great War and then by the Great Depression. These proposals eventually lead to the introduction of Malay to the technical colleges of Western Australia in the 1930s, though the teaching of the courses would prove tenuous.

The rapid expansion of Indonesian/Malay programs during Second World War is linked to the search for local alliances and the countering of Japanese propaganda but the chapter ends with the fading away of the wartime programs, ironically at the dawn of Indonesian independence. The teaching of the language is abandoned to small language schools and to those individuals passionate about the culture and people of Australia's northern neighbour. At a national level, the teaching of the language in the first half of the 20th century is characterised by needs arising from the misfortunes of war and extreme economic disorder. At an individual level, some key figures were motivated by a fascination with the myriad of cultures in the archipelago, and others by their awakening to the injustices endured by its peoples under colonial rule.

The ambiguous origins of the post-war programs are discussed in Chapter 3. While the primary focus is on the Menzies Government's use of language in Cold War diplomacy, changing attitudes are revealed in academic and broader cultural circles that provide new leadership in Australia's approach to its neighbours. As a consequence, the teaching of Indonesian/Malay in the Australian education system during the 1960s would spread far more rapidly than was originally envisaged by the Menzies Government.

The expansion of the language programs, however, did not occur at a constant pace and numerous setbacks were experienced over the next three decades. In chapter four, Coppel presents the University of Melbourne's Indonesian program as a case study of the teaching of the language at an Australian university. Indonesian in this context is set apart from most other languages as it is incorporated not into foreign languages but into area studies to act as a critical tool for exploring the political and social development of the new neighbour. The internal bureaucracy of the university, government language policy vacillations, staff partnerships and conflicts are discussed in this chapter as part of the everyday dynamics determining the fortunes of the new program.

In terms of teaching a successful language program, a fundamental concern is surely the development of suitable teaching materials. For most mainstream foreign languages such as French, German, Italian or even Japanese and Chinese there is a diverse range of established texts from which teaching staff can expand upon or add their own approach. In contrast, when Indonesian was introduced to Australian universities and schools, few or no suitable texts were available. This was a consequence of Australia being the only country to teach the language as a foreign language from primary to tertiary levels. In Chapter 5, Read and Reeve review the history of Indonesian language texts in Australia and analyse the organisational and methodological requirements of developing suitable teaching materials for a national program.

While much attention is given in this volume to Australia's initiatives in developing Indonesian language programs as a form of cultural diplomacy and to enhance its competitiveness in the region, Indonesia also stands to gain considerably from the popularity of the nation's language outside of its homeland. In Chapter 6, Darudoyo provides an insight into Indonesia's deliberations about becoming a cultural exporter and finds while the country has much to offer, it faces strong competition by established players in the business of globalisation. The experience of *shin hallyu* (the new Korean wave) and the status of Indonesian amongst Southeast Asian nations is explored in order to establish the potential of the Indonesian language as a form of soft power. The question arises as to whether Indonesian can become a *bahasa pergaulan internasional* (international language of fellowship) and thus an important tool in people-to-people diplomacy.

In the final chapter of this section, Hill offers both pessimistic and optimistic assessments of the future of the Indonesian language in Australia. He presents the decline of Indonesian language studies in Australia since the turn of the new century in unambiguous statistics while discussing the key features of the decline that continue to impact upon present day programs. More positively, he points to successful structural changes at universities which have improved the position of their language programs and to impressive growth in student numbers and the variety of offerings of in-country programs. However, this does not negate the need to provide warning of an uncertain future for the teaching of the language in Australia's schools and universities if the lessons of recent history are not learnt.

Section II

As indicated above, this section presents a diverse range of professional perspectives on the teaching and learning of Indonesian in Australia over many decades. These contributions allow a more intimate insight into the people and events involved as well as the personal responses of Indonesianists to the role Indonesian Studies has played in their lives. Their accounts of wonder and delight at first encountering Indonesia, its language and its people, their continuing commitment to the cause of passing on skills and knowledge to future generations, in many ways helps leaven the challenges described in the preceding factual reports. Together they provide an ongoing sense of modest optimism.

Lingard, Robson and Witton provide their reflections on the awakening to Indonesian as the key to a new nation's language and culture on Australian university campuses. With reference to two of the founding institutions of Indonesian Studies in Australia, the Australian National University and the University of Sydney, they outline the atmosphere in which the teaching of the language evolved, student response to the language as a cultural innovation and their own impressions of the pioneering staff who established the programs. Djenar, Foulcher and Hatley and make their respective contributions by addressing specific areas of the curriculum, namely grammar, literature and drama. The three contributors reveal their personal passion about their specialisations and how they gave it expression in their teaching.

Lastly, Harbon and Norris each draw on their experience across the broad spectrum of language education to explore the critical relationship between schools and universities in teacher training and support. They emphasise the importance of inspiring teachers in promoting the cause of language education and those who have inspired them. Given the crowded curriculum and competition between prospective offerings in most schools, without inspired, well-trained teachers the argument for a place for language can be lost before it has started.

Future Histories

The idea for this volume evolved out of the celebration of various milestones in the teaching of Indonesian in Australia that have taken place over the last ten years. These included the 50th anniversary of the teaching of Indonesian in Australian universities in 2006 and the 50th anniversary of its teaching in Australian schools in 2012-2013.[5] During this time a number of universities also held their own anniversary celebrations including the University of Sydney in 2008, Monash University 2013 and Flinders University in 2018.

---

5   While Tintern Girls Grammar introduced Indonesian in 1962, the Victorian School of Languages began preparing Indonesian courses in 1961 (Merlino 1988).

These events naturally brought to the surface a rich institutional history and a range of individual memories, some of which are reflected in this volume.

Unfortunately, it has not been possible to include a complete appraisal of the history of the teaching of Indonesian in a volume of this nature, so emphasis has been given to early encounters with the language, case studies in its teaching and the insights of experienced educators. With many important stories left untold, it is hoped that this volume will inspire greater research into the major milestones and individual histories related to the teaching of Indonesian/Malay in Australia. This may well be made more efficient by bringing together researchers in the history of Asian languages. In Europe, for example, the Research Network for the History of Language Learning and Teaching (HoLLT) was established in 2015 as part of the AILA (L'Association Internationale de Linguistique Appliquee/International Association of Applied Linguistics). Histories derived from this group of researchers are providing an in-depth context for the traditions and approaches that have developed for the teaching of languages over several centuries of pedagogy in Europe. There are perhaps lessons to be learned from HoLLT when approaching future research on Australia's language teaching traditions.

The challenges ahead for the Indonesian language in Australia remain considerable. In schools the crowded curriculum can squeeze out what some may still view as exotic, unnecessary subjects, as can competition from more strongly backed languages. Universities are also seeking popularity for their discipline areas and Indonesian in particular has not done well in the shift in interest from area studies to globalisation (see Purdy 2012). Ultimately, all levels of education interested in the teaching of Indonesian could do with a boost of the Indonesian 'brand' overseas. The political colours much of what Australians experience of Indonesia in their day-to-day lives and while this is an essential element in the relationship, Australians and Indonesians must also learn to imagine together. This is something that can be done through shared communication with the expectation that it may allow the relationship to settle on firmer foundations.

Language study is critically linked to the type of relationship Australia wants to have with its neighbours and it remains a constant theme in meetings with Indonesian leaders. In President Joko Widodo's 2017 state visit to Australia, the teaching of Indonesian in Australia was given prominence as it had been by his predecessor Susilo Bambang Yudoyono. On this occasion, the president announced an extension of the Balai Bahasa language centres which had already been established in Perth. It is telling that it was this element of the talks that led the report of a number of Indonesian news outlets.[6]

It is not possible within the framework of this book to answer the question of how Australians can be made more curious about their neighbours. However, in reflecting on the learning and teaching traditions of Indonesian/Malay in Australia the question can be established as important one in stimulating Australians to take the language journey to the near north.

References

Aji, Y. B. 2017. 'Jokowi akan Perbanyak Pusat Bahasa Indonesia di Australia', *METROTVNEWS.COM*. February 26. Available from http://news.metrotvnews.com/politik/nbwe9A6K-jokowi-akan-perbanyak-pusat-bahasa-indonesia-di-australia.

Bostock, W. 1973. 'Monolingualism in Australia', *The Australian Quarterly* 45 (2), pp. 39–52.

Fitriani, E. 2012. *Australia & Negara-negara di Kepulauan Pasifik Selatan: Observasi dan Pandangan dari Indonesia*. Jakarta: Penerbit Universitas Indonesia.

Goldsworthy, D. & Edwards, P. 2001. *Facing North: A century of Australian engagement with Asia*. Carlton South, Vic.: Melbourne University Press.

Joint Standing Committee on Foreign Affairs, Defence and Trade. 2004. *Near Neighbours – Good Neighbours: An inquiry into Australia's Relationship with Indonesia*. Canberra: The Committee.

Merlino, F. 1988. 'The Victorian School of Languages 1935–1988: A brief history', *Journal of the Victorian School of Languages* 1. Melbourne: Department of Education.

Purdey, J. (Ed.). 2012. *Knowing Indonesia: Intersections of self, discipline and nation*. Clayton, Vic.: Monash University Publishing.

Sales, L. 2013. 'Journalist suggests Indonesia and Australia could communicate better'. *7.30 Report*. September 30. Australian Broadcasting Corporation. Available from http://www.abc.net.au/7.30/content/2013/s3859429.htm.

Sobocinska, A. 2014. *Visiting the Neighbours: Australians in Asia*. Sydney: University of New South Wales Press.

---

6   *METROTVNEWS. COM* led with the headline 'Jokowi akan Perbanyak Pusat Bahasa Indonesia di Australia', 'Jokowi will increase the number of Indonesian language centres in Australia' (Aji, 2017).

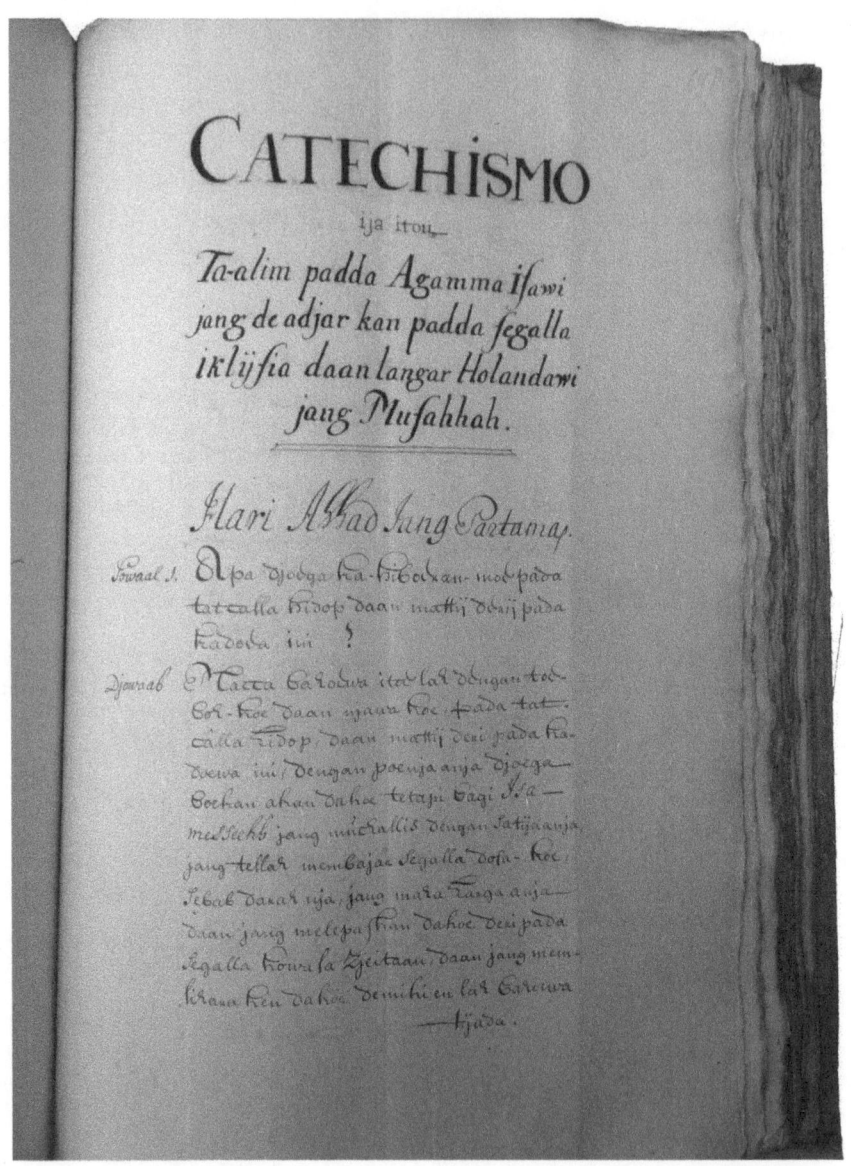

Figure 1: Herbert de Jager's *Maleijtse lees-konst*, a guide for the study of Malay, 1683. The text utilizes grammar descriptions and sample texts from the bible to teach the Malay language and is the oldest Malay language text in Australia.
Mitchell Library, State Library of NSW, RC: 949431 Photo: Paul Thomas.

Section I

Studies in Language and Culture

Chapter 1

THE POLITICAL DIMENSIONS OF LANGUAGE POLICIES

The Case for Indonesian Language in Australian Higher Education

Firdaus

Flinders University

In recent decades, successive Australian prime ministers have expressed the importance of the Indonesian-Australian relationship to an often ambivalent Australian public.[1] However, it is becoming more apparent that Indonesia, along with China and India, is one of the emerging giants of Asia and cannot be easily ignored. This has led to questions regarding the manner by which we should position ourselves to prepare for the immense opportunities and challenges, political and economic, cultural and educational, that this century must surely bring. Australia's role in this part of the world is becoming significant as a developed western country located effectively in Asia, and as a close ally of the United States. What precise form does or should this role take?

For two decades the call for skills in Asian languages or, more recently, the more expansive call for Asian skills, has echoed along the corridors of Australian schools and universities. Politicians have seen these skills as a

---

1   This chapter is a revised work based on an article first published as 'Indonesian Language Education in Australia: Politics, Policies and Responses', *Asian Studies Review*, 37:1, 2013, 24-41.

national priority, albeit on and off, and despite successive studies and reports pointing to a decline in Asian language enrolments. The national policy on Asian languages seems more than ever a pipe dream. To understand the present and plan, we need to look at how we came to find ourselves in today's situation, as well as to look more closely at the factors influencing the dynamics of language education in Australia. Politics and policies, government funding, long-term planning, and behavioural attitudes are among the interrelated forces at work. This paper explores the various roles played by politicians and policymakers, lobbyists, academics, and parents in an attempt to shed light on Asian language education in contemporary Australia.

Although Indonesian is one of the four priority Asian languages in Australia, enrolments in Indonesian language courses have declined steadily at all universities over the last decade. As yet, there is little understanding of the precise factors that contribute to the rise and fall of Indonesian language programs. This paper focuses on the case of Indonesian language teaching, and aims to reflect on the success and subsequent decline of university-level Indonesian language education in the context of both government policies and initiatives undertaken by language educators. Areas of particular interest include the broader social and cultural context, key national policies such as the National Asian Languages and Studies in Australian Schools (NALSAS) strategy,[2] the responses of Indonesian groups in Australia to the formation of the Australian Society of Indonesian Language Educators (ASILE),[3] the birth of the Australian Consortium for In-Country Indonesian Studies (ACICIS)[4] and more recently the New Colombo Plan that was introduced by the Liberal-National Coalition government (Liberal Party of Australia, 2013).

This chapter has three sections. The first considers the evolution of Indonesian language teaching in the context of links between the broader social and cultural milieu and specific political changes. The second sets out the development of Indonesian language study within the national policy framework for languages other than English (LOTE). The final section examines issues from the bottom up, looking at responses from teachers of Indonesian, particularly at tertiary level, and members of the language community.

---

2   First introduced in 1994.
3   Founded at a conference in Adelaide in 1994.
4   Established in 1994 and situated at Murdoch University in WA and Gadjah Mada University in Yogyakarta.

The Broader Social and Cultural Context

Both language education and language policy, like all education, are mostly controlled by government and are hence inevitably intertwined with politics (Slaughter, 2007; Baldauf, 2005; Pierce, 1989). As language education 'shares legroom with politics', it will always be subject to contestation by stakeholders. All language groups wrestle for meaning, access, and power (Carr and Pauwels, 2006; Pierce, 1989). The following cases demonstrate ways in which politics – both domestic and international – and political change can influence national education policy.

In the 1950s, Indonesian language was introduced into Australian university curricula explicitly for reasons of national security. In the context of post-war fears of Communist expansion, the Australian Government thought President Soekarno's leftist tendencies posed a threat to Australia, and so it listed the acquisition of Indonesian language skills as a national priority. It allocated considerable funding to some universities, including the Australian National University, the University of Sydney, and the University of Melbourne, to set up Indonesian language studies programs. This funding, however, ended abruptly in 1965, following the overthrow of the Soekarno regime and the rise to power of the pro-western President Soeharto.

At the secondary-school level, French, German, and some other European languages had traditionally been taught as part of liberal studies or of general intellectual training. This program took on a more utilitarian function in 1945 when the Ministry of Immigration was established with the aim of bringing more European migrants to populate Australia. It changed again with the arrival of a new wave of southern European migrants in the mid to late 1950s. Settlement by these new arrivals triggered debate and challenged traditional language attitudes, as well as injecting a completely new component into domestic politics: the voice of immigrant voters. Politically, there was strong resistance to including the study of languages other than English in mainstream education, but lobbyists worked hard to bring Italian and Modern Greek into Australian schools, capitalising in part on the new political power that came with the expansion of the electorate by migrants. As noted by Slaughter (2007) and previously discussed by Ozolins (1993), by the end of the 1970s these 'new' European languages had secured a firm place in the education system and were even compulsory subjects at matriculation (final secondary year) in some States. These two examples provide stark illustrations of how politics affects language education.

Politics intertwines itself with all aspects of the professional careers of language educators because governments provide the framework within which policymakers operate. Good policy fuels interest and jobs, which generate revenue for education services, so it is not surprising that language groups and others lobby governments to achieve political and economic advantage within their chosen language or field of study.

Another dimension often overlooked is the position of language education within the academic world. Universities pay lip service to the value of language learning in broadening a student's intellectual perspective and enhancing future career prospects, but on the ladder of university prestige, language education occupies the bottom rung. This is because language education is barely acknowledged by many as a true field of study, or at best it is deemed less rigorous. In universities, language teachers and academics in general suffer not only from reduced status, but also from a shortage of opportunities for research and publication. This latter outcome is often a direct result of the size of their teaching load and the nature of the language teacher's role in providing high levels of pastoral care to students. A language teacher is therefore commonly perceived as 'nothing but a technician trained to transmit a fixed canon of knowledge' (Pennycook, 1989, p. 612). This perception reduces the language teacher's authority and status. Language educators receive much less recognition than do language experts (such as pure linguists) or area studies experts (such as Japan specialists or Indonesianists).

Turning specifically to Indonesian language teaching, historically many Indonesian studies programs are located within social sciences faculties, and the above considerations apply. There is a hierarchy of knowledge, with the expertise of Indonesianists (Indonesian area specialists), with backgrounds in the social sciences, ranked above the knowledge of Indonesian language teachers, some of whom are equipped with background knowledge from TESOL, applied linguistics and education. The relationship between the two types of knowledge is often patriarchal (Pennycook, 1989), with one type, such as the expertise of area specialists or linguists, dominating the other. In the case of Indonesian, many social scientists are in the privileged rank; this situation often subordinates language teachers, creating an undercurrent of strain. The lack of mutuality and of a united front in tackling common objectives compromises the success of programs. Despite the evident strengths and weaknesses of both language experts and other faculty members, there has been practically no effort to recognise the differences in the types of knowledge – for example, when appointing staff, assigning workloads, or encouraging scholarly collaboration in research projects – all of which creates a gap that needs to be bridged.

Usually, language educators occupy middle or lower academic ranks. Unless this unsatisfactory state of affairs is addressed – putting language teaching on an equal footing with other academic activities and/or fields of study, and recognising it for its intellectual contribution – language teaching and learning will continue to suffer from low status, not only in universities but throughout the education system.

The Politics of Language within the Framework of National Language Policies

Australia is one of the few countries with an advanced, sophisticated national language policy (Henderson, 2007). Since the 1960s, Australia has produced at least 40 policy papers, from government and non-government bodies, working parties, committees, and organisations, which review and evaluate the need for and advantages of including the study of foreign language and culture in the national curriculum[5] (Henderson, 2007, p. 3).

Australia is known internationally for its effective formulation and modelling of language policies. In 1987, the Federal Government adopted a national language policy following Bob Hawke's[6] election campaign promise to spend $15 million in the first year of the policy's implementation, rising to $28 million per full year (Lo Bianco, 1987; Ozolins, 1993). The Australian Language Policy recommended nine languages for LOTE at primary and secondary levels (Lo Bianco, 1987) – Indonesian, Japanese, Chinese, Korean, German, French, Italian, Spanish and Russian. The government prioritised these languages according to its perception of their importance and the number of speakers of the languages in Australia. The Lo Bianco Report recommended giving space in schools to the emerging Asian languages while maintaining the status of European languages. Lo Bianco's recommendation was adopted by the subsequent Keating Government in 1994 in its National Policy on Languages, through the National Asian Languages and Studies in

---

5   The term 'national curriculum' usually refers to the school curriculum. It affects tertiary education through its influence on language enrolments. The national curriculum reflects public opinion on the importance of languages.

6   Australian prime ministers referred to in this paper, with their dates of office, are Bob Hawke 1989–91, Paul Keating 1991–96, John Howard 1996–2007, Kevin Rudd 2007–10 and 2013, Julia Gillard 2010–2013, Tony Abbott 2013–2015, Malcolm Turnbull 2015-2018 and Scott Morrison 2018-present.

Australian Schools (NALSAS) strategy, but even this move was not without a political element.

In this policy the Federal Government moved beyond considerations of ethnic affairs and multicultural education alone (Ozolins, 1993, p. 248) and Asian languages – Japanese, Chinese, Indonesian, and Korean in particular – were accorded a higher priority. Unlike the previous national language policy, this NALSAS strategy was a cooperative initiative of the Federal, State, and Territory governments.[7] NALSAS was also a result of strong lobbying from the Asian Studies Council (ASC). According to Slaughter (2007), in this way Asian languages received auspicious status and funding. The funding clearly favoured Asian languages (Henderson, 2007, p. 9); this reflected the priority placed by the Australian Government on creating economic ties with rapidly developing Asian countries.

The NALSAS policy was also born in the midst of debates in Australia about multiculturalism, which until then had been sustained by the European lobby and hence closely interwoven with the politics of ethnic issues (Ozolins, 1993). The new NALSAS strategy challenged the concepts and practices of multiculturalism prevailing in Australia at the time, resulting in a significant reduction in funding allocated for European languages as funding shifted more to Asian languages. This followed on the heels of a more general shift towards Asia in Australian public discourse in the 1980s and a consequent closer engagement with the region. It was natural that in due course the shift would extend to language education (Lo Bianco, 2003).

The 1990s thus brought an increase in the status of Asian languages, in the wake of Australia's political and economic realignment towards Asia. The debate over languages in the national educational system flared up again; where it had previously been about the balance between English and the new European languages it was now about the relative claims of European and Asian languages. The Australian Advisory Council on Languages and Multicultural Education (AACLAME) coordinated and promoted European language education, while the ASC coordinated and actively advocated the teaching of Asian languages. Tensions between language lobbyists increased as the competition for limited funding and access to political power intensified, and as the Federal Government became increasingly inclined to prioritise Asian languages. In these circumstances, it was almost impossible for the National Policy on Languages to deal with all of the different interests in a

---

7   Language policy had usually been under the auspices of the National Policy on Languages (NPL).

harmonious and fair manner. The National Policy on Languages was presented as being apolitical, but from its inception it had been coloured both by ideology, including ethnic issues and by the foreign policy pragmatism of the day. To think otherwise would be naïve (McHoul and Mey, 1990). Indonesian, for example, is not a community language, but it was listed as a priority language for reasons of national strategy.

In 1991, the Federal Government, under pressure from advocates for European languages, acknowledged the political implications of its policy and decided to delegate responsibility for language study to the State governments (Viviani, 1992; Henderson, 1999). This move benefited the Federal Government in two ways. By shifting responsibility, it reduced disillusionment with the national policy, particularly on the part of groups advocating for the new European migrants. It also reinforced Australia's political and economic affiliation with Asia by increasing the capacity of young Australians to acquire skills in Asian languages and cultures through the NALSAS strategy.

The Federal Government provided the States with a $300 bonus for each student who learned any of the nine priority languages in Year 12 (the final year of secondary school). This both helped schools to run programs and promote language study, and increased confidence in the Federal Government's leadership in language education. In this way, national policy on Asian languages continued to be implemented, but at State level and at a lower political cost. With these changes came a reorientation of the goals of language study. The former program of 'liberal cultivation of the intellect' promoted by academics in the humanities gave way to government pragmatism: languages were for employment and other economic purposes (Hunter, 1991, p. 9).

Whether the goal of language study should be economic, business-related, political, or intellectual is a matter of constant debate. Shanzer (1996) favoured the intrinsic cultural values of language study, asserting that there was no correlation between economic benefits, such as growth in exports, and language competence in Australia during the 1990s. This stance contradicts more pragmatic arguments, which advocate increasing language competence, including through teacher training, on the assumption that such language skills, especially in Asian languages, are essential for Australia's future economic prosperity and are needed for Australia to take advantage of its geographical location in the Asia-Pacific region. In support of these arguments, we cannot deny that Australia is more than ever engaging vigorously with its neighbours. After China, the ASEAN countries collectively represent Australia's biggest source of two-way trade ($88.7 billion in 2008),[8] and Indonesia is the largest of the ASEAN states in both population and territory (Lindsey, 2010). Additionally, the Liberal Coalition government's New Colombo Plan initiative, is strongly encouraging the in-country study of Asian cultures and languages, a development that I shall return to later. One cannot lightly dismiss the importance of the role played by languages such as Greek and Italian in making Australia receptive to change in language education, but for the future Australia needs to understand and connect more closely with its Asian neighbours because they will have a substantial effect on Australia (Wolfwensohn, quoted in Lindsey, 2010).

So, what does the future hold for language education? One prediction is that in 10 to 15 years, Chinese or Spanish will replace English as the world language. Indeed, at present only 6 per cent of the world's population speak English as their first language (CILT, 2005, p. 4). Approximately 78 per cent of Australians are monolingual speakers of English, and it is difficult to see how a shift from monolingualism to a wide distribution of Asian language skills is achievable without substantial government involvement. It is understandable that in recent decades much has ridden on the implementation of policies such as NALSAS to assist Australia to compete in the modern world. However, Australia now needs to develop policies that promote the study of prioritised languages,[9] as well as the cultures from which these languages spring. The study of cultures and societies is also fundamental to the study of languages, and facilitates a deeper understanding of the world.

Development of Indonesian Language Programs

From the late 1980s onwards, several crucial reports on language teaching in Australia appeared, with great significance for the teaching of Indonesian. Of greatest importance were the Ingleson Report (Asian Studies Council, 1989), the Leal Report (Leal, Bettoni & Malcolm, 1991), and the Rudd Report (Rudd, 1994). These reports criticised the ambivalent attitude of the national framework towards the study of languages other than English. The Ingleson Report asserted that there was a strong tendency to favour European languages in LOTE. It also suggested that it was in Australia's strategic interest to study Asian languages, both as a separate field of study and as an integrated component of other studies. The Leal Report suggested a new

---

8 Two-way trade with Indonesia alone was worth $8.3 billion in 2010.
9 Australia is now the lowest-ranked OECD country for second language skills (Lindsey, 2010).

national framework for language and cultural studies, emphasising quality. It recommended a shift of cultural orientation in Australian education, the funding for which should be provided by the Federal Government, and argued that the government had a responsibility to stimulate teaching of LOTE. The report also argued that it was necessary to subsidise LOTE, and linked this step with the need to improve the level of employment skills in the population.

Both Ingleson and Leal strongly recommended that language study be mainstreamed in the Australian education system, but in contrast to the Ingleson Report, which was positive about Indonesian in universities, the Leal Report was indifferent to the teaching of Asian languages, including Indonesian. The report recommended prioritising Arabic, French, German, Greek, Italian, Russian, and Spanish at the tertiary level – a list that does not contain one Asian language (Read, 2002, p. 48).[10] Leal gave sustenance to the views of the European language lobby by emphasising intellectual and cultural benefits rather than economic considerations.

A turning point for Asian languages, especially Indonesian, occurred in 1994 when the COAG working group,[11] chaired by Kevin Rudd, who was a high-ranking official in the Queensland Government at the time, released a document entitled 'Asian Languages and Australia's Economic Future'. Its focus was the Australian Government's effort to develop and expand the national economy, in particular through relationships with Asian nations. The Rudd Report argued that in order to integrate Australia more closely into the Asian economy, it was vital that young Australians acquire Asian language skills. The Federal Government folded the findings of this report into the NALSAS strategy, which it implemented from 1995 to 2002. The Rudd Report recommended that targets be set whereby 15 per cent of all Year 12 students should study one of four priority Asian languages and that 60 per cent of Year 10s should study an Asian language. From 1995 to 2002, the Commonwealth spent $208 million through NALSAS in the effort to reach these goals.[12] Although the Rudd Report highlighted the importance of both linguistic and cultural understanding, the bulk of the funding focused on the

---

10   In Australian language education the term 'Asian languages' has ethnic, heritage and geopolitical connotations rather than a purely geographical one. The term therefore refers to specific Asian languages in neighbouring countries, some of which have economic and political significance to Australia such as Chinese, Indonesian, Japanese, Korean, Thai and Vietnamese. Of these, the languages currently prioritised nationally are Chinese, Indonesian, Japanese and Korean.

11   COAG is an intergovernmental forum comprising the prime minister, State premiers, and Territory chief ministers.

12   The address of the NALSAS website is <www1.curriculum.edu.au/nalsas/about.htm>.

teaching of languages in schools and on education programs for language teachers provided by tertiary institutions. Only $3.2 million in total of the funding was allocated to the teaching of Asian cultures and Asian studies in general. Nonetheless, Asian studies departments in higher education benefited from this policy, although often indirectly, through funding of 'Asia literacy'.[13] Additional benefits derived from the policy, which encouraged all Asian studies programs to be relevant to the vocational needs of the public and private sectors (Davies, 1993). The benefits included scholarships for in-country language training for top students and teachers, facilitation of language research, and the flow-on effect of providing an incentive for students to study Asian languages and do postgraduate research on Asia. All of these incentives, including added demand on language and teacher-training programs in the universities, benefited the Asian studies departments in particular (Hooper, 1995).

The NALSAS strategy resulted in a dramatic rise in the number of students studying Asian languages, including Indonesian, in Australian schools. From 1994 to 1997, the number of Australian public schools that offered Asian language classes increased by approximately 53 per cent (Henderson, 2007). In 1997–98, 20 per cent of the student population was studying an Asian language, and 25,000 teachers trained or retrained at tertiary level in one of the four priority languages.

This period of successful implementation of the NALSAS strategy created the strong foundation necessary to support long-term success, but it died in May 2002 when Brendan Nelson became Minister for Education in the Howard Government. Nelson cut the government's support for the NALSAS program before it reached its targets. The program was to have continued for at least four more years, attracting a further $240 million in funding, but Nelson argued that it was now the State governments' responsibility to fund language education (Henderson, 2003). Instead of funding the programs, he asked the States to follow Federal Government initiatives. The timing could hardly have been worse, since only a few months later a terrorist attack in Bali killed scores of Australians, creating fear and a nexus in public and official minds between Indonesia and terrorism (Hill, 2012). Together, these factors had a profound impact on Indonesian language programs in Australia.

---

13   'Asia literacy' is a term coined by the Asian Studies Council in its policy statement, *A National Strategy for the Study of Asia in Australia* (Asian Studies Council, 1988), which placed emphasis on the place of Asian countries in relation to Australia's economic future, claiming, 'Asia is central to our trade, our foreign relations and our future'. It called for a stronger focus on Asia in Australian education.

Effects on Tertiary Indonesian Language Programs

Indonesianists, like other Asianists, viewed the Nelson cuts as short-sighted and a loss to the national investment in Australia's human capital. In the early to mid-1990s, more than 20 Australian universities taught the Indonesian language, but this figure had dropped to fewer than a dozen universities by 2004. Concomitantly, there was a net loss of 7.45 Indonesian teaching staff positions in higher education in Australia from 2001–04 (White and Baldauf, 2006, p. 11). Of the remaining universities teaching Indonesian, none had enrolments of more than 30 EFTSL (McLaren, 2008).[14] The period between 1995 and 2001 marked the peak of interest in the study of the Indonesian language. In 2001, there were 628 EFTSL, declining to 478 in 2007. This downward trend is continuing into the second decade of the twenty-first century (White and Baldauf, 2006).

A similar trend is apparent in Australia's schools. For example, in 1994, at the outset of the NALSAS program, there were approximately 90,000 students studying Indonesian at primary and secondary schools, increasing to 316,877 students in 2001, but this number fell by 15 per cent between 2001 and 2005 (Slaughter, 2007). The reduction in student numbers resulted in a decline in the number of language programs, followed by a plunge in the status of the Indonesian language. The last 2010 report of the National Asian Languages and Studies in Schools Program (NALSSP, the Rudd Government's successor to NALSAS) indicated that fewer than 1 per cent of students in Year 12 were studying Indonesian. In the same year, the Asia Education Foundation predicted that, unless action was taken, by 2020 Indonesian would not be studied at Year 12 level at all (Asia Education Foundation, 2010).

The status of a foreign language has an important influence on its popularity. For instance, from the beginning of the 1980s through to 1986, Indonesian was very popular with students, far more so than Japanese or Chinese (Zifirdaus, 1988). The Indonesian economy was booming at the time, like those of other Southeast Asian nations such as Thailand and Malaysia. Students and parents felt that the ability to speak Indonesian would give young people greater opportunities to access the most attractive jobs in both Australia and Asia. Other factors favouring Indonesian included a heightened interest among students at all levels of education in the study of languages other than English (Worsley,

---

14   EFTSL, Equivalent Full-Time Student Load: a unit of enrolment calculation used by Australian universities, amounting to a measurement of the standard annual study workload of a student undertaking a full year of study on a full-time basis, which can vary according to year level and course of study.

1994); the fact that Indonesian utilises the Roman alphabet; and the fact that Bali was already a popular cheap holiday destination for many Australians. The political and cultural environment thus favoured the study of Indonesian in those years. By the mid-2000s the situation had changed dramatically, and Indonesian language was burdened with negative associations and was held in low regard by policymakers, parents, and prospective students.

The political environment, at least in Australia, affects the status of a foreign language. In 2008 the same Kevin Rudd who had written the Rudd Report in 1994 had just become prime minister, and his government committed $62.4 million from 2008–12 under the auspices of the National Asian Languages and Studies in Schools Program (NALSSP). Unsurprisingly, as it was a reincarnation of the previously abolished NALSAS policy, it focused on Chinese, Indonesian, Japanese, and Korean languages and cultures. This policy remained intact as the Australian Government's major language initiative, even after Julia Gillard replaced Kevin Rudd as prime minister in 2010.[15]

NALSSP has four main targets: to fund education departments in every State; to create partnerships between universities, schools, businesses, and communities; to fund scholarships and grants in schools; and to fund national projects that relate to this policy. As with the earlier NALSAS program, the long-term economic goal of the new policy was to increase Australians' ability to compete in an internationalising world. However, a question mark hangs over the ability of this program to address tertiary education. Universities did not receive any significant direct funding through this policy to address problems and rectify their decline in enrolments. Indonesian teaching programs would have experienced far greater change had funding been directly allocated for language programs and had universities been free to establish their own programs without having to fulfil the conditions and prerequisites of the federal Department of Education and other government bodies (Lian, 1997). Jeffrey (2004) remarks that if the Australian Government had been serious about its commitment to Asian language programs, it would have needed to provide only around $300,000 per institution annually to employ three full-time teachers plus administrative and technical staff.

Every foreign language has its own political dimensions, which form a type of linguistic culture (Slaughter, 2007), but according to Schiffmann (quoted

---

15   The most significant variation between the old and the new programs is that in the new White Paper released on 28 October 2012 by PM Julia Gillard, Korean language has been replaced in the list of core languages by Hindi. The media release is available at <http://www.kpmg.com/AU/en/IssuesAndInsights/ArticlesPublications/Documents/australia-in-the-asian-century-opportunities-challenges.pdf>.

in Slaughter, 2007, p. 318) the policymakers have consistently overlooked this issue. Global changes such as the Asian Financial Crisis, political instability following the fall of the Soeharto regime, and the rise of anti-Islamic sentiments in response to acts of terrorism[16] have drastically reduced the popularity of studying Indonesian, despite Indonesia's efforts and achievements in reforming its institutions and its high levels of economic growth in recent years. These events have deepened the anxiety Australians feel towards Indonesia. Such perceptions have historically always been present, although possibly at a subconscious level, 'formed by an unfortunate history and cemented by present fear and ignorance' (Lindsey, 2010). The negative attitude in Australian society has re-emerged, and this has affected the teaching and learning of the Indonesian language. The reality of foreign language study, according to Baldauf (cited in Slaughter, 2007, p. 135), is that 'if I don't like you, I won't study your language'. Unfortunately, this affects Indonesian language education.

Another factor is grounded in Australian domestic politics during the era of the Howard Government (1996–2007). In the middle years of his government, John Howard often exploited sensitive international situations for domestic political benefit. The *Tampa* crisis of 2001, which involved asylum seekers on boats originating from Indonesia, was a prime example. During this period, the Howard Government launched a populist slogan on border security: 'We will decide who comes to this country and the circumstances in which they come'. This slogan created the popular impression that his government had little time or sympathy for Indonesia,[17] even though it maintained good relations with its neighbour at a government-to-government level.[18] Fear of Islam and a backlash against terrorist attacks reinforced the notion of Indonesia as a threat in the minds of many ordinary Australians. Anti-Indonesian rhetoric was recycled and disseminated through a number of popular media such as talkback radio, newspapers, and television. Such rhetoric often bordered on the sensational and lurid, further strengthening Australian antipathy towards Indonesia. Ties between Indonesia and Australia are more often frosty than not; this reinforces on the negative attitudes.

---

16 Among terrorist incidents targeting westerners, including Australians, were the infamous Bali Bombing (2002), attacks in Jakarta on the Marriot Hotel (2003) and the Australian embassy (2004), and a bombing at Jimbaran, Bali, in 2005.

17 The speech is available at <http://museumvictoria.com.au/immigrationmuseum/discoverycentre/identity/people-like-them/the-white-picket-fence/john-howards-2001-federal-election-policy-launch-speech/>, accessed 1 December 2012.

18 Australia developed a reasonably good relationship with the Indonesian Government in the wake of the Bali Bombing in 2002 and the tsunami in 2004.

Thus, unhealthy attitudes towards Indonesia once again permeated Australian society, contributing to a further decline in the popularity of the Indonesian language. Schools found that they had few students interested in studying Indonesian; the government issued warnings that emphasised the risks of travel to Indonesia;[19] so that even those parents who had once viewed the language favourably began steering their children away from studying Indonesian (Australian Council of State School Organisations and Australian Parents Council, 2007). Travel restrictions placed on study tours removed the opportunity and incentive for students to experience immersion in the language and its culture.[20] This has strongly militated against the survival of Indonesian language programs, which were already suffering from economic constraints at both school and government levels (Slaughter, 2007, p. 316). Other languages, such as Japanese and Chinese, which have also lost the support and funding provided by the NALSAS program, are not experiencing the same effects. Although these languages, particularly Chinese, experience similar fluctuations because of political developments, neither has suffered like Indonesian. At school level, enrolments in Indonesian have been declining by 10,000 students every year since 2005 (Kohler and Mahnken, 2010). As what happens at school level always affects tertiary enrolments, the decline at universities seems to be comparatively widespread too (see Figure 1).

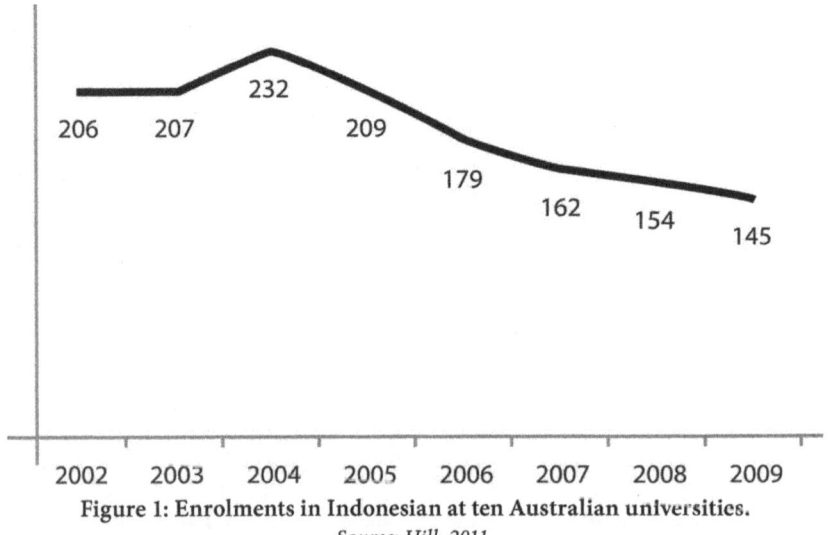

Figure 1: Enrolments in Indonesian at ten Australian universities.
Source: Hill, 2011.

---

19 The media release is available at <http://www.foreignminister.gov.au/releases/2002/fa149_02.html>, accessed 4 December 2012.
20 The travel restriction has since been upgraded to 'Travel with Care'.

Hill, Lindsey, and Perry predict a decline in expertise in this area in coming generations due to the lack of a strategic, long-term plan to replace current levels of skill and knowledge. At the tertiary level, Australian Indonesianists constitute an internationally renowned resource, but the majority of them are baby boomers, many have already retired, and others will in 5 to 10 years. These experts are unlikely to be replaced, because there is no planning for this in the universities. Australian universities will not be producing Indonesianists because the programs lack both funds and graduates, particularly PhD graduates. Instead, Indonesian departments face decline and abolition, and one by one they are closing down. Moreover, this development also represents a threat to the future of teacher training. When there are no longer any students of the Indonesian language or, worse still, when there are no remaining Indonesian departments, school students will have no opportunity to train as teachers. No group of people is so intimately acquainted with Indonesia as the Australian academics working in this field. To fail to halt this university decline would be to squander a body of knowledge and expertise that constitutes a national and international asset.

Ken Ward, a former diplomat and intelligence analyst, has pointed out that a democratic Indonesia is actually more complex to deal with than that of the Soeharto era. 'Australia's need to understand Indonesia is as great as ever', Ward commented (quoted in McDonald, 2007), adding that 'Indonesia is growing ever more complex, yet fewer Australians are becoming attracted to the study of Indonesia than in the past'. McDonald concluded, 'Foreign relations isn't always about diplomats, soldiers, police, academics, or journalists, but about ordinary citizens'.

Policy and politics are intricately intermingled. Policy needs a long-term vision and should be reviewed from time to time as new developments arise. Politics on the other hand is often unpredictable, but government (perhaps in collaboration with business) in Australia needs to act. A short-sighted national plan for language education that suffers from a lack of vision will cost Australia dearly in the future.

In 2013 Julia Gillard was replaced as Labor leader and PM by Kevin Rudd, before that government lost a federal election in September to the Liberal Coalition. On taking office, the new coalition government unsurprisingly overturned many policies of the previous administration; like every incoming government, it wanted to put its own stamp on politics and policies.

In 2013, prior to the election, Tony Abbott and Julie Bishop, then opposition leader and shadow foreign minister respectively, declared that if they won office, their government would focus on the economy and diplomacy on our region (CMAX Advisory, 2013). Indonesia, being Australia's nearest neighbour, would be accorded the highest priority, and the government would strengthen relations that had deteriorated under the Gillard government, especially after the ban on live cattle exports in 2011. One of Tony Abbott's first actions on taking office was to visit Indonesia in October 2013. During this visit a very significant announcement was made: the New Colombo Plan (NCP) Initiative. This reciprocated the Colombo Plan of 1949–57, under which the Australian government sponsored thousands of students from southern and SE Asia to come to Australia to study and train at Australian tertiary institutions (Department of Foreign Affairs and Trade, 2005).

The plan aimed to foster better relations and understanding between Australia and its neighbours in the Asia-Pacific region by sending Australian undergraduates to study in the Asia-Pacific as an integral component of their degree course. The government promised funding to the tune of $100 million over five years. The plan replaced the previous Labor government's Asian Century policy that the coalition had castigated as 'an exercise in vanity' (CMAX Advisory, 2013). The Asian Century white paper was scrapped, and disappeared from the government's website.

The NCP aims to support 300 young Australians aged 22 or under to study in the Asia-Pacific region in 2015 (Liberal Party of Australia, 2013). A pilot project was implemented for 2014–2015 with four outbound countries (Indonesia, Singapore, Hong Kong and Japan) designated for the first tranche. Though the NCP started with tester and short-term courses, the long-term goal is study abroad for a semester. Teething problems aside, the plan has begun in a promising way: Indonesia turned out to be the most popular country, chosen by 90 out of 300 outbound students (Lane, 2014a). Whether this pattern will continue it is too early to decide.

This social engineering via the New Colombo Plan is based on pragmatism. It openly acknowledges that Australia and its Asian neighbours need each other for reasons of both security and economics, now and increasingly in the future. We are interdependent despite intermittent disagreements and tensions; the Snowden revelations about spying being just one of the most recent embarrassments (Wesley, 2013). Tony Abbott proclaimed that if Australians wanted to make their way in the world, they could not rely on other people speaking their language (Scott, 2012).

The NCP offers a significant advance in international understanding. It should foster stability in diplomacy, politics, economics, and security. It constitutes a significant shift from the previous 'command and control' approach, and for this the Liberal Coalition government deserves recognition and plaudits, because its initiative is targeted, manageable, and contained. Like the original Colombo Plan, this one seems set to foster good people-to-people relations, educate young future leaders about Australia's neighbours, and in all likelihood minimise the impact of occasional mishaps and provide a firm foundation for deeply-grounded and cross-cultural mutual respect.

In terms of relations with Indonesia, one can hope that this scheme will increase the number of Australian students exposed to the country and its culture and who come back wanting to learn more. Given that Indonesia has demonstrated to the world its ability to conduct a successful exercise in open, fair democracy (their most recent election was in July 2014) and that it is growing in economic prosperity, the stage seems set for a turning of the tide of public opinion, but only time will tell. This will, with luck, translate into higher enrolments in higher education. The Plan amounts to an investment in better relations between the two countries. Nothing deepens intercultural respect and mutual understanding better than the exchange of people, knowledge, and skills (Meld Magazine, 2012). Graduates of the Plan will come away with deeper insights into Indonesia, just like the many Indonesian students who gained their higher degrees at Australian universities and who now occupy important decision-making positions. It is a truism that the young generation will provide the future leaders of Australia. If future leaders from both countries have better insights into one another from both, we are certainly on the right path.

One distinctive feature of the NCP is that, while it aims specifically at higher education students, it is not limited to undergraduates on arts or education courses. The plan applies to any field of study with relevant content. The attraction is the broad scope of the target audience; the danger is of another 'exercise in vanity' in which program implementation lacks sustainability and accountability.

The New Colombo Plan apart, how have Australian academics responded to the challenges confronting them? Individual academics at the tertiary level in Indonesian studies and languages have taken steps to consolidate their programs, to minimise loss of enrolments, and to introduce new ways to energise their programs, with varying degrees of support from their institutions. The following section highlights a few initiatives in higher education undertaken by academics themselves.

Responses and Initiatives from Indonesian Language Educators

The first step in a national response from Indonesian educators was the formation of an organisation of Indonesian language experts in Australia. The need for such a body was recognised at the 1992 ASAA conference,[21] at which the support and public endorsement of the late Professor Jamie Mackie was instrumental (Firdaus, 1994). From this move came a professional body known as the Australian Society of Indonesian Language Educators (ASILE). This society provides a forum for Indonesian tertiary academics and secondary school teachers to meet and share issues in their professions at an annual (later biennial) conference. This was the first significant initiative by Indonesianists or language educators to consolidate their expertise. Now, more than ever ASILE is branching out to Indonesia; its two latest conferences in 2012 and 2014 were held in Indonesian with the collaboration of Indonesian linguists and universities.

Another initiative at this time was the formation in 1994 of ACICIS (the Australian Consortium for 'In country' Indonesian Studies) organised and led by David Hill of Murdoch University. The consortium coordinates high-quality semester-long study programs for Australian students at Indonesian partner universities. With most of the Australian universities that taught Indonesian as members, ACICIS built bridges between universities to use limited resources to greatest effect. ACICIS has quickly gained popularity and has developed programs in Islamic business, journalism, development studies, and teacher training, as well as short-term programs, among others.

Both organisations have flourished and have become nationally renowned within the Indonesian academic community, providing teaching and learning forums on Indonesian language. They differ, however, in one important respect. ACICIS has received significant funding for its operations and has a structured administration with board members. ASILE operates without funding and has a loose structure; it survives virtually independently.

There was another major stakeholder response in 1992: TIFL (Teaching Indonesian as a Foreign Language). This project was designed to modernise the stilted and limited materials then available for tertiary education. Departing from the traditional audio-lingual materials, TIFL adopted a communicative approach. The innovative educator David Reeve of the University of New South Wales led the project, which offered authentic materials

---

21   Pengembangan bahasa Indonesia di Australia agar lebih komunikatif. *Kompas*, 26 August 1992, p. 12.

carefully developed for Australian students and reformed Indonesian language teaching in classrooms throughout Australian universities (see Chapter 5 this volume).

A similar project, the Regional Universities' Indonesian Language Initiative (RUILI), established in 2007 and led by Phil Mahnken of the University of the Sunshine Coast, brought another major curriculum development, this time using the Internet. Collaboratively, members of RUILI, from the University of New England, the University of the Sunshine Coast, the University of Tasmania, and Charles Darwin University, developed online materials with a grant from the federal Department of Education.[22]

As textbooks and language teaching materials must be constantly upgraded to keep up with developments, these are precisely the responses needed, specially crafted to improve the environment of Indonesian teaching in Australia. The role of people who run Indonesian programs and the support they receive from senior university decision-makers (faculty executive deans, deans, and vice-chancellors) are vital. With their strong support, Indonesian programs have a much greater chance of survival. At the same time, when they lack vision, as they often do, language programs will be detrimental and even under threat, as exemplified by La Trobe (just survived), UNSW (closed), and a near miss at Flinders University (survived).[23]

Online program development started in the early 1990s and, at around the same time, universities began to offer cross-institutional enrolments. In South Australia, for example, Flinders University has been offering this type of enrolment since 1990, making Flinders the sole provider of Indonesian language education in South Australia. The aim was to reduce competition and increase collaboration between universities with differing expertise in various languages. This has boosted enrolments, strengthened Indonesian language programs, and assisted the language program to reclaim a position that might otherwise have been lost. This type of response from universities is not without its challenges. Staff must travel between universities and between campuses, losing both time and work momentum, as well as negotiating the administrative systems of more than one institution: their credit units, room

---

22 Responses from secondary teachers of Indonesian are channelled through ASILE and through regional teachers' associations.

23 In 2013 the Indonesian Program at Flinders University, under the auspices of Faculty of Social and Behavioural Sciences since its conception in the 1970s, was in danger of being closed down due to 'financial liability'. However, thanks to the leadership of the university's deputy vice-chancellor, Prof. Andrew Parkin, the program survived after being moved to a new Faculty of Humanities, Education, and Law, in which all other languages are located.

bookings, and conflicting timetables. Many of these tasks are invisible in workload plans, yet they eat into the time available for research and publication, not to mention staff morale. Deakin University has addressed the issue by allowing promotion based more on teaching record and less on research and publications. Some other universities, such as Monash, La Trobe, and Flinders, have developed similar work flexibility, whereby staff can choose the focus of their contribution: teaching, research, or a balance of the two. Others have yet to follow suit.

For a long time the Indonesian government either did not see itself as one of the stakeholders in this process or failed to recognise the value of supporting its language and culture programs overseas. With the 1998 reformation, Indonesia became more liberal and progressive, a change reflected in the appointments of Dr Agus Sartono and later Dr Aries Junaidi as cultural attachés in Australia. These men fostered grassroots understanding between Indonesia and Australia and enthusiastically supported Indonesian language programs by opening up dialogues, attending ASILE conferences, and disseminating updated information on Indonesia's economy and transition to democracy. The Indonesian government also collaborated in establishing Balai Bahasa (Indonesian cultural and language centres) in Perth in 2009, Canberra in 2011, and Melbourne in 2014 (Department of Education, 2014). Support also comes in the form of scholarships for travel to Indonesia. Their aim is to boost Indonesia's image in Australia and to promote positive exchanges and relationships between the two cultures and peoples, in particular through education. Even though continuing funds are not available in the way they are from other countries for target languages, this moral support, previously absent for so long, has invigorated teachers of Indonesian language and culture in Australia.

No major language-teaching venture in Australia has been successful without the assistance of the home country. Japan, China, Germany, and France, for example, have all invested substantially in the development of cultural institutions for teaching their languages overseas. This support is no mere gesture of goodwill. It is a carefully considered investment. The government of the home country usually involves private institutions in that country, sharing the costs and the long-term benefits. China's Confucius Institutes, jointly funded and run by local universities and Hanban, a Chinese government body, are a recent example of an overseas governmental cultural institution teaching their languages overseas. Fortunately, Indonesia is now realising that they need to follow suit if their language and culture is to be more widely known and understood, and to play an important role internationally.

Conclusion

We cannot look at the state of Indonesian language programs from only one perspective. First of all, education involves politics. As domestic politics and political relationships between countries change, so language education changes. Secondly, at least in Australia, language education is governed by national policies and initiatives.

There are additional factors that influence the changing patterns of language education. National politics, global political trends, funding, the status of the language, and stakeholders' contributions and responses all play a significant role in language education. Often, when trying to grapple with these shifting circumstances, we tend to investigate only one aspect and not the full situation. Because the decline of Indonesian language teaching in Australia has become a major concern, it is critical that we see these challenges from within our own domain first, focusing not only on the external factors but, more importantly, on ourselves. Have we examined the system sufficiently critically? Can we respond by working in a smarter manner? How can we do things differently? Indonesian has been taught in Australia for more than half a century. Its popularity has fluctuated, but now the situation is serious. We cannot risk having no plan and taking no urgent action; new strategies need to be explored within existing constraints. When all concerned educators of language or area study, at secondary and tertiary level, form a united front, presenting arguments in a strategic and coherent manner, their voices may be heard more clearly.

It is important that Australia does not waste time arguing over language policy, for example choosing between European and Asian languages. Australia must plan its future in the light of its needs and global trends. Just which languages are prioritised can change over decades, because the world keeps changing and Australia needs to change with it. This is not to say that language diversity must be eliminated, or that we should turn our backs on Europe in favour of Asia. What it does mean is that some languages, such as Asian languages, need to be assigned priority in order to meet national goals and needs. To achieve optimum results, both governments and academics need to develop an action plan.

The top-down approach taken by government and the bottom-up one of educationalists share some common elements, but there is still a gap between them. The most recent response from below was a national Indonesian language colloquium, held in Perth in February 2011 and organised by that fervent advocate of Indonesian language in Australian universities, Professor David

Hill of Murdoch University, with funding from the Australian Learning and Teaching Council. For three days around 50 Indonesian educators from all over Australia, representing universities, secondary schools, and other institutions, discussed the challenges they face.

Among the recommendations from the group was that more Year 12 Indonesian language students should concurrently enrol in university-level language study. This would enable students to obtain results at first-year level equivalent to 25 per cent of the first-year load. The group also proposed the notion of language entitlement: the principle that language learning is the educational right of every student. A further recommendation was the formation of an Indonesian reference group involving all staff with relevant teaching and research interests, making use of modern communications technology to highlight universities' engagement with Indonesia and the achievements and diversity of Indonesian-related activities, and allowing easy access to both internal and external university communities. Such a project would require strong support from senior administrators in universities. The colloquium also advocated the establishment of a key centre (an Indonesian think tank) to facilitate research on Indonesia and to supervise graduate students, with the aim of producing future scholars to succeed older staff in Australian universities. The group noted that substantial ongoing government support would be required for such a centre to be viable. Other suggestions included a national provider for external Indonesian, a national proficiency rating scale for Indonesian, and a national body for the promotion of Indonesian. All of these concepts reflect the passion and optimism of those attending the colloquium, and their hope for a better future for Indonesian language education in Australian universities.

Whilst this event was constructive, communication remained confined to relevant Indonesian academics. It needs to embrace others, particularly senior decision-makers in universities and government. It is important for policymakers to be actively involved in this kind of forum, to gain insights and to work together to complement discussions on pertinent issues faced by teachers. This would present a rare opportunity to reconcile differing approaches and minimise inefficiency. The collaborative endeavour required would include reconnecting the social sciences with the humanities, where most European languages are located. The survival of language programs at tertiary level must be the common goal. The Brisbane universities (Griffith University, Queensland University of Technology, and the University of Queensland) have formed an alliance called the Language Hub to give students more opportunities to incorporate language studies into their degrees.

The Hub constitutes a recent model of collaboration in language teaching and maximising resources.

This model has been adapted, with some regional universities starting along these lines in late 2013. These regional universities, Charles Darwin, La Trobe, Flinders, Griffith, James Cook, Newcastle, and Murdoch universities, have come up with the solution of adapting more modern technology and shared teaching to language classes with low enrolment, in an attempt to support Asian language teaching and to minimise running costs rather than closing down entire language programs. This group called itself IRU (Innovative Research Universities) with the objective of streamlining cross-institutional enrolments and creating something like the Language Hub in Brisbane. The plan involves, among other things, providing online facilities enabling IRU students to undertake cross-institutional language learning studies, the sharing of teaching resources through online delivery; and formation of an Asia Bound collaboration for country language study. In addition, this initiative provides a platform for raising the profile of language learning and airing related issues within IRU universities; as well as lobbying for changes or clarifications to the AQF[24] if needed.

One thing that needs to be stressed is that the initiative is a positive direction towards rescuing language study at tertiary level. Having said that, this kind of shared curriculum was tried before with RUILI materials and UNSW materials in the 1990s; and also with ANU materials developed by George Quinn, specifically for the Indonesian language. To a certain extent, the idea has worked, but factors such as the sustainability of the program; variation in teachers' approaches, and the provision of financial and technical support are crucial in determining whether this kind of initiative will succeed.

Support from within educational institutions is crucial. Tenured language staff appointments are an absolute requirement. With a stable workforce, language teaching would be more visible, ensuring the survival of programs. In particular, language teachers would have career paths opened up to them. Furthermore, language teaching needs to be recognised as a field like any other academic field. Language teaching staff should be better qualified, and economic disparity removed. It is not enough to engage native or other fluent

---

24 Australian Qualifications Framework, the national policy for regulated qualifications in the Australian education and training system. It incorporates the quality assured qualifications from each education and training sector into a single comprehensive national qualifications framework. Details are available at <http://www.aqf.edu.au/aqf/about/what-is-the-aqf/>, accessed 27 August 2014.

speakers of the target language if they lack appropriate qualifications; this undermines the professionalism of language teaching.

Ideally, the study of languages, including prioritised languages, should be compulsory at all educational levels. This idea may encounter some resistance, as it has in the past, but it should be pursued, particularly at tertiary level, with consistent support from government. Such a commitment would make a potent contribution to Australia's future, not only in achieving economic well-being, but also through intellectual benefits, such as enhanced appreciation and understanding of global society.

Language learning has profound social, political, and cognitive benefits. It nurtures tolerance, it promotes understanding, and it boosts confidence. Language teaching constitutes an immense future investment for Australia. In her speech to the United States Congress on 10 March 2011, the then prime minister Julia Gillard acknowledged Indonesia as one of the recently-emerged major powers. The Liberal prime ministers that followed expressed similar sentiments, with Malcolm Turnbull making it 'a personal foreign policy objective' to strengthen ties with Indonesia in his 2016 Lowy Lecture,[25] and in 2018 Scott Morrison declaring 'the first place a new prime minister visits is Indonesia'.[26] Australia has laid the foundation of an investment in Indonesian studies. To fail to build on that foundation would not merely be a great loss to Australia; it would be a loss from which Australia might never recover.

Acknowledgments

I should like to thank Julia Read, David Reeve, Sue Sheridan, and Paul S. Thomas, who contributed generously of their time and expertise by providing commentary on previous drafts of this article.

---

25 The full text of Turnbull's 2016 Lowy Institute lecture is available at: http://www.malcolmturnbull.com.au/media/2016-lowy-lecture1.
26 Scott Morrison lands in Indonesia for first overseas test. *SBS*, 31 August 2018. Available at <https://www.sbs.com.au/news/scott-morrison-lands-in-indonesia-for-first-overseas-test>.

References

Asia Education Foundation. 2010. 'The current state of Chinese, Indonesian, Japanese and Korean language education in Australian schools: Four languages, four stories'. Available at: https://www.google.com.au/url?sa=t&rct=j&q=&esrc=s&source=web&cd=2&cad=rja&uact=8&ved=0ahUKEwj7n5iR06vMAhXJipQKHbLeCl8QFggiMAE&url=https%3A%2F%2Fdocs.education.gov.au%2Fsystem%2Ffiles%2Fdoc%2Fother%2Fthe_current_state_of_chinese_indonesian_japanese_and_korean_language_education_in_australian_schools.rtf&usg=AFQjCNFiOA9NrabSc0oz5IOrj1PiQX3TWQ&sig2=7sUnYDIzVdx802fjOxeF8g, accessed 26 April 2016.

Asian Studies Council. 1988. *A National Strategy for the Study of Asia in Australia*. Canberra: Australian Government Publishing Service.

Asian Studies Council. 1989. *Asia in Australian Higher Education: Report of the Inquiry into the Teaching of Asian Studies and Languages in Higher Education*. Sydney: University of New South Wales.

Asian Studies Council. 2005. *After the Tsunami: The Urgency of Maximising Australia's Asia Knowledge: Renewing and Repositioning a National Asset*. Canberra: Asian Studies Association of Australia.

Aspinal, E. 2009. 'Lost in translation'. *Inside Story*. Available at: http://inside.org.au/lost-in-translation, accessed 24 February 2009.

Australian Council of State School Organizations and Australian Parents Council. 2007. 'Attitudes to study of languages in Australian schools'. Available at: http://www.acsso.org.au/files/1214/4842/3589/attitudestowardsthestudyoflanginausschools.pdf, accessed 26 April 2016.

Baldauf, R. B. 2005. 'Language planning and policy research: An overview'. In *Handbook of research in second language teaching and learning*, edited by E. Hinkel. Mahwah, NJ: Lawrence Erlbaum. pp. 957–970.

Baldauf, R. B. & White, P. 2010. 'Participation and collaboration in tertiary language education in Australia'. In *Languages in Australian Education*, edited by A. J. Liddicoat & A. Scarino. Newcastle upon Tyne: Cambridge Scholars. pp. 41–69.

Carr, J. & Pauwels, A. 2006. *Boys and Foreign Language Learning: Real Boys Don't Do Languages*. New York: Palgrave Macmillan.

CILT. 2006. 'ELAN: Effects on the European economy of shortages of foreign language skills in enterprise'. Available at: http://ec.europa.eu/languages/policy/strategic-framework/documents/elan_en.pdf, accessed 26 April 2016.

CMAX Advisory. 2013. 'Engagement with Asia under the Abbott government'. Available at: http://www.cmaxadvisory.com.au/public-policy-briefs/engagement-with-asia-under-the-abbott-government, accessed 26 April 2016

Davies, G. 1993. 'Valuing the other: Institutional investment in Asian studies'. *Asian Studies Review* 16 (3), pp. 9–16.

Department of Foreign Affairs and Trade (DFAT). 2004. *Australia and the Colombo Plan 1949–1957*. Barton, A.C.T.: Department. of Foreign Affairs and Trade,

Firdaus. 1994. 'Teaching Indonesian at tertiary and secondary levels: Constructive planning for a coordinated future'. Available at: http://wacana.usc.edu.au/1/firda.html, accessed 25 April 2016.

Fitzgerald, S. 1995. 'Ethics and business'. In *Living with Dragons: Australia Confronts its Asia Destiny*, edited by G. Sheridan. Sydney: Allen and Unwin. pp. 7–66.

Foulcher, K. 1990. 'Indonesian studies in search of a model'. *Asian Studies Review* 13 (3), pp. 3–6.
Garnaut, R. 1989. *Australia and the Northeast Asian Ascendancy: Report to the Prime Minister and Minister for Foreign Affairs and Trade*. Canberra: Australian Government Publishing Service.
Goot, M. 1990. 'Speaking in tongues: Survey of opinion on the teaching of Asian languages'. *Australian Cultural Studies* 9, pp. 117–125.
Henderson, D. 1999. 'The Rudd Report: An anatomy of an education reform'. Unpublished PhD thesis. Griffith University, Australia.
Henderson, D. 2003. 'Meeting the national interest through Asia literacy: An overview of the major stages and debates'. *Asian Studies Review* 2 (1), pp. 23–53.
Henderson, D. 2007. 'A strategy cut short: The NALSAS strategy for Asian languages in Australia'. *Electronic Journal of Foreign Language Teaching* 4 (suppl. 1), pp. 4–22. Available at: http://e-flt.nus.edu.sg/v4sp12007/henderson.pdf, accessed 16 May 2007.
Hill, D. 2005. 'They are not talking our languages'. *The Australian*, 20 July, p. 18.
Hill, D. 2007. 'Return to Asian studies'. *The Australian*, 23 May, p. 38.
Hill, D. 2011. 'Indonesian in Australian universities: A discussion paper'. *Proceedings of the National Colloquium on the Future of Indonesian in Australian Universities, Murdoch University, Perth, 9–11 February*, pp. 1–33. Available at: http://altcfellowship.murdoch.edu.au/Docs/ALTC_NTF__Discussion_Paper.pdf, accessed 4 March 2011.
Hill, D. 2012. 'Indonesian language in Australian universities: Strategies for a stronger future. National Teaching Fellowship Final Report', 2nd edition. Murdoch University, April 2012. Available at: http://www.murdoch.edu.au/ALTC-Fellowship/_document/final_report/ALTC_NTF_Indonesian_in_Australian_Universities_FINAL_REPORT.pdf
Hooper, B. 1995. 'Asian studies in Australia: Trends and prospects'. *Asian Studies Review* 18 (3), pp. 71–80.
Hunter, I. 1991. 'Personality as a vocation: The politic rationality of the humanities'. In *Accounting for the Humanities: The Language of Culture and the Logic of Government*, edited by I. Hunter. Brisbane: Griffith University Institute of Cultural Policy Studies. pp. 7–66.
Jeffrey, R. 2004. 'Languishing languages'. *The Australian*, 20 October, p. 38.
Jeffrey, R. 2005. 'ASAA's 2004 language survey'. *Asian Currents*, February, p. 1. Available at: http://asaa.asn.au/asian-currents-html-archives/2005/asian-currents-05-02.html, accessed 25 April 2016.
Kohler, M. & Mahnken, P. 2010. 'The current state of Chinese, Indonesian, Japanese and Korean language education in Australian schools: Four languages, four stories'. Available at: http://apo.org.au/resource/current-state-chinese-indonesian-japanese-and-korean-language-education-australian-schools, accessed 25 April 2016.
Lane, B. 2014. 'Indonesia the go-to nation for Colombo'. *The Australian (Higher Education)* 21 May, p. 33.
Leal, R. B, Bettoni, C & Malcolm, I. G. 1991. *Widening Our Horizons: Report of the Review of the Teaching of Modern Languages in Higher Education*. Canberra: Australian Government Publishing Service.
Lian, A. 1997. 'Australian LOTE policies and universities'. In *Globalisation and Regional Communities, Geoeconomics: Implications for Australia*, edited by D H McMillen. Toowomba: University of Southern Queensland Press. pp. 362–367.

Liberal Party of Australia. 2013. 'The Coalition's policy for a New Colombo Plan'. Available at: http://www.liberal.org.au/latest-news/2013/08/30/coalitions-policy-new-colombo-plan, accessed 20 January 2014.

Lindsey, T. 2007. 'Relaxed, complacent and risible'. *Australian Literary Review*, 7 March, pp. 18–19.

Lindsey, T. 2010. '"Preposterous caricatures": Fear, tokenism, denial and the Australia-Indonesia relationship'. *Dialogue* 29 (2), pp. 31–43. Available at: http://www.apo.org.au/research/price-fear-dialogue-2010-volume-29-number-2, accessed 16 September 2010.

Lo Bianco, J. 1987. *The National Policy on Languages*. Canberra: Australian Government Publishing Service.

Lo Bianco, J. 1995. 'Asian or multicultural: Does Australia have to choose?' *Journal of the Catholic Education Office* 14 (1), pp. 14–20.

Lo Bianco, J. 2003. 'A site for debate, negotiation and contest of national identity: Language policy in Australia'. Available at: http://www.coe.int/t/dg4/linguistic/Source/LoBiancoEn.pdf, accessed 23 February 2010.

McDonald, H. 2007. 'A long-term relationship requires ability to speak'. *Sydney Morning Herald*, 28 April. Available at: http://www.smh.com.au/news/world/a-longterm-relationship-requires-ability-to-speak/2007/04/28/1177459990931.html, accessed 20 April 2009.

McHoul, A. L. & Mey, J. L. 1990. 'On the limits of language planning: Class, state and power'. In *Language Planning and Education in Australia and the South Pacific*, edited by R. B. Baldauf & A. Luke. Clevedon, Avon: Multilingual Matters. pp. 25–46.

McLaren, A. 2008. 'Asian language enrolments in Australian higher education, 2006–07'. Unpublished report dated 10 April 2008. Available at: https://www.griffith.edu.au/__data/assets/pdf_file/0008/145790/ASAA-Language-Stats-Summative-Report-April-2008.pdf, accessed 26 April 2016.

Meld Magazine. 2012. 'Australians falling behind in Asian language education'. Available at: http://www.meldmagazine.com.au/2012/02/australians-language-education/, accessed 23 February 2014.

Menzies Research Centre. 2013. 'Coalition commits to New Colombo Plan'. Available at: http://www.menziesrc.org/news/item/new-colombo-plan-paper-and-policy, accessed 20 January 2014.

Ozolins, U. 1993. *The Politics of Language in Australia*. Cambridge: Cambridge University Press.

Pennycook, A. 1989. 'The concept of method, interested knowledge, and the politics of language teaching'. *TESOL Quarterly* 23 (4), pp. 589–618.

Perpitch, N. 2009. 'Language funds risks being lip service'. *The Weekend Australian*, 27–28 June, p. 2.

Perry, L. 2004. 'Language cuts will be costly'. *The Australian*, 8 June, p. 25.

Pierce, B. N. 1989. 'Towards a pedagogy of possibility in the teaching of English internationally'. *TESOL Quarterly* 23 (3), pp. 401–420.

Read, J. 2002. 'Innovation in Indonesian language teaching: An evaluation of the TIFL tertiary curriculum materials'. Ph.D. thesis, University of Wollongong, Australia.

Rudd, K. M. 1994. *Asian Languages and Australia's Economic Future*. Canberra: National Languages and Literacy Institute of Australia.

Sartono, A. 2007. 'Understanding Indonesia: Does it really matter?' Available at: http://wacana.usc.edu.au/asile/agus_sartono.pdf. Accessed 26 April 2016.

Shanzer, M. 1996. 'Goals for Asian language teaching in Australian universities'. *Babel* 31 (2), pp. 16–23.

Slaughter, Y. 2007. 'The rise and fall of Indonesian in Australian schools: Implications for language policy and planning'. *Asian Studies Review* 31, pp. 301–332.

Sydney Morning Herald. 2014. 'Tony Abbott is testing the friendship with Indonesia'. Available at: http://www.smh.com.au/comment/smh-editorial/tony-abbott-is-testing-the-friendship-with-indonesia-20140608-zs14b.html#ixzz372Mx0OSy, accessed 10 July 2014.

Tamatea, L. 2002. 'Indonesian language education and the limitation of tolerance'. In *Worlds of Learning: Globalization and Multicultural Education*, edited by S Garbutcheon. Altona, Australia: Commonground Publishing. pp. 169–185.

Viviani, N. 1992. 'Uni fails in educating Australia for Asia'. *Australian Campus Review Weekly*, 7–13 May, p. 4.

Wesley, M. 2013. 'Australia-Indonesia diplomatic crisis: this, too, will pass'. Available at: http://www.theguardian.com/commentisfree/2013/nov/23/australia-indonesia-diplomatic-crisis-this-too-will-pass, accessed 25 April, 2014.

White, P. & Baldauf Jr., R. B. 2006. 'Re-examining Australia's tertiary language programs: A five year retrospective on teaching and collaboration'. St Lucia, QLD, Australia: Collaborative Structural Reform Research Project, UQ.

Worsley, P. 1994. *Unlocking Australia's Language Potential. Profiles of 9 Key Languages in Australia. Vol. 5: Indonesian/Malay*. Canberra: National Languages and Literacy Institute of Australia.

Wykes, O. & King, M. G. 1968. *Teaching of Foreign Languages in Australia*. Hawthorn, VIC: Australian Council for Educational Research.

Zifirdaus, I. 1988. 'Factors inhibiting the development of Indonesian language study'. *Babel* 23 (3), pp. 15–18.

Chapter 2

EARLY EXPLORATIONS OF THE MALAY LANGUAGE IN AUSTRALIA

Paul S. Thomas

Monash University

The extensive history of the Malay language in Australia stretches across nearly three centuries of human contact between the people of the Australian continent and those of the Malay Archipelago. It makes the various forms of the Malay language that have been used in Australia arguably its oldest foreign language, bringing into question whether it should be considered 'foreign' at all.

This chapter traces the early presence of the language in Australia identifying four key areas of purpose: first, as a means of traditional trade and negotiating peace between Indigenous Australians and Indonesian traders, 1780-1906; second, as a lingua franca in Malay towns in northern Australia, 1860s-early 20th century; third, as a tool to promote commerce during the depression, 1930s; and fourth, as a tool for intelligence gathering and propaganda in the Second World War, 1940s. While the presence of the language was continuous, its standing amongst European Australians ebbed and waned. It was commonly dependent upon shifts in cultural, economic and political circumstances. This resulted in the language being viewed variously as an asset in economic expansion and regional security or conversely as a language of the coolie, the pearl diver, or the houseboy with little use other than for the issuing of orders.

For the language to be seen as strategic and of academic curiosity, Australia needed to take an independent view of itself and of its place in the region. This was not something European Australia felt comfortable doing. Australia's

19th and early 20th century vision of the region was filtered by British interests in Southeast Asia and its own aspirations to be accepted as a European culture, part of an Empire whose heart was well beyond the islands to the north. Nevertheless, when under pressure, the country sought out new relationships with its near neighbour and relied on intermediaries, interpreters of culture and language, to assist. These were often drawn from adventurers and enlightened individuals, who were somehow attracted to the culture of the islands and pioneered the relationship. They had, however, already been preceded by Indigenous Australians who had established their relationship with the peoples of the archipelago before European settlement.

The Arrival of the Trepangers and Their Language

The coming of the Malay language to Australia is linked to the arrival of various ethnic groups from the archipelago recorded in Australian history as Indians, Malays, Macassans, Koepangers, Manilamen[1] and Indonesians. This variety of nomenclature, to some extent, contributes to the lack of a clear identity for Indonesians or Malaysians in Australian history. Consequently, their presence in many accounts of Australian history can be blurred before the Second World War, particularly in contrast to other Asian nations such as the Chinese, Japanese and Indians. They are, however, the oldest of any non-Aboriginal people on the continent with Aboriginal rock art of Indonesian praus being dated to at least the 17th century (Taçon et al., 2010).

While this early contact may have been sporadic, the arrival of the trepang[2] fishing fleets in the mid-18th century (see Macknight, 2011) to the land they referred to as Marege and Kayu Jawa[3] brought regular contact which enabled an exchange of both goods and knowledge. The complexities of these exchanges and the need to negotiate access to Aboriginal labour and lands necessitated the use of either a common language or of interpreters who had experience with both cultures. It therefore points to the trepangers from the eastern archipelago as the first conveyers of Asian languages to Australia, including Malay and the Makasar language.[4]

---

1   Though the term 'Manilamen' was coined for migrant workers from the Philippines, there was often some confusion in its use and at times it could be used for any person from the archipelago.
2   A marine invertebrate also known as sea cucumber.
3   'Marege' north east coast of Australia, 'Kayu Jawa' north west coast of Australia.
4   Although the home port of the fleets was Makassar, the crews were commonly of diverse ethnic and linguistic backgrounds.

The role of the Malay and Makasar language in Aboriginal cultures on the north coast is still to be fully determined, but in addition to their use with the trepangers and traders, the languages were of some use as a lingua franca between different indigenous linguistic groups or with anyone considered an outsider (Urry and Walsh, 1981; Harris, 1986, 2007). It is unfortunate that most of the linguistic studies in Arnhem Land were not started until the 1970s, over 60 years after the fishery had been closed and more than a hundred years after European interference in the trade. This makes it difficult to ascertain changing patterns in the use of the languages between groups, their use by whole clans as opposed to individual Aboriginal or Indonesian interpreters, and the geographical spread of the languages over time.

It is possible that the use of Malay was more frequent in first contact situations and where the crews of the praus were mixed. Use of the Makasar language could have grown as more long-standing and personal relationships developed with the crew and *nakhoda*,[5] captains of the vessels, from Makassar itself. What can be established is that from the remnants of Austronesian languages in Arnhem Land languages, the Makasar language is more dominant over forms of Malay. Nevertheless, within the Yolngu dialects, the Malay influence is evident in words Australian school students would recognise from their Indonesian texts e.g. *babi*, pig, *kelapa*, coconut, *jalan*, path, *perahu*, boat, *balanda*, white men, derived from 'Dutchman' (based on Evans, 1992).[6]

In determining individual skills and the emergence of Indigenous interpreters, it is clear that there were different degrees of contact with the trepangers that would have influenced language ability considerably. First, there were those individuals who initiated contact with the outsiders. If patterns were followed similar to contact with Europeans, individuals would have come forward to initiate communication, they would not have needed to be a chief or headmen, but their association with the outsiders would have afforded them a new status in their cultural group and as a consequence assisted the transfer of language.

Second were Aboriginal women who were taken as wives or partners, sometimes forcibly, by the trepangers. This appears to have been a major point of conflict between Indonesians and Aborigines, but there are also indications that peaceful agreements were reached and of relationships that were more formalised (see Swain, 1993). In these cases, a greater degree of language

---

5   A title given to captains of the prau.
6   Spelling has been adjusted to contemporary Indonesian spelling.

exchange is likely to have taken place, multilingualism being a common characteristic of indigenous cultures in Australia.

The third group requiring higher levels of language were those who regularly worked with the trepangers on processing the catch. Finally, the fourth, and perhaps most significant group, were those who not only worked with the trepangers but sailed with them to the islands including the port of Makassar.[7] It is not clear what the motivation of those who invited the Aborigines on-board was, as we cannot assume the trepangers were simply in need of labour. What can be stated with some certainty is that those who made the journey to Makassar and stayed in the sultanate over one or more seasons would have greatly enhanced their ability to act as interpreters. On their return to Marege, they would have had the potential to act as interpreters and cultural intermediaries, which would have been extremely valuable in the negotiation of peace, cultural exchange, and trade between the two peoples. Concepts, which would have been too abstract to comprehend before their journey would have been much easier to put into words after witnessing everyday life in Makassar. These Aborigines were potentially the major source for Malay and Makasserese words entering the languages of northern Australia. The status afforded to them as travellers, the affinity with their own culture, and their ability to explain words to others based on their experiences, creating an easier path for cultural and linguistic influence to flow.

At the turn of the 19th century, European, Asian, and Aboriginal history would intersect off the north coast of the continent. The discovery of the trepang trade by Europeans added an additional layer of complexity to the communication as the industry's potential was considered as the basis for British expansion to the north coast of the continent.

European Entry into the Trepang Trade

When Mathew Flinders departed Sydney in 1802 on his historic journey to circumnavigate the continent, he took on-board as his interpreter an Aboriginal man known as Bungaree (see Smith, 1992). Flinders had no idea of the geographical limitations of Bungaree's language, but he was aware that there would be times where he would need to negotiate a peaceful passage through native lands. However, before his journey's end Flinders

---

7   See Russell, 2004 for a general review of Indonesian and Indigenous interactions. The earliest record of Aboriginal sailors comes from the diary of Collet Barker who reported Aborigines on board praus visiting Fort Wellington in 1828 (in Mulvaney and Green, 1992, p. 159).

found the need to call on another crewmember to act as his interpreter for a completely unexpected encounter with a people whose presence in Australia the British had no knowledge. The crewmember was Flinders' Javanese cook known as Williams. We know little about Williams; either how long Flinders had known him or where he boarded the ship. However, his ability in English and Malay together with Flinders' previous voyages suggests he may have been born or spent some time in Cape Town (Thomas, 2013, p. 72), where the Dutch had brought servants and exiles from their East Indies colonies.[8]

Over two days Williams acted as Flinders' interpreter while he met with six of the *nakhoda* from the fleet. Through these discussions, Flinders was able to produce a detailed report on the nature of their business in the northern waters, which then became a major reference for all interested in the industry for nearly a century. In terms of the presence of the Malay language in Australia, it is the first extensively recorded conversation in the language and confirmed the use of Malay amongst the trepangers as a lingua franca.[9]

In 1818 the trepangers were once again encountered off the north coast of Australia, this time by an expedition led by Phillip Parker King to the North West Coast. Bungaree also accompanied this expedition as a cultural intermediary and although there was no Malay interpreter, King was provided with two official letters, one translated into Javanese and the other into Malay (see Figure 1). The letters requested safe passage and explained the nature of the expedition. Unfortunately, they did not prove useful when approaching the praus:

> Our anchor was weighed immediately, and we steered towards their sternmost vessel, in order to communicate with her, and to show her a letter with which we had been kindly provided by Sir Thomas Stamford Raffles, written in the Malay language, and explanatory of our occupation. On running alongside the proa, the letter was displayed, but they appeared frightened and unwilling to bring to, and repeatedly pointed towards the headmost proa in which their Rajah sailed.[10]

When eventually they were able to make direct contact with the Indonesians after enticing them on board, King and his men had little alternative but to

---

8 The British had taken control of the Cape from the Dutch in 1795 but would return it to the Dutch in 1802 after the peace agreement between France and Britain.

9 Thomas (2013) provides a breakdown of each of the exchanges that Williams interpreted for and a summary of the information obtained.

10 King, 1825, 16 April 1818.

communicate via a few words of Malay augmented with a good deal of sign language:

> My inquiries were made partly by signs and partly by a few terms in the Malay language that we had collected from Captain Cook,[11] and from Labillardiere's account of D'Entrecasteaux's voyage. Aer (water) was among the foremost of our inquiries, to which we added the terms for pigs, sheep, fowls, and coconuts, (vavee, doomba, mannu, and nieu). Everything but water was plentiful and could be supplied by paying for them in rupees or bartering them for gunpowder. On repeating the question for water, their constant reply was, trada aer! trada aer! (no water, no water). No misunderstanding could have taken place, for on our inquiry, thinking it was for present use, they brought us some to drink.[12]

The failure of the letters was in part due to the lack of knowledge by the Europeans about the diversity of the written form in the Archipelago. The Malay letter was written in Jawi, a modified Arabic script, a script rarely used in the Eastern archipelago at the time. Literacy in any script was also limited, though we know from Flinders' encounter that there were those on-board who could write; in the meeting between Flinders and one of the *nakhoda* Pu' Baso', his son recorded the origins of Flinders' vessel. While not written in New South Wales, the letter represents the oldest use of a Malay translation in Australia (see Figure 1). Both Javanese and Malay letters are now preserved in the State Library of New South Wales.

European contact with the trepangers came to a height with attempts to establish a northern settlement, which could act as both a military garrison and trading post. The first attempt occurred in 1824 on Melville Island and was known as Fort Dundas. From the British perspective, the primary motivation for the settlement was defensive,[13] nevertheless many earlier settlers in New South Wales had much greater hopes that such a settlement might stimulate development of the north and provide trading links to India.

Whatever the motivation, the settlement's initial viability would rely on attracting Indonesian traders along with the fishing fleets. Governor Brisbane of New South Wales reminded the captain commanding the expedition to Melville Island, Morris Barlow, of the 'necessity of not molesting these

---

[11] Cook had called at Batavia (Jakarta) in November 1770 after charting the East Coast of New South Wales and compiled a short word list in Malay.

[12] King, 1825, 24 October 1818.

[13] Concerns were primarily about possible Dutch or French claims on New Holland's north coast.

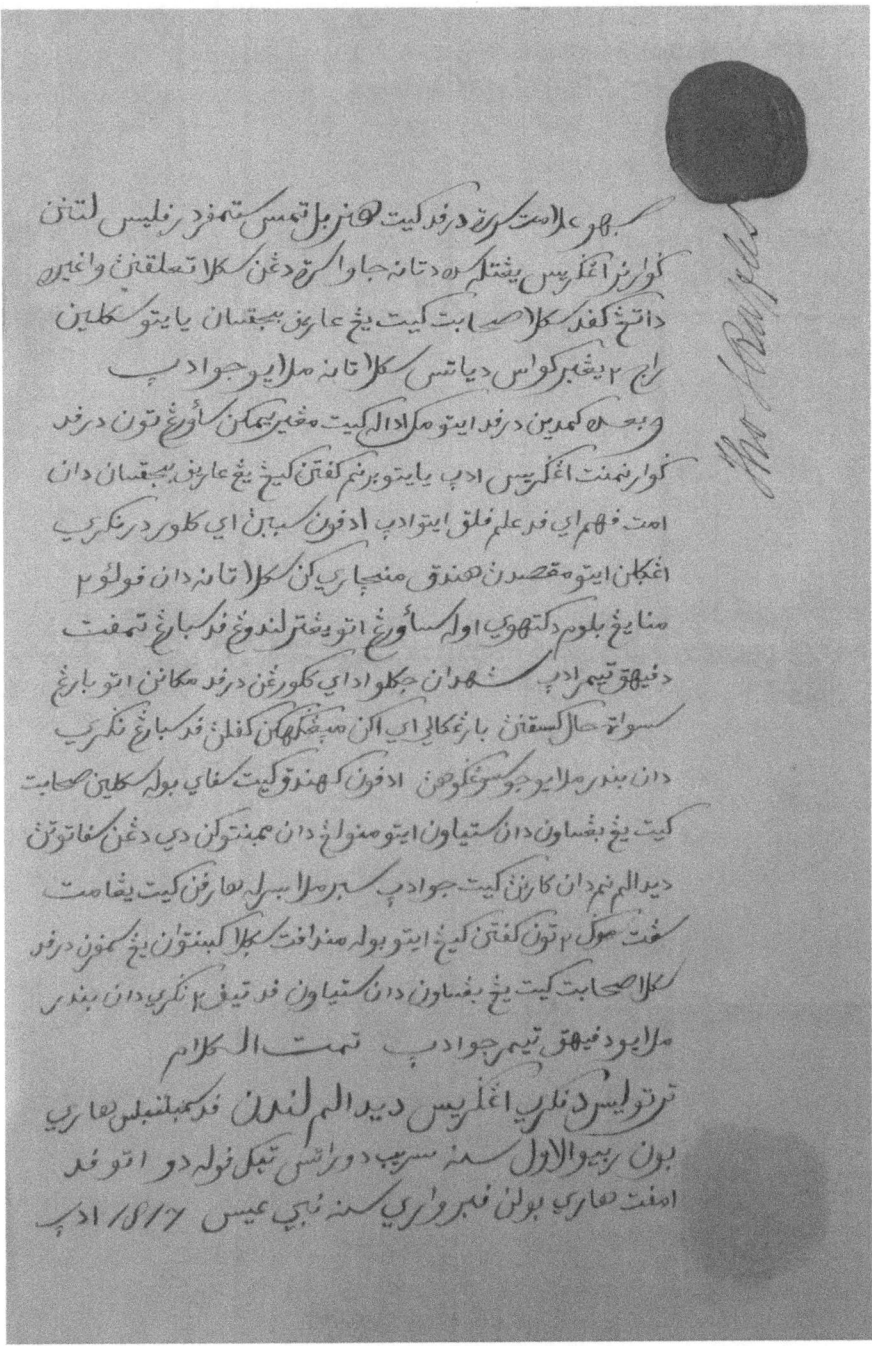

Figure 1: Document of safe conduct written in Malay in 1817 and carried by Phillip Parker King.
Dixson Library, State Library of NSW [DLMSQ 303]. Photo: Paul S. Thomas.

traders'.[14] Brisbane understood that the settlement was likely to be in competition with Dutch trade and wished to prove British superiority in the treatment of the 'Indians': 'let the Indian taste on the shores of New Holland for the first time in his life the sweets of private prosperity ... let the liberty of the settlement be laid open to all'.[15]

He also instructed the new settlers on to how they should interact with the 'Indians': 'learn their language, their customs, their usages, their institutions and pay a respect to them all'.[16] Brisbane was nevertheless clear about the superior nature of the British civilisation, considering the 'Indians' of the Eastern Archipelago as 'half civilised'.[17] Seen from Brisbane's perspective, this was a positive trait, the inference being that these were people with potential, they were people the British could do business with and the aim was to welcome them to the British Empire's great civilising project. It would be over a century before another government official would call on Australians to learn the Malay language.

While Fort Dundas was destined to fail due to its poor location,[18] two further attempts would be made: Fort Wellington in 1827, and Port Essington in 1838, both on the Cobourg Peninsula. In each case, it was clear from the appointment of Malay interpreters that the primary trading language would need to be Malay rather than the Makasar language (See Harris, 1985; Thomas, 2013). Malay was the language that the British had experience with; British colonies on the Malay Peninsula and Sumatra had used it since their inception. Additionally, it was considered the principal trading language of the archipelago and there were already British officers learning it in a variety of posts as far afield as Sri Lanka.

At Fort Wellington the Malay Interpreter Oodeen was appointed Government Interpreter, having arrived in Sydney as a convict with his family from Sri Lanka in 1817.[19] Over the two years that Oodeen was present in the settlement, he interpreted on a number of occasions and had fully expected to continue to live there permanently with his family; however,

---

14   Letter to Cpt. Morris Barlow from Gov Thomas Brisbane Government House Parramatta, 14 August 1824. Colonial Secretary's papers, in Reel 6013; 4/3512, NSWSR.
15   Colonial Secretary's papers, in Reel 6013; 4/3512, NSWSR.
16   Colonial Secretary's papers, in Reel 6013; 4/3512, NSWSR.
17   Colonial Secretary's papers, in Reel 6013; 4/3512, NSWSR.
18   The trepang fleets generally sailed much further to the east.
19   See Thomas (2012) for a full account of Oodeen's life and role as an interpreter in New South Wales.

the settlement was abandoned in 1829. At Port Essington George Windsor Earl, a linguist who had originally come to Western Australia to be a wheat farmer, was appointed (see Reece, 1992; Jones, 1994). Although he travelled regularly from the settlement, he was a champion for northern development. Alongside his interpreting, he was also interested in Aboriginal custom and provided the only description of Aboriginal use of the Makasar language at that time (Earl, 1846, p. 244).

It was also at Port Essington in 1845 that Ludwig Leichardt, the German explorer, completed his 4,000 km overland trek from Queensland and coincidently provided a description of the Malay spoken on board the schooner *Heroine* which called there. He had boarded the schooner at Port Essington for his return to Sydney and found on board a mixed crew, many of whom were Indonesians. Intrigued by their language, he described it in the following way:

> I had several times opportunity of hearing the Malay language spoken in a passion, and I was struck with its power and yet with its melodious flow. Spoken by an intelligent man possessing a good organ, it must be a beautiful language. I remember well the impression which the Italian language spoken by the Romans made on me-it was soft and yet powerful. The Malay is not quite so soft, seems not to be quite so rich in vowels as the Italian, but yet rich enough to be melodious.[20]

The description is a rich and rare description of the language in colonial Australia and many learners of Indonesian/Malay today would relate to this first impression of the language.

Ultimately, what kind of future Malay might have had in these settlements is hypothetical as by 1849 the last of the settlements, Port Essington, was abandoned. This was in part due to a lack of support, sickness, poor planning and because the British saw no further defensive role for a garrison on the north coast (Powell, 2000). By the middle of the 19th century Britain had declared its sovereignty over the whole of the Australian continent and there was no one to challenge it in the region. The New South Wales colonists' dreams of a northern port to link India and the archipelago with Australia were of no consequence, nor were the promises made to the trepangers and traders. The trade once again became the sole business of the Aborigines and the peoples of the archipelago.

As a consequence of the closing down of the trading posts, Australian colonists turned away from the idea of communicating directly with their near

---

20   Leichhardt in Webster, 1986, p. 54.

neighbour. The islands became the 'Far East', exotic, and distant from the burgeoning southern settlements. The failure of the settlements also ended the opportunity for the Malay language to have any major role in the Australian colonies. Nonetheless, by the early 1860s small permanent settlements did begin to emerge across the north, not as trading posts but based on specific local resources including pearls, sugar cane, and grazing. The Malay language would find a home here but only at the very fringe of European settlement.

Bahasa 'Coolie' and the Language of the Australian Kampong

In the mid-19th century, thousands of Chinese gold seekers began to arrive in southern Australia's great Gold Rush. Consequently, unease began to develop amongst other miners that the Chinese, through their hard labour, might now be considered overly competitive. This, in turn, resulted in pressure for restrictions to be placed on the number of Chinese arriving.[21] As these restrictions began to be applied, a seemingly contradictory move in the north of the continent took place that sought out Asian labour to overcome the resistance of Europeans to working in the tropical regions of Australia.[22]

During the 1860s to early 1880s a series of towns sprung up in the tropical north including Cossack, 1863, and Broome, 1883, on the west coast, Darwin, 1869, and Normanton, 1867 on the north coast and Thursday Island, 1877, Cairns, 1876, Innisfail, 1879, and Mackay, 1862, along the east coast (see Figures 2 & 3). All of these towns would acquire within a short period of their establishment an associated Malay kampong[23] or what the Europeans referred to as Malay Towns. The men[24] living in these kampongs would work as domestic servants and in a variety of industries, including sugar cane, mining, pearling and fishing.

---

21 A tax on every Chinese landed had already been imposed by 1857 in the state of Victoria.

22 The Northern Territory also began to apply a head tax in 1886. This was partly due to obligations under an 1880 conference of colonial premiers, but other Asian races such as the Malays were not included.

23 Some of these 'kampongs' were no more than simple work camps, but in the towns mentioned they existed for a time as distinct features of the town.

24 Early records of Indonesian women on the Australian mainland are rare; however, in what is now the Australian territory of the Cocos Islands, many women were employed in the 19th century. Their presence ensured that these kampongs would become a permanent feature of the islands' life, as would the Cocos Malay language (See Adelaar, 1996).

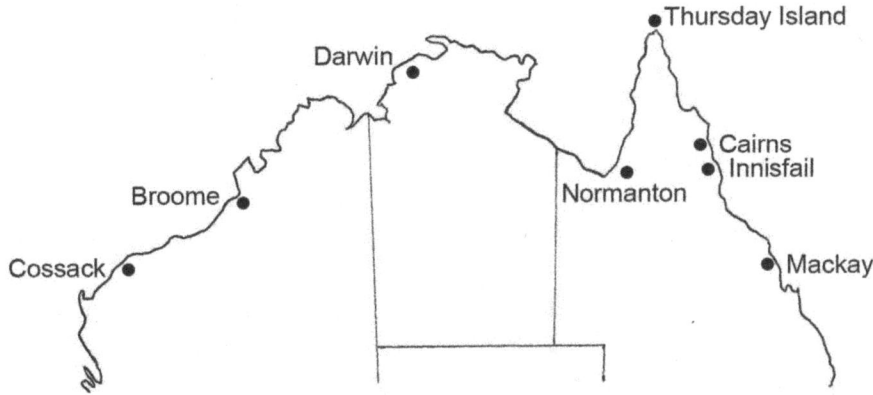

Figure 2: Malay quarters or 'Malay towns' were located in a number of northern Australian settlements in the 19th and early 20th centuries. While these communities on the mainland faded away, Malay communities established on the Cocos Islands and Christmas Island continue today.
Map: Paul S. Thomas.

Figure 3: Malay Town, Cairns 1922.
Reproduced with permission from Cairns Historical Society.

With the expansion of the pearling industry, Aboriginal and Indonesian/ Malay pearlers were joined by Filipinos, Melanesians and, most significantly, the Japanese. The languages that accompanied this inflow of nations no doubt made communication difficult at times, but several linguistic solutions began to arise which included pidgin Englishes, sometimes leading to creoles, and the dominant lingua franca of the archipelago, Malay, which produced its own pidgins. The Malay Towns were obvious settings for language exchange, as they often became the default residence for all those that did not fit into the categories of European, Chinese or Japanese. Malay was well adapted to being picked up, moulded, and used as the speakers saw fit, as it had served this purpose for centuries across the archipelago. Now it had become Australian frontier language. The *Northern Territory Times and Gazette* of 1883 in its report on the population of the Gulf town of Normanton stated that 'the remaining coloured races are composed of Malays, Singhalese, African niggers, and Indian Coolies, the Malay language being pretty generally spoken by all these'.[25]

In Broome, a Malay pidgin developed amongst pearlers in the early 1900s and was used by Filipinos, Koreans, local Aborigines and even the Japanese, with whom the Malays sometimes had tense relations. The nature of the Malay pidgin no doubt varied according to the speaker and would have evolved over time. Commenting on the changes that occurred to Malay in Broome, one Japanese diver reported that the main influence before the War was from Koepangers (Timorese) but that after the war Malays[26] arrived, which was confusing because of the similarities in vocabulary. This was no doubt a reference to differences in dialect between the Malay of Timor and the Malay from the west of the archipelago, including Singaporean and peninsula Malay (Hosokawa, 1987). It should be added that some of the European captains of the luggers also learnt Malay, but fundamentally this was the language of the 'coolie'. In the pecking order of the north, Malay occupied a low rung on the ladder. The idea that the language should be the subject of serious study in these communities would have been an odd proposal, though Malay words such as *jalan*, *ikan*, *tuan* (street/walk, fish, master/boss), drifted in and out of most of the population's vocabulary, including the Europeans.

With the federation of Australian states in 1901, the Commonwealth Parliament legislated against the importing of Asian labour. Many Indonesians/Malays returned to their islands, though some exceptions were made notably for those working in the pearling industry. We know little of their concerns about the growing tide of racism in Australia as few letters or diaries appear to have survived. However, in a letter to the editor of the *Advertiser* in 1896,

---

25   Normanton. *Northern Territory Times and Gazette*, 26 May 1883, p. 3.
26   'Malays' here is a reference to those from the eastern archipelago and peninsula Malaya.

a reader using the pseudonym *Orang Malayu*[27] expresses their concerns about the exclusion of Asian labour, if only from an economic point of view:

> Australia at the moment is suffering from a severe attack of anti-colored-labor fever. If this should subside, and it is recognised that tropical Australia can only be developed in the same manner that other tropical countries are developed, the future of Port Darwin will take care of itself, and it will grow into an important coaling station. If the present policy be persevered in our grand harbor will remain empty and grass will continue to flourish in the streets of the capital of the Northern Territory, which is a standing disgrace to Australia. In the meantime it is not right that South Australia should alone pay for the luxury of indulging in racial prejudice.[28]

With few Malay women present in the mainland towns,[29] the remaining Malay community evolved into a mixed community and the grass did indeed flourish in the streets of Port Darwin as predicted. However, new factors began to take hold that would kindle interest in the first formal study of Malay, namely, the expansion of trade and tourism would assist in the ushering in of more modern views concerning the relevancy of language study in Australia.

Signs of Change: 'The Plea' for Eastern Languages

In 1914, on the eve of the outbreak of the First World War and a half a world away, the *Northern Territory Times and Gazette* reviewed a book, *The Malay Manual*, edited by F. H. Freese. The paper encouraged those readers who wished to tour the Malay Archipelago to consider studying the language and it chided those Europeans living in the archipelago who did not:

> The average man limits his vocabulary to hotel uses, and considers that when he is able to say – "Boy! Bring me a small whiskey soda." Boy! Bawa sama sahya [sahaya] tengah whisky soda", his knowledge is complete.[30]

---

27 Literally 'Malay person'. There is no evidence to show the writer is actually Malay, but the letter expresses the dilemma for the Northern Territory if an 'anti-colored-labor' policy is continued.
28 Orang Malayu, [Letter to the Editor] *Advertiser*, 24 April 1896, p. 5.
29 Australia would acquire the Cocos Islands in 1955 and Christmas Island in 1958. Malays were employed on both island groups in the 19th century but, significantly, there was a much greater balance of women and men in these populations compared to the Malay towns of the mainland.
30 News and Notes. *Northern Territory Times and Gazette*, 30 July 1914, p. 18.

The article is interesting in its reference to early tourism to the archipelago, but is perhaps more important for its advocacy of a language that should be taken more seriously.

Just as tourism between the two countries began to develop it was severely hampered by the outbreak of the First World War. However, the exigency of war and the disruption it caused to traditional trading patterns within the British Empire stimulated the debate on the teaching of Asian languages in Australia. Before the War's end, Japanese would be introduced to the University of Sydney and the Royal Military College, Duntroon (Zainu'ddin, 1988), though the situation for Malay was more complex. Formally, the Dutch East Indies was neutral and this should have ruled out any military need for either Dutch or Malay. In reality, this was not quite the case and patrols did venture into the archipelago keen to track German shipping and other activities. Subsequently, this need to gather intelligence necessitated the occasional use of Malay interpreters who could work both independently and in conjunction with other agents.

One mission run out of Thursday Island was assisted by the British Vice Consul at Makassar and employed an interpreter named Batcho Mingo. Mingo lived with the Malay community on Thursday Island until ordered aboard a French warship in October of 1915. He was then transported to Dili, Timor where he joined the Australian destroyer flotilla. During his duty, he was struck down with malaria and typhoid, reported to the Dutch authorities, but still managed to survive the War. After the War, he was given exemption from the Aliens Restriction Act and permitted to settle permanently on Thursday Island in recognition of his service.[31] This was a significant achievement, as many Indonesians working for Australian forces in the Second World War would not be given the same opportunity.

The disruption in Empire trade during the War was to have a more significant influence on the debate for modern languages, as business needed to consider a less Eurocentric emphasis on its commercial interests.

The issue of trade and languages found a natural forum in 1916 at the 13th Australian Chambers of Commerce Conference in Brisbane, where discussions took place concerning promotion of trade with the East. By the end of the conference, the delegates had passed an ambitious motion, moved by the delegate from Newcastle, Major O'Neil, 'that the conference should support a Chair of Eastern Languages in the various universities'.[32] Shortly thereafter,

---

31 National Archives of Australia, A1608 B15/1/1.
32 Chambers of Commerce, the Brisbane Conference. *Adelaide Advertiser*, 19 May 1916.

letters were prepared and sent to the Australian universities informing them of the Chambers' proposal. This was the first call in Australia for a coordinated effort in the teaching of Asian languages and was made all the more remarkable by the list of languages attached to the proposal: Russian, Japanese, Spanish, Dutch, Chinese and Malay.[33]

The inclusion of Malay as a university subject was not a unique idea in the world at the time; it was taught in France by the Ecole National des Langues et Civilisations Orientales Vivantes as early as 1841,[34] at Cornell University in the United States by 1887 – though this program later lapsed – and at the Tokyo Gaikokugo Daigaku in Japan by 1908 (Read, 2002). Naturally, the British and the Dutch also had Malay programs for their colonial civil servants, though not all were taught within a formal academic environment. It was, therefore, a great stimulus to the study of Malay and other Asian languages in Britain when the School of Oriental Studies[35] was founded, coincidentally, in 1916. The School aimed to greatly enhance the education of its colonial administrators and at the same time develop scholarship in the area (Hartog, 1917). Similarly, in the Netherlands, a centre for the education of colonial officers developed within Leiden University and it too developed into a leading centre for the study of languages of the archipelago. Both these universities would be influential in the latter establishment of Indonesian studies in Australia in the 1950s (see Chapter 3, this volume).

Meanwhile, as Australia had no colonies of its own, with the exception of Papua,[36] the possibilities for teaching Malay and other Asian languages would clearly depend on trade. With this in mind, the Dutch Consul General in Melbourne, supported by the Belgian Consul, put their support behind the Chambers of Commerce proposal and likewise sent letters to the universities. When the correspondence arrived at the universities, it was met with mixed reactions. The establishment of university chairs was costly, and while the Chambers' proposal was admirable, there was no indication of possible financial support. The University of Tasmania was quite blunt in their response, passing a motion that acknowledged receipt of the communications, but stating any possibility of such a department 'was out of the question at present'.[37]

---

33 Professorial Board, Melbourne University, 3 August 1916. MUA, Book 10, Nov. 1914 – Aug. 1920.
34 Now the Institut National des Langues et Civilisations Orientales.
35 Since 1938, the School of Oriental and African Studies (SOAS).
36 Papua became an external territory of Australia in 1904 and Australia would take control of German New Guinea in 1914.
37 University Council. *Mercury*, 26 July 1916.

Melbourne University, or more specifically its Professorial Board, gave the proposal more consideration. The Dutch Consul General had pointed out that Dr Lodewyckx, who was already on the university's staff as a lecturer in German but was a native of Belgium, would be a competent teacher of Dutch. The Board agreed and recommended his appointment. As for the other languages, including Malay, the Board resolved to 'call the Council's attention to the increasing need of Education in languages which [are] important especially from the point of view of Australian commerce ... and suggests that the Council should make provision whether by appointment of instructors or otherwise'.[38]

In the midst of some to-ing and fro-ing between committees the idea of a Chair of Eastern Languages seems to have evaporated at Melbourne, but Sydney continued to be interested. It was perhaps inevitable that with no financial support from the government or private institutions, the general proposal for languages was destined to falter. It was not, however, before there was an attempt to stimulate some public debate on the matter.

Supporting the teaching of modern languages, both Eastern and European, the wife of the Governor of South Australia, Lady Galway, presented public lectures in Melbourne and Adelaide in 1916 (see Figure 4). In Melbourne, Lady Galway's lecture was sponsored by the Council of Public Education. The Victorian Minister of Education lent his support by stating, 'if it could be demonstrated that there were remunerative positions in the Federal service or commercial life for men who could speak Russian, Japanese, Spanish or Dutch, there would be no difficulty in establishing classes.'[39]

Malay would not feature in these public debates, though this was possibly due to the belief that Dutch would suffice for the Dutch East Indies. There was also a good deal of ignorance concerning the importance of Malay in the archipelago and Lady Galway undoubtedly needed to highlight those languages which would lend prestige to her cause. Her primary focus was on convincing the universities of the value of teaching of any modern languages.

> Lady Galway's lecture managed to fill the Melbourne Town Hall and appears to have been a major social event with the Governors of Victoria, Tasmania, and South Australia attracting a parade of other dignitaries to listen to 'A Plea for the Teaching of Foreign Languages'. Although Lady Galway was a speaker of French, German, Italian and some Russian, she gave some emphasis to the importance of Eastern languages:

---

38   Professorial Board Minute Book, 3 August 1916. MUA, 97/59.
39   Items of Interest: Foreign Languages. *Argus*, 14 September 1916, p. 9.

Figure 4: Lady Galway, 1915. As wife of the South Australian Governor she was able to pursue her campaign for the teaching of modern languages through public meetings in both Adelaide and Melbourne.
State Library of South Australia, B 62951.

The war had forced us to look ahead. A great and powerful Eastern ally had taken over protion [portion] of trade which was previously in the hands of the enemy. Was not a chair of Oriental languages a pillar of this country's growing edifice [?].[40]

Lady Galway was not without her critics. In an article for the *Argus*, provocatively entitled 'The Cult of Modern Languages',[41] University of Melbourne's classics professor Thomas Tucker dismissed the need to teach languages as part of any formal education, believing such a pursuit to be devoid of any intellectual challenge and best left for private tuition or business colleges: 'it may appear a harsh thing to have said that "intellectually" the mere ability to speak a language amounts to nothing. Yet anyone who has become acquainted with polyglot interpreters, couriers, waiters, and hall porters must realise that observation is true'.[42]

---

40 Foreign Languages. *Argus*, 30 September 1916, p. 20.
41 The Cult of Modern Languages. *Argus*, 7 October 1916, p. 4.
42 The Cult of Modern Languages. *Argus*, 7 October 1916, p. 4.

Arising from the debates and proposals for chairs in Eastern languages, we can see the fundamental factors inhibiting the introduction of Asian languages at the time were a lack of suitable staff, poor immediate demand, a lack of sustained coordinated political support, and a lack of funding. Also evident was the academic conservatism directed at all modern languages, but particularly Asian languages. This opposition was fuelled by an overemphasis on the practical purposes of languages; the focus on trade over cultural and scholarly pursuits. This would become a persistent theme for both Indonesian and other Asian languages.

As an indication of the relative importance of these factors, it should be noted that the University of Sydney's appointment of James Murdoch as a lecturer in Japanese in 1917 was made possible through funding provided by the Department of Defence (Zainu'ddin, 1988). Although the principal motivation for the funding was concern over Japan's growing power in the Pacific, it also has to be seen in the context of the discussions of 1916. Murdoch made reference to the Chambers of Commerce when outlining the purpose of teaching Japanese at the University of Sydney, noting they were interested in 'a number of young men capable of driving bargains and carrying on business in Japan' (Murdoch in Zainu'ddin, p.47, 1988). With funding from the Commonwealth and Murdoch's strong scholarly credentials, any conservative concerns about languages, Eastern or otherwise, appear to have been overcome. A year later, Murdoch would become Australia's first Professor of Oriental Studies.

In the case of Malay, there were no immediate prospects for funding. The patrolling of the maritime border between the Dutch East Indies and Australia was limited, and economic ties lacked any sophistication partly due to British influence on the Australian economy and Britain's presence in Singapore and the Malay Peninsula. Within a decade, however, desperate economic times brought on by the Great Depression would force Australia to look to its near horizon.

The 1930s: An Educational Experiment

Through the 1920s, Australia's limited view of the world was encouraged by the concentration of trade and the close political relationship with the United Kingdom. The Australian Prime Minister of the time, Stanley Bruce, encouraged even further strengthening of the relationship as means of expanding Australia's population and commercial interests. The islands to the north became ever more the exotic fantasy, now witnessed on movie screens through newsreels, and the occasional film. This led to a great ignorance of the changing political landscape in the archipelago. The University of Melbourne's Dr. Lodewyckx remarked in 1930 that 'it is somewhat remarkable that in Australia we disregard almost completely what is happening at our very doors in Java and in the Dutch East Indies generally'.[43]

By the late 1920s, it became clear that Bruce's reliance on Britain for economic development was not succeeding. The Great Depression was a painful experience for most Australians and inflicted a considerable cost on the nation; the pressure to find new trading partners was now constant. The possibilities that lay to the north were enhanced in the 1930s by significant improvements made to transport between Australia and the archipelago through both the introduction of air services[44] and an increase in shipping. This in turn added considerably to the numbers of Australians travelling to the archipelago.

With a renewed interest in trade, it was not surprising that the next proposal for the teaching of Malay would also come from one of the chambers of commerce, though this time at a more provincial level, namely the Perth and Fremantle Chambers of Commerce.[45] Unlike the 1916 proposal, a more regional approach was formulated which would see the language introduced into the technical colleges in Perth and Fremantle, with the University of Western Australia as the examining body (see Klarberg, 1997). The proposal's success was partly due to the Vice Chancellor of the University of Western Australia, H.E Whitfield, who was known as one of the leaders of a particularly progressive period in Western Australian education (Klarberg, 1996). He was optimistic about the potential for Malay, describing the proposed certificate in the language as one which:

> Would be useful for a clerk or commercial traveller or other business man employed trading with the Malay States. Business in the Dutch East Indies and the Malay States was generally conducted in the Malay language whether the speakers were Englishman, Dutchman or members of the other native races.

---

43 Nationalism and Communism, Unrest in the Dutch East Indies. *Argus*, 15 February 1930, p. 7.

44 QANTAS and the Dutch airline KNILM developed services between Australia and Batavia in 1930s, though the Dutch believed Australia was holding back their plans to extend the air service. Report to the Prime Minister, Latham, 1934. A981, 1934-1934, NAA.

45 Perth Technical College, Foreign Language Courses, 1934, in 'Talking Business, Proposed Course in Malay', in 1838-1, UWAA.

I think that everything should be done to equip those who are opening up trade relations with our nearest neighbours in the north with the knowledge of the language most used for business transactions.[46]

While Whitfield expressed great hope for Malay as a language of trade, he appeared to underestimate the difficulty of teaching the language: 'I am informed that the actual number of words in the Malay language is comparatively small.'[47] Perhaps this was reflective of his classical training at the University of Sydney, but a cautionary note appeared in a letter to the University from the Director of Education for the Straits Settlements and the Federated Malay States:

> I might explain that the Malay has a habit of "talking down" to Europeans. His mode of expression to all but the most fluent Europeans is quite different from what it would be to a fellow country-man. The Malay language is highly idiomatic and in talking to Europeans the Malay generally drops the idiom to a very great extent. I might add that it is my opinion practically impossible for anyone to pass the conversational test in Standard III without having had considerable practical experience in conversation with Malays in their own country and indeed the similar test in Standard II presents considerable though not insurmountable difficulty to learners ... [48]

Concerns about what standard the students could hope to reach and what form of Malay was to be taught soon emerged and were taken up by the University's appointed chief examiner, P.K Hazlitt, who thought students were being taught 'Baba Malay'.[49] Hazlitt, a former police commissioner in Kedah on the Malay Peninsula, believed this form of Malay to be ungrammatical and in his opinion should 'be decidedly frowned upon by the examiners for the standards required by the Malayan Governments'.[50] He urged the University 'to set the hallmark of a certificate of competency on this very excellent solution to the Singapore Tower of Babel'.[51] From Hazlitt's comments and the

---

46   'Talking Business', Proposed Course in Malay, 1932. UWAA: 1838-1.
47   Ibid.
48   Director of Education for the Straits Settlements and the Federated Malay States to the University of Western Australia, 4 January 1933. UWAA: 1838-1.
49   The Malay dialect of the *peranakan*, the Chinese Malay mixed race of Malaya.
50   Examiners Report, 19 December 1935. UWAA: 1838-1.
51   Ibid. The reference here is to the use of Malay as a lingua franca between the Chinese, Indians and Malays in Singapore.

correspondence with the education authorities in the Malay States, it is clear that the kind of language the University's chief examiner wanted to be taught was a Malay that would be useful in the Malayan Civil Service.

This view is reinforced when assessing the tasks in the examination where students were requested to translate non-technical reports or petitions from a Malay subordinate. At times, the curriculum drifted even further from Whitfield's broader view of commercial engagement reflecting more a means of communicating with the Malay 'coolie' as the following translation task from the Standard 1 examination illustrates:

> 1. I want the office cleaned properly once a week. It is not enough to sweep it out. You must get some coolies from the town overseer and order them to wash the floor with disinfectant. I will give you a letter to the Overseer on Friday and you can do this job on Saturday morning before the office opens. Do you quite understand? I shall inspect on my arrival in office.[52]

As an indication of the links between Western Australia and the archipelago at the time, the new course engendered some debate in the local press in regards to what should be the preferred form of Malay taught. In a letter to the editor using the pseudonym *Tuan Ingris*,[53] the writer pointed out that there were a number of residents in Perth who had had spent several years in the East Indies and were familiar with various forms of Malay. Offering his opinion:

> I would like to endorse the remarks of previous writers that the teaching should not only be high class Malay but the dialects as spoken by the trading communities in localities widely separated.
>
> ...
>
> But should the customer go into an ordinary shop or "toko", and try to do business in high class Malay, it is quite possible he would have to get an educated Malay to interpret for him, especially if it is a Chinese "toko".[54]

He also called upon the Malay speaking residents of Perth to form a language club where interested parties could learn the different dialects of Malay.

---

52 Malay Examination Standard I, 8 December 1932. UWAA: 1837-1.
53 Literally, 'Master English' or 'Mr. English', here, clearly written by a European Australian.
54 Malay Examination Standard I, 8 December 1932. UWAA: 1837-1.

Materials for teaching Malay were difficult to come by in the 1930s, but Perth Technical College prescribed Shellabear's *Malay-English Dictionary*, first published in 1902, and Khan's (1920) *Malay Self-taught by the Natural Method*. Malay was offered at the College via two levels, Standard I and Standard II, with the second level offering instruction in Malay literature, history and commerce.[55] Given that the curriculum was based on the curriculum of the Malay States, any comments on the Malay found in the Dutch East Indies would have been dependent on the language instructor's experience. This knowledge, however, would have been of little use in the examinations.

The examinations continued into the mid-1930s, but ceased well before the War. The program's failure no doubt related to a number of factors, including the apparent disconnect between the curriculum and the commercial aims for which the program was initiated. The program had also failed to be accepted as a formal area of academic study at the University. The University of Western Australia's role was simply to offer Malay as a subject for public examination; Malay was not even approved as part of a qualifying examination for the University, nor would the University offer it as a standard public examination certificate.

The discontinuation of the program in Western Australia occurred despite continued calls for trade with the Dutch East Indies. In an address to the Sydney Rotary Club in 1933, Mr R.J. Morehead, who had just returned from a trip aboard the trade ship *Nieu Holland*, called for Australia to develop commercial relations with the East, especially the East Indies. He specifically mentioned the link between trade and a knowledge of languages prioritising Malay over Dutch: 'In Indonesia the three languages current are Malay and, Dutch, and English in that order, and it is imperative that trading representatives of Australia should have a knowledge of, at least, the first mentioned, and would also find a working acquaintance with the second an advantage'.[56]

The Commonwealth Government while interested in trade also began to be aware of the strategic importance of the archipelago to the continent's defence. Reporting to parliament after a goodwill mission to the 'East', including the Dutch East Indies, Deputy Prime Minister and Trade Minister J.G. Latham in 1934 stressed that:

> Australia has a special relationship with the Far East. The continent of Australia is actually in the geographical area often described as "the

---

55   Perth Technical College, Foreign Language Courses in 1838-1, UWAA.
56   Technique of Trade. *Sydney Morning Herald*, 22 June 1933, p.8.

East". The risks attendant upon any disturbance of peace or actual outbreak of war in that region are of the greatest moment to our people. Our trade relations with Eastern countries are most important to our welfare.[57]

The substance of this 'special relationship' was unclear, and no mention was made of language study other than the recommendation 'that a number of Australian naval officers be trained in the Dutch language'.[58] To the Navy's credit, the recommendation was taken seriously and, as a result, some Australian naval officers did study Dutch (Bussemaker, 1996). Furthermore, the government appointed a Dutch speaking commissioner, Mr H.A Peterson, to Batavia (Jakarta) in 1937.[59]

In spite of Latham's visit, it was clear that neither the government nor Australians in general were keeping abreast of important political developments in Indonesia. It was a similar situation in the country's universities where the term 'Indonesia', if used at all, was more likely to be found in courses such as anthropology or geography.[60] The frustration of the lack of real progress began to be expressed by individuals such as Winifred Ponder (see Figure 5), a writer, adventurer and Fellow of the Geographical Society in London who believed there needed to be an awareness of the link between trade, good relations, and an understanding of culture and language. Writing in Brisbane's *Courier Mail* in 1934 she stated:

> ... there is talk of trade commissions and of advisory committees, and every now and then some fortunate individual is financed by patriotic public bodies and dispatched in quasi-official role to "report", returning armed with sheaves of statistics and recommendations – and all is exactly as it was before![61]

This was a direct jab at Latham's mission, which she referred to as making 'a polite social call' on the Far East.

---

57   J.G. Latham, Australian Eastern Mission, 1934 report to the Parliament of Australia, page 3. NAA: A981, 1934-1934.
58   Confidential Report to the Prime Minister by J.G. Latham, 1934. NAA: A981, 1934-1934.
59   New opening for public service. *Canberra Times*, 26 November 1937, p. 4.
60   The University of Sydney's Anthropology 1 included 'Indonesia' as a topic along with Micronesia. Sydney University Calender 1931.
61   Ponder, 1934, p. 10.

Figure 5: Queensland based adventurer, writer and interpreter Winifred Ponder, was a strong critic of the government's lack of attention to Asian languages, including Malay which she spoke.
The Telegraph, Brisbane, Tuesday 14 January 1941 p. 8.

In her article Ponder emphasised that language was 'the key' and drew up an impressive list of languages that might be considered:

> The truth is, of course, that the only sort of trade "commission" that would have the least hope of achieving useful results in even the Far East as a whole, would be one including persons capable of conversing fluently in Japanese, Chinese, (at least three dialects), Malay, Hindustani (for Indian traders are everywhere), Anamese, Dutch, and French.[62]

She added, '... only through the medium of language can true contact with any nation or people be established'. Perhaps Latham, if he had read the article, would have found the question of language far too daunting. Ponder conceded that to put such a multilingual mission together 'would give the selectors more trouble than any team yet chosen for the Ashes'.[63] Ponder travelled and wrote extensively on Java and Malaya and her interest in the Malay language led her to be particularly critical of the linguistic ability of the English in the East, 'but it has to be confessed that the Malay spoken by all English people, except those who have learned it compulsorily, is about on a par with our very worst schoolroom French' (Ponder 1935, p. 264).

In Queensland, Ponder was not alone in believing something needed to done in regards to Asian languages. The Governor of Queensland, Sir Leslie Wilson, seeing the growing trade with the region, argued Australian children in some schools should be taught 'Eastern languages' instead of European languages. He was supported by the director of Education in Queensland, Mr B. J. McKenna, who emphasised the changing perceptions of distance due to the recently established air services between Asia and Australia 'Air travel has swept away barriers of distance' and, as a result, he believed the languages of Asia were becoming more relevant to Australians: 'In addition to Japanese the question now arises whether we should not teach Dutch and Malay as well'.[64]

In spite of these occasional calls for support, the prospects for the teaching of Indonesian/Malay in Australia's educational institutions appeared minimal; there were no real champions for scholarship in the language, no colonial service in need of it, and no war to demand it. This was, however, about to change.

---

62 Lost Opportunities in Eastern Trade. *Courier-Mail*, 28 February 1934, p. 10.
63 Ibid.
64 Australians Learn Malay "More Useful than French". *Straits Times*, 21 June 1936, p. 12.

The 'Near North' Comes South: Language as an Ally

In January 1941, the Australian Prime Minister Robert Menzies[65] arrived in Batavia and was greeted by Australian Commissioner H.A Peterson. On route to London, Menzies, the first Australian Prime Minister to visit the Dutch East Indies, had come to meet Governor General Tjarda van Starkenborgh Stachouwer for discussions on security issues. While a hurried visit, he was impressed by Tjarda: '... this man possesses strength of character' (Martin & Hardy, 1993, p. 23). Menzies was also impressed by the Governor General's English, 'speaks perfect English', so there was little need to test Peterson's interpreting skills.

Tjarda expressed a pessimistic view of Japanese intentions on the Indies and Menzies offered to take Dutch concerns to London; Menzies believed the Dutch would resist any incursions by the Japanese, though he acknowledged they were short of supplies. Tjarda clearly took some hope from the meeting and informed the Dutch Minister of Colonies that Australia was prepared to go to war with Japan should Dutch territory be taken. On arrival in London, however, Menzies was told bluntly by Vice-Admiral T.S.V. Phillips that 'we should not go to war with Japan over their occupation of any part of the Netherlands East Indies' (Bussemaker, 1996).

While this should have directed Australia's focus to the war in Europe, it was clearly not in Australia's interests to simply ignore the changing circumstances to its north: cooperation between the East Indies and Australia would need to be upgraded. With this in mind, the need to train interpreters and translators in Dutch and Malay began to be explored by the Australian military and Australia's Department of External Affairs. By July 1941, External Affairs was able to confirm to the military that Malay would be introduced to the University of Sydney;[66] this preceded Australia's declaration of war on Japan in 1941 by some months. Once the War had escalated to the Pacific, the Australian Military moved to have its own language instruction for military servicemen and women. The Malay program commenced in 1942 and was based at the Western Australian Lines of Command in Perth.[67]

Malay was also taught in several other states where intelligence officers trained including Queensland (see Figure 6), Northern Territory, and Victoria; these programs were predictably unknown to the public. Melbourne was the

---

65   Menzies first term as Prime Minister ran between 1939 and 1941.
66   Letter from Minister of External Affairs to Colonel Hodgson. NAA: A981/ AUS63.
67   Teaching of Malay, Report by D.A.D. West Australia Lines of Command Area on Potential Instructors in Malay. NAA: MP74211, 89/4/420.

USEFUL SENTENCES.

What is your name ?	APA NAMA ?
What is your nationality ?	BANGSA APA ?
Where do you come from ?	DATANG DARI MANA ?
Where do you work ?	MANA KERJA ?
I can speak little Malay. Speak slowly like this and I can understand.	SAYAH BOLEH CHAKAP SADIKIT MALAYU SAHAJA. CHAKAP PERLAHAN BAGINI SAYA BOLEH ERTI.
How far is the village from here ?	KAMPONG BERAPA JAUH DARI SINI ?
What is the news ?	APA KHABAR ?
Did you see any Japs on the road ?	ADA NAMPAK ASKAR JEPON TENGAH JALAN KAH ?
How many Japanese did you see ?	BERAPA ORANG JEPON NAMPAK ?
How were they armed ?	APA JENIS SENJATA-NYA ?
When did the Japanese pass ?	BILA ORANG JEPON SUDAH LALU ?
Where did they go ?	DIA PERGI MANA ?
Were they walking quickly ?	DIA JALAN LEKAS KAH ?
How far away are they now ?	DIA ADA BERAPA JAUH SEKARANG ?
Did they say anything ?	DIA CHAKAP APA-APA ?
We want to meet the chief man or head of the village	KITA MAHU JUMPA PENGULU ATAU KAPALA KAMPONG.
About how many men live in the village ?	LEBEH KURANG BERAPA ORANG TINGGAL DI KAMPONG ?
Do the village people like the Japs ?	ORANG DALAM KAMPONG SUKA ORANG JEPON KAH ?
What Jap formations are in the town and what are they like, well or sick and tired looking ?	APA PASOKAN JEPON DI PEKAN DAN APA RUPA NYA ? ADA SIHAT ATAU SAKIT LAGI PENAT ?
Go into the town and get all the news about the Japs.	MASOK PEKAN DAPAT SAMUA KHABAR DARI-HAL ORANG JEPON
Hurry back and tell us what you saw.	LEKAS BALEK. KASI TAHU APA SUDAH NAMPAK .
Do not tell other people that we are here . If the Japs here, they certainly will come to look for us	JANGAN CHAKAP SAMA ORANG LAIN KITA ADA SINI. KALAU JEPON DENGAR TENTU DIA DATANG CHARI KITA
Can you do that ?	BOLEH BUAT ITU ?
Why can't you get news ?	KENAPA TA' BOLEH DAPAT KHABAR ?
Do you know where the Japs store their ammunition and petrol ?	ADA TAHU DI-MANA ORANG JEPON SIMPAN MINYAK DAN PELURU ?
Can you show us the bridge in the town.	BOLEH TUNJOK JAMBATAN DALAM PEKAN ?
Is that bridge used much by the Japs?	JAMBATAN ITU, ORANG JEPON ADA PAKAI BANYA KAH ?
How many feet long is it? What sort of bridge is it.	BERAPA KAKI PANJANG-NYA. APA JENIS JAMBATAN ITU ?

Figure 6: Page from a Malay course taught at the Fraser Commando School, Fraser Island, Queensland.
National Archives of Australia: A3269, Q1/B.

headquarters for the Allied Intelligence Bureau, which coordinated a range of intelligence bodies many of which required interpreting and translating services including Indonesian and Malay.[68] While these duties could be undertaken by Indonesians evacuated to Australia by the Dutch, there was also a need for some Australian personnel to gain knowledge of the language. Malay, for example, was taught at intelligence training camps at Mt Martha in Melbourne's southeast and at the School of Eastern Interpreters which opened in February 1944. The School's name, however, was intentionally misleading as the primary focus was on 'building an organization, in clandestine work and in espionage and intelligence.'[69]

In the space of 12 months, the teaching of Indonesian and Malay had gone from a total absence to being taught in several states and in the field (see Figure 7), such was the focus of war. This rapid implementation of language programs relied heavily on the presence of suitable staff in Australia; they were primarily drawn from former British colonial officers, with varying degrees of Malay, who had retired or had been evacuated to Australia at the outbreak of the War.

The most important of these men were James Pearce and Arthur Wedderburn Hamilton. The two men would produce their own Malay language texts used by both military and civilians, and they would oversee the design of the programs in their respective institutions.

Figure 7: Australian military studying Indonesian/Malay.
Left: at sea, 1945, Townsville-Morotai, Captain C.S. Morrison, an intelligence officer, conducts classes in Malay aboard the troopship *USS General H.W Butner*.
Right: An Australian soldier practicing his Malay in Balikpapan, July 1945.
Australian War Memorial, 090766 and 018935.

---

68   Some differentiation between Indonesian and Malay began to be made in Melbourne at this time, with propaganda materials prepared in both forms of the language.

69   Unpublished notes by Ivan Southall for a book on the history of SRD - Services Reconnaissance Department in World War Two. NAA: Canberra: A10851/10.

Arthur Wedderburn Hamilton had been a probationary officer in Malaya, learning his Malay in a number of locations, though primarily in Penang. He became deeply interested in the Malay language and published twenty-three papers in the *Journal of the Straits Branch of the Royal Asiatic Society* (Brewster and Reid, 1989). He would also publish the first Malay language text in Australia, *Malay Made Easy* published in Sydney in 1940 with a revision in 1944 to include notes on Dutch East Indies Malay.

In 1941, Hamilton was the natural choice to establish the Malay program at the University of Sydney, as he had lobbied hard for a Malay program to be introduced and there were few other candidates available at the time with his extensive experience. While Hamilton was keen to point out the importance of learning Malay for the War effort, he also saw a long-term future for the Malay language in Australia. Writing in 1941 to the Minister of External Affairs, Frederick Stewart, he stated that:

> The men of the A.I.F. in Malaya in scattered jungle operations will find it invaluable to have a smattering of the native tongue and should the field of operations extend to the Dutch islands the same tongue would act as a means of communication with their Dutch allies.

But he continued:

> Furthermore, with the advent of more peaceful conditions there is bound to be a great increase in commercial relations between Australia and the Netherlands East Indies and to enable Australian businessmen to take full advantage of the native markets some knowledge of bazaar Malay would be requisite.[70]

Although the program was taught only as part of an extension program, and therefore not accredited for university study, Hamilton's long-term goal was for Malay to join Japanese and Chinese in a new School of Oriental Languages at the University of Sydney. The University had for some time been open to the idea and, as already mentioned, appointed a Professor of Oriental Studies in 1918. This seemed an ambitious proposal, but there were others who were also lobbying for acceptance of Malay at the University, namely, former Directors of Education in New South Wales Ross Thomas and Thomas Daily Mutch.[71]

---

70 In Brewster and Reid, 1989, p. 25.
71 Teaching of Malay. Hamilton letter to Lt. Col R. B. Madgwick, 17 Nov. 1942. NAA: MP74211, 89/4/420.

Mutch is of particular interest, as besides being a politician he was also a journalist and an historian with a passion for the early Dutch explorers of Australia. Significantly, Mutch's preference was for the establishment of what he referred to as Pacific Languages at the University of Sydney, and in 1942 he lobbied the Minister for External Affairs, Dr Evatt, for five thousand pounds to start the program immediately.[72] While the proposals did not proceed, it seemed to indicate the direction that the teaching of Indonesian-Malay might head in the post-war years.

In Perth, James Pearce soon became the prime candidate for the directorship of the Malay program under the Western Australian Lines of Command, which began in 1942.[73] He was a former British colonial officer who had been a lecturer in Malay at the Teachers Training College in Singapore before being evacuated to Australia. During the First World War, he had been in the infantry and had also served as a major in the Federated Malay States Volunteer Force.

Pearce was not a lobbyist for Malay in the way that Hamilton was, though he understood its long-term importance. He also saw the importance of status in the military, and in his reply to the Australian Military was insistent that he be given appropriate rank. While the military had some doubts about his requests for officer rank, they had no doubt about his language ability, writing in their report:

> There seemed to be general agreement among gentlemen consulted that Pearce's knowledge of Malay and experience in teaching of Malay and organization of instruction in Malay were considerable.[74]

Upon his successful recruitment, Pearce was given the rank of Captain and by October 1942 the Army Education Service reported it had timetabled a total of 51 classes with 1,036 personnel and 10 instructors, of which 7 were full-time.[75]

While working on the program, Pearce was able to develop materials which he published in 1944 as the *A Simple but Complete Grammar of the Malay Language*. Like Hamilton's work, Pearce's publication was meant to be a practical guide for the general learner of Malay rather than an academic

---

72 Teaching of Malay. Letter from Secretary of NSW State Advisory Committee, Department of Education to Lieut. Talty, Australian Services Education Council, Department of the Army, 31 December 1942, NAA: MP74211, 89/4/420.
73 Teaching of Malay. Report by D.A.D. NAA: MP74211, 89/4/420.
74 Ibid.
75 Teaching of Malay. Instruction in Malay Language. 3 Australian Corps. 2/10/1942. NAA, MP74211, 89/4/420.

work. Pearce also shared Hamilton's optimism for a greater role for Malay after the War, pointing out:

> Opportunities in trade, opportunities to securing posts as officials and as commercial representatives, will be plentiful. To those who are able to spend holidays in these parts, a knowledge of the language will be the 'Open Sesame' to intimate relationships with the people, and a certain way to full enjoyment of all there is to do and to see.
>
> Who knows how close will be the relationship between Australians and Malays in the post-war era?[76]

Predicting that Australians could be 'close' to Malays was a dramatic shift in thinking from the pre-war years when the military seemed far more equivocal about close relationships with the 'natives'. When the HMS Pelandok called into an Australian port in 1940, for example, a number of photos were taken of the visiting Malay crew together with the white Australian troops, but the photos were banned for showing 'undignified fraternisation between white troops and natives'.[77]

The Second World War, however, was a period of rapid change in Australia's view of its region and the following quote from the RAAF's own guide to the Malay language *Elementary Malay* (1940), demonstrates elements of both old and new attitudes:

> The Malay, generally, has a quiet dignity, in boarding him, coupled with a naturally happy disposition. He is easy to get on with, and will, in most cases, show respect for and willingly assist the white man. They are an independent race, and in a different class altogether from the prevalent idea of a "native" being a coolie—someone to order about.
>
> ... Many Malays are good motor car drivers, and their sober habits make them reliable. They are an easy-going and rather lazy race ...
>
> Much was done by the British and Dutch to protect Malay interests, provide education facilities, improve methods of cultivation and raise the standard of living. There is no doubt that the great majority of the Malays will welcome the return of the white man.[78]

---

76 Pearce 1944, p. 3.
77 Australian troops mix with Malay sailors. NAA: PA25, CRS A11663.
78 RAAF, 1944, p. X.

The text attempts to redefine the relationship between the Malays and Australians with the rejection of the terms 'native' and 'coolie', though one awaiting the 'white man's' guidance. It also demonstrates either some form of self-censorship or substantial ignorance of the political situation in Indonesia at the time. The 'welcome return of the white man' was more a belief than a reality and one that was soon to be shaken. It is not surprising, in this context, that none of the instructors considered for the Perth program were Malays or Indonesians. Instead, 'Malay boys' from ships that called at Fremantle were commonly used for conversation; an experience much appreciated by the students.[79]

With Hamilton teaching alone in Sydney, the only native speaker tutors were in the intelligence services. A number of Malays/Indonesians were working with the Allies at the time as translators, interpreters and assisting with Allied propaganda. This also made them available to assist with language tutoring. Samuel Jacob was of particular note in this regard.[80] Jacob was well qualified to act as a tutor and had the appropriate background for both the Australian and Dutch intelligence agencies. Not only had he been a Dutch language schoolteacher in Eastern Indonesia before being evacuated to Australia, but he had also proved his loyalty to the Dutch by suppressing a small uprising in Dobo in Eastern Indonesia, for which he received a bravery award from the Dutch Government.[81]

After his evacuation to Melbourne with his family, he took up a broad range of duties with the Dutch Civil Administration, including an editorial position with *Penjoeloeh*, the Indonesian language news magazine, and it was at this time that he began teaching Indonesian language to the Allies.[82] The urgency for cooperation during the War and the nature of tasks that Indonesians such as Jacob now performed created a new partnership with Australians that deviated substantially from the boss and coolie relationship that dominated before the War. It provided a more equal need to communicate with each other and for some Australians stimulated their curiosity about the North.

While the War years demonstrated some signs of an awakening to the importance of the language in the context of regional security, neither Pearce nor Hamilton was in a position to secure the future of Indonesian/Malay in

---

79 Teaching of Malay. Department of the Army Minute Paper 8 July 1944. NAA: MP74211, 89/4/420.

80 Some of Jacob's activities are recorded in the following court case involving the deportation of his wife: Mrs. Annie O'Keefe, High Court of Australia's proceedings, 1949. NAA: A432, 1942/127.

81 *Penjoeloeh* 7 March 1944.

82 See Brawley, 2012 for further details of Jacob's wartime activities.

Australia. To begin with, there were many weaknesses in the manner that the wartime programs had been structured. The military courses in Perth were purely voluntary and many personnel found they were transferred before they could complete the course. The complexities in the training, management and deployment of highly skilled translators and interpreters had also not been fully considered. As a result, few fluent interpreters were produced and they were not always available in areas of most need.

At the University of Sydney, the Malay program suffered from being too closely associated with the war effort, and little had been achieved to broaden its appeal to students or to increase its academic position within the university. Before the end of the War, these weaknesses would contribute to the demise of the Malay programs in Australia.

At War's End: A language of the Left, Idealists (and Love)

It should have been expected that with the proclamation of Indonesian independence at the end of the War, the language would have had some basis for establishing itself as a regular feature in the training of the military and in Australian universities as part of the country's new diplomatic efforts in the region. Australia still had troops in both Malaya and in Indonesia and the new Prime Minister, Ben Chifley, took a surprisingly independent stance in regards to its support for the Indonesian Republic.

Nonetheless, strong budgetary pressures forced the government to look at reducing military spending as quickly as it could. The Indonesian/Malay language programs in Perth had already been wound back in 1944. It was hoped that any additional training that was needed could be done by correspondence and prospective students were directed to the Perth Technical College.[83] This appears to have been a revival of earlier plans for a correspondence course first mooted in the early 30s, but there is no evidence that it went ahead. The Chifley Government also put on hold a proposal made during the war for a national school of administration and international affairs in which oriental languages, including Indonesian, would be studied (Burns, 1944, p. 2).

Meanwhile, Sydney's dream of a School of Oriental Languages was fading and post-war austerity measures had little time for Hamilton's Malay program, which declined from 16 students to 5 in 1945.[84] A number of the students had been given Government positions, including postings with the

---

83   DAD Education, HQ, Victoria L of C Area, Request for Classes in Malay. NAA, MP74211, 89/4/420.
84   Extension Board Annual Reports. SUA: G12/25.

United Nations Relief and Rehabilitation Administration, ironically proving the success of the program. With little prospect of new students, the Vice Chancellor requested the program be discontinued. The Extension Board continued the program for one more year,[85] with Hamilton's employment being terminated in December 1946.[86]

As with the University of Melbourne, the University of Sydney saw more of a future in Dutch, including it in its undergraduate program after the War. The loss of Malay must have been a great disappointment to Hamilton, who had written with considerable passion about the future of the language in Australia. After leaving the University, he moved to Perth and played no further formal role in teaching or lobbying for the language.

A review of what was achieved during the War reveals little long-term planning and a lack of coherent policy between what the government might believe the future relationship between Indonesia, Malaya and Australia would be and its education policy. It would be another decade before consideration would be given again to the teaching of Indonesian/Malay in Australian universities.

While the teaching and learning of Indonesian/Malay declined, it did not disappear altogether. Some trade unionists and other left wing supporters of the new republic began attending ad hoc classes or were tutored by Indonesians who had managed to remain behind. There were also a number of Australian war brides who had married with Indonesians (Lingard, 2008, pp. 237-248) and who were interested enough to learn the language from either their husbands or from members of the remaining Indonesian community. In the immediate post-war period, to learn Indonesian appears to have become a somewhat passionate, subversive affair.

The *Canberra Times* reported Darwin residents were 'very disturbed that a treasonable cell in direct contact with Indonesia' was operating there. Australian Member of Parliament for the Northern Territory, Mr A. M. Blain, claimed 'Communist fellow travellers[87], believed to be on the public pay roll were teaching the Malayan language to Communists at Darwin … in preparation for the time when the Communist south-eastern drive comes through Indonesia and menaced our northern shores.'[88]

---

85 Minutes of Extension Board. SUA: G12/18.
86 University of Sydney Staff Cards. SUA: G3/254.
87 A reference to Sugoero Atmaprasadja who had campaigned against the Dutch and been interned in a prison in Marauke before escaping to Australia, see Onnie Lumintang et al 1997.
88 *Canberra Times*, 16 September 1948, p. 3.

This political dimension can be further illustrated by some of the organisations that were established at the time. The Australian-Indonesian Association (AIA),[89] for example, had a clearly defined political agenda in regards to its support for Indonesian independence. They also took an interest in the language and culture of Indonesia, its members first learning the language from the community, when and where the opportunity arose. Eventually, the Association began to conduct its own classes in a more structured way and included night classes taught by Robert Go in Melbourne commencing in 1947.[90]

In this period, individual effort was more prominent and some who had studied the language during the War would put considerable time into learning and maintaining it. William Cammeron, for example, had first learnt Malay as an infantry man when based in Morotai and Labuan Islands. He was a dedicated language student, impressively learning Malay both in the Latin and Jawi script. After the War, he continued to exchange letters in Malay with other Australian servicemen who he had met in impromptu Malay study groups, but it was his interest in politics where he considered putting his language skills to proper use.

Cammeron was one of a number of Australian servicemen who sympathised with the Indonesian Republicans after the War. While on service in Japan, he endeavoured to correspond with Indonesians in Australia so he could improve his Malay and 'at the same time I shall offer my services to the Indonesian Republic'.[91] In order to contact the Indonesians, he wrote to Professor Elkin at the Department of Anthropology at the University of Sydney, but was advised by the Department that most of the remaining Indonesians in Australia were all 'loyalists' working for the Dutch.[92]

In Japan, he also decided to switch from writing his diary in English to writing Malay in the Jawi script (see Figure 8). This gave him further practice in Malay; it also allowed him to make a record of some of the people he was meeting with in Japan, including communist contacts. Eventually, his strong political commitment led him to join the Australian Communist Party, though by the late 1950s he would become disillusioned and resign his membership.[93]

---

89 AIA was formed in 1944 by trade unionists, political activists and intellectuals to support Indonesian independence, and had branches in the major capital cities. See Kartomi, 1981.
90 Australia Indonesia Association Monthly Newsletter No 2. 1 September 1947. MUA: 67/13.
91 Cammeron Personal Diary, 2 June 1946, in Cameron Family Collection.
92 Letter from Anthropology Department, University of Sydney, Cameron Family Collection.
93 Ian Cammeron, Personal Communication, 2009.

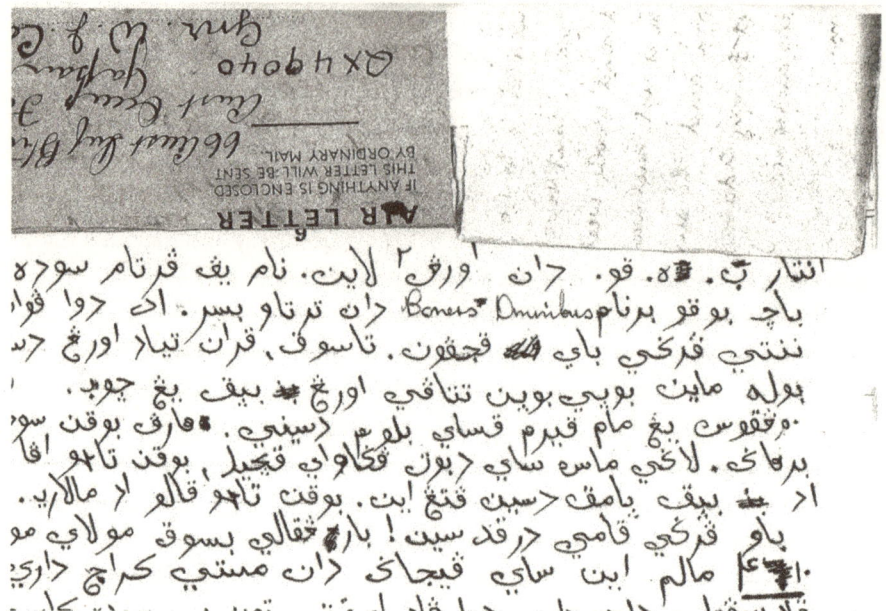

Figure 8: Extract from William Cammeron's Malay language diary written in Jawi script, 1946.
Photo Paul S. Thomas, Cammeron Family Collection.

More widely known was Molly Bondan, who was one of the Australian women married to an Indonesian at the end of the War. Her husband was a political prisoner, Mohammad Bondan, who after being released in Australia worked with both the Australian military and the Dutch sponsored *Penjoeloeh* magazine along with Samuel Jacob.

Molly Bondan had been a founding member of the AIA in 1944, and through it became exceptionally active in supporting Indonesian independence (Hardjono and Warner, 1995, p. 33). When, in 1947, her husband decided to return to Indonesia, she did not hesitate to follow. While in terms of her language ability she was poorly prepared, only having a few words on her arrival, she was quick to rectify this starting up a language exchange with a new friend, Trimurti, the Minister for Social Affairs in the Republican Government (Hardjono and Warner, 1995, p. 74). On moving to Jakarta, Molly would become one of the key English translators of President Soekarno's political writing, working on both his speeches and on translations of his books.

Conclusion

While political activism attracted intelligent and passionate supporters for the cause of Indonesian independence, and in some cases its language, it was not successful in kindling the interest of the broad spectrum of Australian society in matters Indonesian. In the immediate post-war period, there was a tendency for a polarization of opinion on the Indonesian independence issue, often based more on concerns about growing union power than on what was actually taking place in the country. Occasional personal stories, such as the repatriation of Indonesians from Australia, did create public and media sympathy for individuals caught up in the post-war confusion. However, the interest remained with individuals not with the new nation.

Outside of the politically active groups, occasional classes could be had in private language schools such as Berlitz, which had started Malay classes during the War in Melbourne's Collins Street and the College of European and Eastern Languages in Sydney's Elizabeth Street,[94] but for the most part Indonesian/Malay remained a truly exotic language.

The future of the language in Australia appeared to be in a political and cultural limbo requiring Government and academic leadership. The rapid introduction of the language during the War exposed a number of problems conceptually and academically of what the Indonesian/Malay language was and where it should be placed within tertiary education. For some academics, the Indonesian form of the language simply did not exist because they saw no classical past and no modern literature in it. This perception was usually drawn from ignorance about the manner in which the national language was being developed and its relationship to classical Malay.

Many of the areas where the language was dynamic and spreading such as journalism and popular culture were not seen as appropriate areas of university study. Disciplines such as applied linguistics, communications and translation studies, which could have helped explore the modern language, were yet to be established. The objective of introducing the languages also seemed to be overly pragmatic; universities were not prepared to be a training ground for interpreters and translators. What was required perhaps was a greater understanding of the Indonesian language as a manifestation of a growing political identity and a weathervane for the direction the culture was heading.

In reviewing this early history of Indonesian/Malay in Australia, what is most remarkable is the long and continuous presence of the language on the

---

[94] Advertising in Melbourne's *Argus* and *Sydney Morning Herald*, in the immediate post-war period suggest Malay classes were irregular.

continent and its regular inclusion in the early proposals for Asian languages in Australia. However, outside of Indigenous Australians' relationship with the archipelago and dedicated individual study, interest in the Indonesian/Malay language was primarily motivated by political, economic, or military crises where Australia had to reassess its position in the region. This indicated that Australia was most likely to engage with its immediate neighbour only under exceptional circumstances and when it viewed itself more independently. These exceptional circumstances would come in again in 1949 when the United Nations recognised Indonesian independence from the Dutch and the country became an area of concern during the Cold War.

Archives

NAA - National Archives of Australia
NLA – National Library of Australia
AWM - Australian War Memorial
SUA – The University of Sydney Archives
MUA – Melbourne University Archives
UWAA – University of Western Australia Archives
NSWSR – New South Wales State Records

References

Adelaar, S. 1996. 'Malay in the Cocos (Keeling) Islands'. In *Reconstruction, Classification, Description: Festschrift in Honor of Isidore Dyen*, edited by B. Nothofer. Hamburg: Abera Network. pp. 167–198.

Brawley, S. 1995. *The White Peril, Foreign Relations and Asian Immigration to Australasia and North America 1919-78*. Sydney: University of New South Wales Press.

Brawley, S. 2012. 'The spirit of Berrington House: the future of Indonesia in wartime Australia, 1943–1945'. *Indonesia and the Malay World*, 40 (117), pp. 175–192.

Brewster, J. & Reid, A. 1989. 'A. W. Hamilton and the origins of Indonesian studies in Australia'. In *Observing Change in Asia*, edited by R. J. May & J. O'Malley. Bathurst: Crawford House. pp. 22–32.

Burns, C. 1944. 'School of Oriental Studies part of a wide federal plan'. *Argus*, September 7. p. 2.

Bussemaker, H. 1996. 'Australian Defence Cooperation 1940–41'. *Journal of the Australian War Memorial*. 29, November. Available from: http://www.awm.gov.au/journal/j29/herman.asp, accessed 12 April 2010.

Earl, G. 1846. 'On the Aboriginal tribes of the northern coast of Australia', *Journal of the Royal Geographical Society of London*, 16, pp. 239–251.

Evans, N. 1992. 'Macassan loanwords in top end languages'. *Australian Journal of Linguistics* 12 (1), pp. 45–91.

Hamilton, A. 1940. *Malay Made Easy*. Sydney: Australasian Publishing Company.

Hardjono, J. & Warner, C., (Eds.). 1996. *In Love with a Nation: Molly Bondan and Indonesia, Her Own Story in Her Own Words*. Picton, NSW: C Warner.

Harris, J. 1985. 'Contact languages at the Northern Territory British military settlements 1824-1849'. *Aboriginal History* 9, pp. 148–169.
Harris, J. 2007. 'Linguistic responses to contact: Pidgins and creoles'. In *The Habitat of Australia's Aboriginal Languages: Past, Present and Future*, edited by L. Gerhard & I. G. Malcolm. Berlin; New York: Mouton de Gruyter. pp. 131–151.
Hartog, P. J. 1917. 'The origins of the School of Oriental Studies'. *Bulletin of the School of Oriental Studies* 1 (1), pp. 5–22.
Hosokawa, K. 1987. 'Malay Talk on Boat: An account of Broome Pearling Lugger Pidgin'. In *A World of Language: Papers Presented to Professor S. A. Wurm on His 65th birthday, Pacific Linguistics*, C-100, edited by D. Laycock & W. Winter. Canberra. pp. 287–296
Jones, G. 1994. 'Out of the shadows: George Windsor Earl in Western Australia', *Indonesia and the Malay World* 22 (64), pp. 265–278.
Kartomi, M. 1981. 'The first AIA: The Australian-Indonesian Association'. *Australian Indonesian Association Journal*, August, 8–11.
King, P. 1825. *Narrative of a Survey, Volume 1*. John Murray: London.
Klarberg, F. 1996. 'A precursor to multiculturalism: Western Australia accredits secondary school languages 1920-1936'. *Journal of Intercultural Studies* 17 (1–2), pp. 53–68.
Klarberg, F. 1997. 'Asian languages in Australia: The accreditation of Japanese and Malay as public examination subjects'. *Asian Studies Review* 20 (3), pp. 80–90.
Lingard, J. 2008. *Refugees and Rebels: Indonesian Exiles in Wartime Australia*. North Melbourne: Australian Scholarly Publishing.
Macknight, C. 1976. *The Voyage to Marege': Macassan Trepangers in Northern Australia*. Carlton: Melbourne University Press.
Macknight, C. 1986. 'Macassans and the Aboriginal past'. *Archaeology in Oceania* 21, pp. 69–75.
Macknight, C. 2011. '"The view from Marege": Australian knowledge of Makassar and the impact of the trepang industry across two centuries'. *Aboriginal History*, 35, pp. 121–43.
Martin, A. & Hardy, P., (Eds.). 1993. *Dark and Hurrying Days: Menzies' 1941 Diary*. Canberra: National Library of Australia.
Mulvaney, J. & Green, N. 1992. *Commandant of Solitude: The Journals of Captain Collet Barker 1828–1831*. Melbourne: Miegunyah Press.
Onnie Lumintang, O.P. Haryono S., Gunawan R., Nurhajirini, D.R. 1997. *Biografi Pahlawan Nasional Marthin Indey dan Silas Papare*. Jakarta: Departemen Pendidikan dan Kebudayaan
Pearce, J. 1944. *A Simple but Complete Grammar of the Malay language*. Central Press: Perth.
Ponder, W. 1934. 'Lost opportunities in eastern trade'. *Courier-Mail*, February 28. p. 10.
Ponder, W. 1935. *Java Pageant*. London: Seely, Services and Co.
Powell, A. 2000. *Far Country: A Short History of the Northern Territory*. Carlton South: Melbourne University Press.
Read, J. 2002. 'Innovation in Indonesian language teaching: an evaluation of the TIFL tertiary curriculum materials'. Ph.D. thesis, University of Wollongong, Australia.
Reece, R. 1992. 'The Australasian career of George Windsor Earl'. *Journal of Northern Territory History* 3, pp. 1–23.
Royal Australian Air Force Head-Quarters. 1944. *Elementary Malay*. Melbourne: Royal Australian Air Force.
Russell, D. 2004. 'Aboriginal-Makassan interactions in the eighteenth and nineteenth centuries in northern Australia and contemporary sea rights claims'. *Australian Aboriginal Studies* 1, pp. 3–17.

Smith, K. V. 1992. *King Bungaree: A Sydney Aborigine Meets the Great South Pacific Explorers, 1799–1830*. Kenthurst, NSW: Kangaroo Press.
Swain, T. 1993. *A Place for Strangers: Towards a History of Aboriginal Being*. Cambridge: Cambridge University Press.
Taçon, P. S., May, K., Fallon, S. J., Travers, M., Wesley, D. & Lamilami, R. 2010. 'A minimum age for early depictions of Macassan praus in the rock art of Arnhem Land, Northern Territory'. *Australian Archaeology* 71, pp. 1–10.
Thomas, P. S. 2013. 'Interpreting the Macassans: Language exchange in historical encounters'. In *Macassan History and Heritage: Journeys, Encounters and Influences*, edited by M. Clark & S. K. May. Canberra: ANU E Press. pp. 69–93.
Webster, E. M. 1983. *An Explorer at Rest: Ludwig Leichhardt at Port Essington and on the Homeward Voyage 1845–1846*. Melbourne: Melbourne University Press.
Zainu'ddin, A. 1988. 'The teaching of Japanese at Melbourne University, 1919–1941'. *History of Education Review* 17 (2), pp. 45–62.

Chapter 3

TRANSLATION AS PERSUASION

The Menzies Government's Sponsorship of Indonesian Studies during the Cold War

Paul S. Thomas

Monash University

Introduction

On 19 December 1949, Robert Menzies' Liberal Party was elected with its primary focus on domestic issues, but within eight days of taking office Australia would have a newly independent nation at its doorstep. Menzies, in opposition, had rejected the Indonesian 'rebels', preferring to place his trust in the Dutch to rule the East Indies after the Second World War. Now, as the new Australian Prime Minister, he needed to both accommodate the fledgling Indonesian Government and develop an influential relationship with the new nation's people or risk the bilateral relationship being subsumed into the Cold War politics of the day. In the negotiation of this new relationship, the introduction of the Indonesian language to Australia's tertiary institutions was proposed as a tool to enable the government to translate Australia's message of democracy for the Indonesian people and demonstrate an ability to take a cultural approach to any problems that might arise.

As discussed in the previous chapter, until the 1950s attempts to introduce Indonesian, or Malay, had not been sustained. The language lacked academic acceptance and efforts to introduce it had occurred at times when Australia had little or no diplomatic representation in the region. However, after the Second World War, Indonesia's proclamation of independence, its subsequent successful revolution and the emergence of the Indonesian Communist Party, coincided with Australia's development of strategic anti-communist alliances and the establishment of Australian diplomatic missions in the region. This moved the study of Indonesian language, politics and culture from a fringe interest into a strategic priority.

This chapter considers the government's response to its lack of capacity to project itself as an exemplary democracy in the region in the context of Cabinet Decision 262 — the decision that funded the introduction of Indonesian language studies to tertiary institutions in Australia in the 1950s. It has been argued that the decision had little to do with the promotion of cultural understanding between the two nations, but rather represented ' a concerted effort to train future intelligence, military and External Affairs officials in the language and customs of a potential enemy nation' (Phelps, 1996, p. 216). However, I propose that the government was more equivocal in its approach to Indonesia, as it was at least partially aware of conflicts between the short-term Cold War objectives and the need to build a long-term bi-lateral relationship. Adding to the complexity of the motivation and implementation of the strategy were varying opinions within the government, idealism within the nascent diplomatic corps, and the diverse objectives of the academics and institutions who would design the programs. This effectively presents a more multifaceted view of both the pragmatics of the programs and the political machinations behind the decision. Overall, the government was extremely uncertain about Indonesia in the 1950s. The lack of knowledge about Indonesia's past, present and potential futures meant it could not be categorised as friend or foe with any conviction.

Previous accounts of the introduction of Indonesian studies in Australia have been largely descriptive or academic reviews of the discipline (see Aveling, 1998; Robson, 2008; Reid, 1981; Worsely, 1994) and have not dwelt on the motivational forces behind the introduction of the programs. Additionally, little attention has been given to the priority of translation as the government's immediate activity; the means by which it hoped to communicate Australian political values to the Indonesian people. However, what is evident in these previous accounts is the manner in which the programs, once introduced, developed independently and set forth academic processes that at times distanced the programs from the government's guidance and immediate objectives.

Menzian Narratives on Indonesia and Asia

The Australian Government's position on Indonesia in the 1950s was coloured by its prime minister's uncertain views on the country and his narratives on Australia's relationship with Asia in general. In his first term as prime minister, 1939-1941, Robert Gordon Menzies talked of the need for Australians to view the countries to its north differently from that of Great Britain: 'what Great Britain calls the Far East is to us the Near North.'[1] He summed up his view of Australia's immediate region as consisting of 'primary responsibilities and primary risks',[2] flagging the need for Australia to regard 'herself as a principal, providing herself with her own information and maintaining her own diplomatic contacts with Foreign Powers.'[3] Concerned that this could be misconstrued as a completely independent policy, he stressed that Australia 'must, of course, act as an integral part of the British Empire.'[4]

In the same speech, the Dutch East Indies was singled out as one of the countries with which Australia wanted to have closer relations. This naturally meant the colonial government and when, in 1939, the prime minister prepared a speech for the first short wave broadcast of Australia Calling, later Radio Australia, it was translated into Dutch rather than Indonesian or Malay (Hodge, 1992, p.93). Dutch broadcasts became a regular feature from 1940, though with the outbreak of the War Indonesian broadcasts would follow. Similarly, in his 1941 visit to the Dutch East Indies (see Chapter 1), Menzies appears to have only consulted with the Dutch elite.

Ten years later, as Australia recovered from the War, the Menzies Government adjusted its 'Near North' narrative to substantially different circumstances, but retained the notion that Australia's proximity to Asia brought with it both threats and responsibilities. Cold War politics meant that Chinese communism now replaced Japanese militarism as the major threat from the north, while Australia's desire to take up its responsibility in the region was expressed through the establishment of a diplomatic presence of its own for the first time. In a 1951 newspaper article, the Minister for External Affairs R. G. Casey, recently returned from a visit to Southeast Asia, stated:

---

1   Report on Prime Minister Menzies' inaugural radio broadcast. New leader talks to nation. *Argus*, 27 April 1939, p. 1.
2   New leader talks to nation. *Argus*, 27 April 1939, p. 1.
3   New leader talks to nation. *Argus*, 27 April 1939, p. 1.
4   New leader talks to nation. *Argus*, 27 April 1939, p. 1.

> My visit has given point to the term "The near North" as distinct from what Britain and America call "The Far East." No point in South-East Asia or the East is more than 24 hours by air from Sydney ...

He also noted:

> Militant Communism is on the march in all the areas to our north, yet it appears improbable that any country of South-East Asia will "go Communist" of its own accord. (Casey, 1951, p. 2)

While the government's concerns regarding the 'Near North' can be viewed as a defensive reaction to a perceived threat, it was clear that Southeast Asia was more open to influence. Indonesia in particular needed to be addressed directly. After the War, Menzies had remained supportive of the Dutch and was antagonistic towards the Labor Government's bias to the Republicans, clearly voicing his view:

> That we, a country isolated in the world, with a handful of people, a white man's country with all the traditions of our race, should want to set ourselves apart, by saying to our friends here and there, as in the case of the Dutch, who have been great colonists and our friends, 'out with you, we cannot support you'. (Menzies, 1947 in Goldsworthy, 2002, p. 24)

Even after considerable diplomatic gains by the Indonesian Republicans, Menzies remained remarkably consistent in his preference for the Dutch; as late as November 1949, he accused Chifley's Labor Government of doing 'everything it can to drive the Dutch out of the Netherlands East Indies' (Menzies in Patterson, 1949, p. 9). However, eight days after Menzies return to power on the 19 December 1949, he demonstrated his pragmatism as a politician in an open letter to the Indonesian people whose independence had just been formally recognised by the United Nations:

> The Australian Government and people send to the Government and people of the United States of Indonesia warmest congratulations and best wishes on the occasion of the inauguration of the Republic.
>
> As a near neighbour, Australia has deep and constant interest in the well-being and prosperity of Indonesia, and we look forward to the most intimate and friendly relations with you.[5]

---

5   Australia Recognises New Republic. *Sydney Morning Herald*, 28 December 1949, p. 1.

As evidence of Australia's limited view of its own horizon before the Second World War, neither the Dutch nor the Indonesian people had generally been referred to as 'neighbours',[6] but after the War the term began to be used frequently, primarily by the political left, to garner support for Indonesia's independence. Now, the new conservative Government had found 'neighbour' a positive way of expressing its acceptance of the new state on its doorstep. Unlike the somewhat anonymous 'Near North', a 'neighbour' was less likely to be portrayed as threatening and, therefore, signalled a far more positive narrative which emphasised the willingness of Australia to work together with Indonesia (see Sobocinska 2014, p.3). Shortly after Menzies' message of congratulations, the Dutch short wave broadcasts, commenced before the War, ceased while Indonesian language broadcasts, commenced during the War, continued.

The government would now need to juggle these seemingly contradictory, and at times overlapping, political narratives in its expression of the bilateral relationship. Together, they formed the essential context in which the government approached its cultural and political policies towards the new state.

Countenancing a Cultural Approach

Committed to the pragmatics of the relationship, the government was obliged to assess its available resources and strategies to move the relationship forward and to develop the promised 'intimate and friendly relations' with a country which it remained poorly informed. A possible approach that an Australian Government might take had already been aired by the Australian journalist Graham Jenkins on his return from Indonesia in late 1946. He proposed nine points, which he referred to as national necessities, including the exchange of diplomats, the provision of loans for trading purposes, and the setting up of defence ties. With specific reference to language, he proposed Australia should:

> Open an office of the Information Department to flood the country with information in the Malay language about our resources, democratic institutions, and way of life; simultaneously, extend and improve Radio Australia programmes beamed on Indonesia so that short-wave listeners may hear about us for 8-12 hours each day and become interested in the affairs of their neighbour. (Jenkins, 1946, p. 2)

---

6   In a rare early reference, University of Western Australia's Vice Chancellor, H. E. Whitfield did describe the people of the archipelago as our 'nearest neighbours' in his press interview regarding the introduction of Malay in 1934 (see Chapter 1).

This suggestion alone would have required a considerable number of professional translators, clearly a challenge for a country which at the time did not have a single university or technical college teaching Indonesian. However, Jenkins (1946, p. 2) also proposed the teaching of each other's languages:

> Promote cultural and educational ties as suggested by Sjahrir[7] by giving free places in our secondary schools and universities to Indonesian students; exchange teachers to improve Indonesia's knowledge of the English language; include Malay in the curriculum of Australian secondary schools so that we may better understand our neighbours; encourage tourists.

While Jenkins' idea of flooding Indonesia with translations of Australia's 'way of life' and its democratic institutions may have seemed over enthusiastic, it proved predictive, to a degree, of how the Menzies Government would approach their cultural initiative. However, the motivation behind the Menzies government's actions diverged from Jenkins' altruistically inspired recommendations.

The first opportunity for the Menzies government to initiate an Indonesian and Malay Studies program came through a proposal for a School of Oriental Studies. The universities in Sydney and Melbourne had for some time made attempts to establish Oriental Studies and this included the teaching both Chinese and Japanese (see Zainu'ddin, 1988). As referred to in Chapter 1, the Curtin government had given consideration to a National School of Public Administration and International Affairs in Canberra which was to include Oriental studies (Burns, 1944, p. 2), but the cost and the need to focus on the War effort did not allow its establishment. Only as the post-war recovery became a reality and Australia finally began to build up its diplomatic presence in Asia was the idea approached more seriously again.

In 1950, the Menzies' Government set up a Commonwealth Committee of Inquiry to consider Federal funding of a School of Oriental Languages. The recommendations of the committee were that the School be set up in Canberra and that it focus on four languages Japanese, Chinese, Russian and Hindustani, though there was some indication that Indonesian and Malay might be added as 'subsidiary studies' (Brewster and Reid, 1989). The reason for the low priority given to Indonesian/Malay is not clear, but it appears that the decision was driven by academics who drew on established models in Europe where Indian,

---

7   Sutan Sjahrir, Indonesian Prime Minister 1945-1947 and founder of the *Partai Sosialis Indonesia*.

Japanese and Chinese studies carried more prestige and had a more substantial body of academic work behind them. The universities were generally less interested in an engagement with Australia's neighbours or the government's immediate needs, than reflecting the established European approach.

In the public realm, there were those who were concerned that Australia's unique position in the region needed to be considered in any Government funded School of Oriental Studies. An editorial in *The Argus* of 1951 argued for a more rapid development of Australia's expertise on Pacific and Asian affairs commenting:

> It is rumoured that there will be a school [of Oriental Studies] some day in the National University at Canberra. But "some day" is a long way off. As for Malay, Indonesian, and other Far Eastern studies, not to mention the languages of India, there seems to be no provision whatever.[8]

External Affairs did raise the issue of Indonesian/Malay with the Committee on more pragmatic grounds. In an 1952 article published in Singapore's *Straits Times* reporting External Affairs Minister Casey's announcement of the School of Oriental Studies, it was claimed that previous training of officials had omitted major languages and that 'in the proposed school, Malay and Arabic will have as much importance as Chinese and Japanese' (Stanley, 1952, p. 6). While this may have been directed at the local readership, it was nevertheless some indication of the differences between academics who wished to follow established scholarly pursuits and a government that needed to quickly upgrade the ability of its officers to work in the region.

When the School of Oriental Languages was finally established at the Canberra University College in 1952, neither Malay nor Arabic were included. Initially, it was a somewhat rudimentary affair, teaching only Chinese; its head, the Swedish scholar Professor Hans Bielenstein, was a specialist in Chinese. Even under these circumstances, the need to develop translation and interpreting skills was pitted against 'true' academic study when the School drew criticism for being merely a 'school for training interpreters'.[9] The Minister for the Interior, Mr Kent Hughes' commented that 'an intensive study of Asian history would be more valuable than "a smattering of the language"'.[10]

The comments were made in ignorance of the standards of language required of a professional interpreter. Hughes also failed to grasp the point

---

8 What Do We Know About Asia? [Editorial] *Argus*, 6 January 1951, p. 2.
9 CU Doubts Decision on Oriental School. *Canberra Times*, 31 May 1952, p. 4.
10 CU Doubts Decision on Oriental School. *Canberra Times*, 31 May 1952, p. 4.

that translating and interpreting skills were exactly what the government immediately required. Rather than be overly concerned about the Minister's remarks, the principal of Canberra University College, Professor Herbert Burton, exploited the comments to argue for a more robust program: 'the study of oriental languages ought to be spread over several years, and that it should be accompanied by studies in the history and institutions of the countries concerned'. He added that: 'it is reassuring to know that Mr Kent Hughes' support can be counted on in achieving this objective.'[11]

Burton's comments were partly made out of frustration with the early arrangements made for the School and the desire to progress the language courses to a fully integrated undergraduate program. He would get to pursue these aims further through the Commonwealth Advisory Committee on Oriental Languages. In 1954, it was reported to the Committee that the Vice Chancellors' conference had recommended that the School of Oriental Studies be a strong school located in one place, Canberra. They proposed that the main areas of studies should be the Far East – Japan and China, together with Southeast Asia, the Islands, India, Pakistan and Ceylon. The Vice Chancellors' proposal was clearly based on the model of the School of Oriental and African Studies (SOAS) in London. In fact, they challenged the government to fund the new school appropriately or consider providing sufficient scholarships for students to go to London to study at SOAS.[12]

SOAS was a natural model for the Australian universities, but it had the potential to marginalise or even ignore the teaching of Indonesian. The SOAS model only prescribed a minor role for Malay and as Anthony Johns, ANU's first senior lecturer in Indonesian Studies and a former student of SOAS, would recall was 'overtly hostile to any recognition or status given to Indonesian/Malay.'[13] Australia's view of Asia had been coloured by the British academic experience and there was little understanding of how Malay as a contemporary national language, now increasingly referred to as Indonesian, had developed so rapidly.

While the Government may have been tempted to allow the School to evolve slowly and thereby accept a delay in the introduction of languages such as Indonesian, new developments began to take place in terms of the strategic architecture for the region that would require it to bring Indonesian to the top of the agenda.

---

11 CU Doubts Decision on Oriental School. *Canberra Times*, 31 May 1952, p. 4.
12 Advisory Committee on Oriental Languages, 5 November 1954. NAA: A705, 208/44/1, Part 3.
13 Personal correspondence, 22 May 2007.

Language as a Cold War Strategy: The Manilla Pact

During Minister for External Affairs R. G. Casey's visit to Indonesia in 1951, Indonesia was in the process of its only serious crackdown on the Indonesian Communist Party (PKI) of the period. After what Casey had witnessed in other parts of Southeast Asia, this left a positive, if somewhat distorted, impression on him (Casey, 1951). Casey concluded that Australia needed a new initiative to increase goodwill between Australia and Southeast Asia and that it would require a much broader involvement with non-Government institutions, including unions, churches and universities. He does not mention language specifically, but it is clear he was referring to a much greater involvement than Australia had previously attempted with Southeast Asia. Clouding this proposal was Casey's concern about defence. In the government's view, any action to increase goodwill would need to be assessed from its ability to act as strategy to persuade Indonesia's leaders of the flaws in communism and thereby lessen any menace to Australia.

Australia's capacity to act on its own in the region was severely limited, but if it could work together with its allies the possibility of securing an influential role in the region would be much more likely. With this objective in mind, Australia entered a new regional security arrangement in September 1954 with the signing of the Manila Pact, which brought into being the Southeast Asia Treaty Organization (SEATO).[14] The treaty obligated Australia to implement strategies that would counter communist subversion in the region and, as one of the champions of the Pact, Australia was keen to be seen as taking swift action.

Less than three months after its signing, in December of 1954, Australia brought together representatives from the Departments of External Affairs, Defence, and the Prime Minister's Department in a conference in Canberra to consider strategies which Australia could implement to fulfil its treaty commitments.[15] The general consensus of the deliberations was that a series of non-military activities would best serve the nation and that the focus should be on countering China's influence on Southeast Asia. It also helped that such activities were within Australia's capacity to deliver in the short-term.

The range of activities from the 1954 conference was diverse, but two proposals related directly to the utilisation of language: first, that Indonesian

---

14 The signatories were Australia, France, Great Britain, New Zealand, Pakistan, the Philippines, Thailand and the United States.
15 Conference on Cold War Planning at Canberra, 20 December 1954, NAA: A7936, B/4/2 PART 1.

should be introduced to both universities and schools; second, that the government should greatly expand its Indonesian shortwave broadcasts via Radio Australia. This was not dissimilar from what had occurred during the War when Indonesian/Malay radio broadcasts had been introduced for the first time for propaganda purposes and language programs were established for the training of translators and interpreters to assist in the War effort. However, in this new proposal before cabinet, the teaching of language was to engage far broader sections of the community. The cabinet believed that these and the other non-military activities being considered might well be more important and more fruitful than military measures'.[16] However, it conceded that there might also be a need for languages in future military operations.

The key minister managing the language strategy within the Menzies Government was Casey and shortly after the proposal was made, he lent his support to the idea:

> One thing that clearly emerges from an examination of possible Australian activities, not only in the cold war but in possible future military operations, is the shortage of Australians with a knowledge of Far Eastern languages. Very few Australians know Indonesian, the language of our nearest neighbour. An attempt may well be made to institute Indonesian and Malay (which are closely akin) as university subjects in Australia. [17]

Aside from the motivations behind the government's proposal, it represented a complete reversal of fortunes for Indonesian and Malay, which for the first time were now given priority over other Asian languages. Outside of the political context, the introduction of the language would still be confronted with academic resistance, but the government was prepared to support its proposal financially. This would assure serious consideration by the universities.

Cabinet Decision 262 and 'Friendly' Propaganda

By January 1955, Menzies was anxious to move ahead on the Indonesian language proposal and set aside £18,000[18] for the establishment of the programs

---

16 Cabinet Agendum, Australian activities in the Cold War, 5 January 1955. NAA: A1838, 563/6.
17 Cabinet Agendum, Australian activities in the Cold War, 5 January 1955. NAA: A1838, 563/6.
18 Review of Cold War Activities, 1955, in Cold war activities - Policy. NAA: A1838, 563/6.

in Australian universities. He called on Casey to manage the implementation of the initiative, though it was agreed that it would be the Office of Education's director, W. M. Weeden, who would approach the universities in Sydney, Melbourne and Canberra.[19] Weeden had been on both the Government's Commonwealth Advisory Committee on Oriental Languages and the committee set up by External Affairs to implement Cabinet Decision 262 on the introduction of Indonesian and Malay studies. Using Weeden as the intermediary made it clear that the government wanted the proposal to be seen as a cultural and educational initiative. The letter that Weeden wrote to the Vice Chancellors assured them 'that the form which courses in Indonesian and Malay Studies would take is a matter for the University to decide',[20] though he also indicated that language should constitute a major area of study and that it should be taught within a degree course in the Arts.

The need for the universities to offer languages within degree courses was problematic in terms of the time it would take for candidates to graduate. The Prime Minister's Secretary, A. S. Brown, wrote to External Affairs arguing that he believed there was an understanding that Weeden could 'at his discretion, discuss the teaching of Indonesian at something less than a Degree course.'[21] He also believed that the RAAF School of Languages' course could be extended not only to External Affairs, but might well be open to members of the Department of Commerce, the Office of Education and other departments.

The Prime Minister's Department seemed to have a greater sense of urgency in the area of language training and this reflected the Cold War environment, which had given weight to the idea of translating Australia's democratic message across a broad front to Indonesia. In practical terms, the government could not wait the three to four years required of a standard degree to have some capacity in translation and interpreting in Indonesian. Brown's argument for a wider use of the proposed RAAF program was therefore reasonable, as it had considerable advantages over the universities: it could be established quickly and efficiently; it could concentrate specifically on translating and interpreting skills; and the relative brevity of the course meant current Government officers could participate with a minimum disruption to their departments.

---

19   Letter Office of Education to Professor S. H. Roberts, Vice Chancellor, University of Sydney, 24 June 1955, SUA: Senate Minutes, G1/1/31.

20   SUA: Senate Minutes, G1/1/31.

21   Letter Secretary Prime Minister's Department to Acting Secretary of Department of External Affairs, 24 February 1955. NAA: A1838, 563/6.

The government's willingness to allow the universities an independent hand in the development of the programs opened the language programs to influences beyond objectives of the government; academic interests and motivation would be the primary force and ultimately the key to the long-term success of Indonesian in Australia. There were also advantages for the government in this hands-off approach, as it did not limit the value of language to being a tool for propaganda, but allowed for the campaign to be interpreted as an earnest attempt in engagement. This was defined as 'friendly propaganda': 'Friendly Propaganda involves the output of ideas from a single centre, ideas which are intended to spread widely so as to reach the greatest number of people'.[22]

This definition was presented to the government in a report commissioned by Casey on the use of propaganda and written by a retired British officer Brigadier Dudley W. Clarke, who had worked with Casey as his chief deception officer in the Middle East during the Second World War (Waters, 1999). In regards to language, he advised Casey that most propaganda to Southeast Asia would involve the use of translations and that he should keep a priority list of nationals who could act as translators. He also endorsed the teaching of Southeast Asian languages in Australia's educational institutions as part of a Good Neighbour campaign 'to build a reputation among Asians for the Australian cultural approach to problems.'[23] While Casey understood the importance more than most in the cabinet of a developing the long-term relationship with Indonesia, his decisions were fired by a deep belief in propaganda as a Cold War tool (see Hodge 1995; Waters 1999) and Clarke's recommendations did not fall on deaf ears.

Indonesian Initiatives with Australia

It is important to consider that while Australia contemplated its strategies in dealing with the relationship, Indonesia was not simply a passive observer and in the mid-1950s began a set of its own diplomatic initiatives. The first was an announcement to the Australian people during a ministerial visit in 1954 that the Indonesian Government had adopted a 'good neighbour policy'[24] with Australia, a policy of non-aggression and positive engagement. The

---

22 Report to the Minister for External Affairs by Brigadier Dudley W. Clarke on the use of propaganda, economic warfare, infiltration of agents and other covert action to counter communist subversion in South East Asia, December 1955. NAA: A7133, 22.

23 Report to the Minister for External Affairs by Brigadier Dudley W. Clarke, December 1955. NAA: A7133, 22.

24 Good Neighbour Policy. *Canberra Times*, Thursday 13 May 1954, p. 2.

second was a 1955 proposal for a Treaty of Friendship with Australia which, aware of Australian sensitivities, it put cautiously and unofficially through the United States and India.[25]

Australia had never signed a bilateral treaty; however, the Indonesian treaty was more difficult to reject, given its objectives of establishing goodwill with the new nation. James Plimsoll, Assistant Secretary Department of External Affairs, wrote to the Secretary of the Prime Minister's Department, Allen Stanley Brown, warning against rejecting such a proposal and explaining that the Indonesians already had a friendship treaty with Afghanistan, Burma, Egypt, India, Pakistan, the Philippines, and Thailand and the treaty had more significance to the Indonesians than perhaps the department had recognised.[26] While Brown was generally a supporter, he thought it prudent not to express any detailed comments on the treaty. Differing from both these views, Menzies and Casey could see little usefulness in it and Casey, in particular, began to consider alternatives.[27]

The treaty that Indonesia was proposing covered a number of areas but of most relevance to language studies was Article 6:

> The two governments agree, in the spirit of friendship and goodwill, to examine and develop means of expanding trade, culture, educational and other contacts between the two respective countries.[28]

Given the considerable reservations held by those in power in Australia at the time, and the fact that the Indonesian elections were due in September 1955, any formal discussions on the treaty were delayed. Following the elections, the possibility of a treaty faded but some form of bilateral agreement, which expressed goodwill, was still kept alive by diplomats from both sides. This would eventually result in discussions on the more innocuously titled 'Cultural Agreement'. The agreement sat well with the Australian Government's notion of projecting Australia's cultural and democratic principles to Indonesia and, at the same time, referenced Indonesia's earlier desire for a bi-lateral goodwill agreement.

As various drafts of the agreement were couriered back and forth between Canberra and Jakarta, the proposal became attached to Prime Minister Menzies

---

25   Letter to the Secretary of the Prime Minister's Department, 24 October 1955. NAA, A1209, 1957/5020.
26   Plimsoll to Brown, 24 October 1955. NAA: A1209, 1957/5020.
27   Letter to Prime Minister Menzies, 28 October 1955. NAA, A1209, 1957/5020.
28   Treaty of friendship between Australia and Indonesia, 24 October 1955. NAA: A1209, 1957/5020.

long overdue state visit to Indonesia which was now planned for late 1959. The agreement consisted of twelve articles; with the very first confirming the priority to be given to the teaching of each other's languages. The second promoted the understanding of each other's 'way of life':

> Article 1: The two High Contracting Parties shall foster the teaching in Australia of the Indonesian language and in Indonesia of the English language in educational institutions and otherwise.
>
> Article 2: The two High Contracting Parties shall encourage the teaching and understanding in each country of the history and culture and general way of life of the other. [29]

In spite of the work on the drafts being carried out jointly by Australian and Indonesian diplomats, by the time Menzies was ready to visit Indonesia, the political landscape had changed to such an extent that President Soekarno was less than enthusiastic about the proposal. He perhaps sensed the mixed political motivation behind it and the agreement stalled shortly before the Prime Minister's arrival in Jakarta. It is also worth noting that at the time Soekarno was waging a strong campaign against Western cultural influences and Australia was, in Indonesian eyes, very much a Western nation.

A second attempt to have the agreement signed occurred in 1962, though once again it was rejected; a victim of the continual political tensions between the two parties and the additional stress of growing confrontation over the formation of Malaysia. It was only with a change of presidents from Soekarno to Suharto, and a complete reorientation of Indonesian foreign policy, that the Australian Indonesian Cultural Agreement was finally signed by Indonesia's Foreign Minister Adam Malik and the Australian Ambassador H. M. Loveday on 14 June 1968.[30]

Indonesian Involvement in the University Language Programs

Outside of Indonesia's offer of a treaty, Indonesia also sought to have an influence on the establishment of the Australian Indonesian language programs. In mid-1956, the Indonesian Government offered to provide academic staff to the Australian universities' programs. While appreciative of the assistance

---

29 Indonesian Counter-draft with suggested Australian amendment, 16 July 1959. NAA: A1209, 1968/8418.
30 Personal Papers of Prime Minister Fraser. NAA: M1369, 17.

Australian universities had given to Indonesian students under the Colombo Plan, Indonesia had to some degree been suspicious of the scheme which it believed might be used 'to keep Indonesia from pressing the West New Guinea issue too vigorously'.[31] It saw its offer to become active in the language programs as some way to redressing the imbalance in education.

Indonesia's offer of academic staff required some delicate diplomatic considerations as it involved Indonesia's national pride in respect of providing a chance 'to escape from the status of being the perennial recipient of aid'.[32] It also required some sacrifice on Indonesia's part, as there was a great need for the country's academics to develop the nation's own educational system; Indonesian was still a new language for many Indonesians at the time. The Australian Government's problem was that it could not be seen to be removing the right for the universities to scrutinize or even reject the Indonesian candidates.[33]

The first and only test for the scheme came with the appointment of Amir Hamzah Nasution in 1957 to the Canberra University College. Nasution had been seconded from the Department of Education and Culture (*Kementerian Pendidikan, Pengajaran dan Kebudayaan*), where he had been Head of the Foreign Aid and Project Division of the Bureau of Foreign Relations and UNESCO Affairs (Bastin, 1957). However, when Nasution's term came to end in 1960, he was replaced by Dr S. Soebardi, whom Canberra University College appointed independently. The Indonesian Government appears not to have pursued their original proposal, perhaps content with the appointment of Indonesian nationals at Melbourne and Canberra.

A further gesture the Indonesian Government made to the establishment of the programs was the donation of over 16,000 books to Australian universities in 1957. A portion of the books was presented by the Indonesian Ambassador Dr A. Y. Helmi to the Australian External Affairs Minister Richard Casey (see Figure1).[34] The donation made it clear that the Indonesians still had an interest in the programs and were willing to be active in their promotion. Echoing the journalist Graham Jenkins' earlier idea of flooding Indonesia with books on Australia, Indonesia was also aware that there was something to be gained in projecting itself culturally outward to its neighbour.

---

31 Letter to the Secretary of External Affairs from J.M McMillan. NAA: A11604, 611/12A.
32 Letter to the Secretary of External Affairs from J.M McMillan. NAA: A11604, 611/12A.
33 Letter to the Secretary of External Affairs from J.M McMillan. NAA: A11604, 611/12A.
34 Photographic image and notes. NAA: A1501, A973/1.

Figure 1: The Indonesian Ambassador in Australia, Dr A Y Helmi, handed over a gift of 16,000 Indonesian books to the Australian Minister for External Affairs, Mr Richard Gardiner Casey, in Canberra on 9 April 1957.
National Archives of Australia: A1501, A973/1.

Menzies '*Bahasa*'

While Brown, Casey and Weeden played an active role in the discussions surrounding the decision on the Indonesian language programs, Menzies' personal attitude to the proposal is more obscure. However, in the lead up to his state visit in 1959, the Prime Minister took the novel step of calling on the services of a diplomat, Duncan Campbell, to assist him with some training in Indonesian language and pronunciation in order to incorporate some Indonesian language into his speeches in his upcoming visit. Campbell was amongst the first graduates from the RAAF School of Languages and he recalled his sessions with Menzies in an interview in 1993:

> Now Menzies wanted to make a good neighbourly impression and one morning over in the department onto my desk came a one page piece of paper, cheap lined writing pad, in pencil, and it was exquisitely concise friendly statesmanlike statement in English by Menzies, penned that morning in his bathtub which I gather was often a place where the muse

settled, for me to translate or have translated into Indonesian and then to teach him to say. And it was to be the sort of stock, short, central message of every public utterance he was going to make when he went to Indonesia.[35]

Unfortunately, through their sessions, Campbell realised 'that while Menzies had an astonishing memory, amongst other intellectual attributes … (he) was language -deaf and, to try to teach Menzies to pronounce this speech of, say fifteen lines in Indonesian, proved to be quite beyond me and certainly beyond him.'[36] It should be added that the prime minister was now about 65 years old and so he was clearly presenting himself with a considerable challenge.

Aside from Campbell, Menzies also delegated some of his aides to approach Anthony Johns at Canberra University College to translate comments on the most sensitive issue of the day, West New Guinea. Johns sought assistance from his wife and future ANU lecturer Yohanni Johns and recalls:

> They included the words, 'we have only one area of disagreement, the status of West New Guinea' which Yohanni duly rendered. We were sworn to secrecy. It was necessary to avoid sounds that Menzies would have difficulty in pronouncing, combinations such as 'ng' in initial position, 'ngg', 'nya' and so on.[37]

Plainly, the Prime Minister's intention was not to learn Indonesian[38] but to attempt a direct and personal address to Indonesians and to give legitimacy and sincerity to his own translated voice. He would also use Indonesian in his speech to suggest openness and equality between Australians and Indonesians prefacing his inaugural address on arrival at Jakarta's Kemayoran Airport with (see Figure 2):

> Now sir, you have rather put me to shame because you speak English, if I may say so, better than I do and I'm not able to speak to you in your own language, but I wonder if you would mind me trying just two sentences on you.

---

35   Michael Wilson (Interviewer) & Duncan Campbell (Interviewee), 1 February 1994. NLA: Oral TRC 2981//9.
36   Michael Wilson (Interviewer) & Duncan Campbell (Interviewee), 1 February 1994. NLA: Oral TRC 2981//9.
37   Anthony Johns, personal communication, 22 May 2007.
38   Menzies did not reveal to Campbell any long-term interest in studying the language. Personal Correspondence, December 2009.

He then went on to say:

> *Saudara-saudara, dari rakyat Australia saya membawa salam dan doa untuk masa datang yang gemilang kepada seluruh bangsa Indonesia.*

> [Brothers and sisters,[39] from the people of Australia I bring greetings and hope for a bright future to the whole of the Indonesian nation.][40]

This was the embodiment of translation as a persuasive approach. Menzies symbolic use of the language, no matter how shaky, was a projection of Australian values. In particular, it emphasised openness and equality, which was aimed at contradicting impressions drawn from Australia's White Australia Policy, a policy that sought to preserve Australia's European heritage. In terms of broadcasting a message, it was clearly successful with both Australian and Indonesian papers making mention of it. Melbourne's *Herald* reporting:

> Mr Menzies had also taken the trouble to learn Bahasa, the official language of Indonesia. He spoke the last two sentences of his reply to Dr. Juanda in this language. He has been studying Bahasa with the aid of External Affairs Department officers and a young Indonesian Colombo Plan student during the busy last two weeks for the parliamentary session.[41]

The readers were perhaps comforted by the addition that 'official discussions with Indonesian leaders will be conducted in English'.

Campbell's quite legitimate concerns that Menzies might not even be understood were partly put to rest by the following day's *Pos Indonesia* headline which quoted the Prime Minister directly (see Figure 3).

The initially relaxed approach that Menzies took to the trip, his use of Indonesian, his chatting with journalists allowing them impromptu questions, and his approach to Indonesians in general, led the *Pos Indonesia* to report on Menzies 'rama-tama'[42] (easy-going/friendly) manner. Soekarno and Menzies also managed more than cordial discussions and Menzies attitude to the man he had once called 'a collaborationist', due to his association with the Japanese during the War, appeared to be far more open.

---

39 A literal translation which Menzies would have been unlikely to have used in English, but indicates the warmth of the address in Indonesian.
40 Robert Menzies. [sound recording]: December 1959. December 1959. NLA: TRC 1169/75.
41 *Herald*, 2 December, 1959, p. 2.
42 *Pos Indonesia*, Evening Edition, 2 December 1959, p.1.

TRANSLATION AS PERSUASION

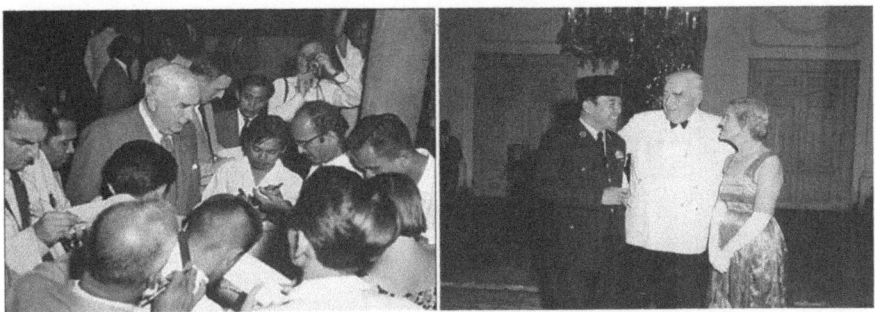

Figure 2: Prime Minister Menzies' state visit to Indonesia 1959.
Left: Menzies at Kemayoran Airport, Jakarta with the press corps. Right: Menzies and his wife Dame Pattie Menzies with President Soekarno at the Istana Negara.
NAA: A1775, RGM9 and A1775:RGM43.

Figure 3: *Pos Indonesia*, 2 December 1959. Headline translation: 'Bringing greetings and hope for a bright future to the whole of the Indonesian nation'.
Monash University library.

Nevertheless, substantial obstacles remained. Menzies was mired down in the Cold War politics of the day and his dedication to the British Commonwealth meant that he struggled to demonstrate a more independent view for Australia, one dissociated from the recent colonial past to which Indonesians remained highly sensitive. This was most apparent on the issue of West Papua. The *rama-tama* atmosphere with the press began to fade when they became frustrated at Menzies lack of willingness to continue to discuss the problem frankly, reporting:

> *Perdana Menteri Menzies dengan suara ngambek berkata: "Soal itu sudah tjukup saja djelaskan. Tuan2 tahu masalah ini amat penting sekali, tapi pun djuga rada pelik".*
>
> [In a petulant voice Prime Minister Menzies stated: "This issue has already had enough clarification. Gentlemen, you know that this is an extremely important problem, but one which is also somewhat complicated"].[43]

The risk for the Prime Minister in evading or dismissing public discussion on the matter was that it would erode the promotion of Australia as an open democracy, the government's primary strategy of persuasion against the ideologies of the extreme left. While the prime ministers' visit was generally viewed as successful from both parties' point of view, few were convinced any real substance had been given to the relationship.

The Universities' Response

While all three universities accepted the Menzies government's offer of funding to introduce Indonesian and Malay language programs, their approach varied. At the University of Melbourne and at Canberra University College, the government's immediate needs were partially addressed by introducing the language programs as extension courses, programs outside of the undergraduate program. This was not unlike what had been offered at the University of Sydney during the War.

Staffing was also unconventional with Melbourne employing a former Indonesian diplomat Zainu'ddin (see Figure 4) who had previously served in Australia. Meanwhile, Canberra accepted an offer from the Indonesian Embassy for their Cultural Attaché, Supangkat, to tutor. This allowed Melbourne and

---

43   *Pos Indonesia*, 8 December 1959.

Canberra to be operational by 1956. In contrast, the University of Sydney's program would be delayed, as the university sought an established academic and a more orthodox approach to the introduction of the language. While that was the intention, its first academic would come from an agricultural college. Fritz Van Naerssen had been working as a sociologist at the State Agricultural University Wageningen, but he had an extensive knowledge of Indonesian languages and introduced the language program in 1958. This was in spite of the Faculty of Arts' advice to delay its introduction while the studies programs were being developed.

Figure 4: Pak Zainu'ddin, who began teaching at the University of Melbourne in 1956, was the first Indonesian tutor employed of the post-war programs.
Photo Zainuddin family collection.

While the staff that were employed were enthusiastic promoters of their subject, the universities in general were somewhat sceptical of the academic value of the language. At Melbourne, the professor of French openly confided to Zainu'ddin that he saw no cultural value in Indonesian at all, that it 'was only good for trade and politics'.[44] When Indonesian finally made it into the University of Melbourne's handbook in 1959 it was placed in group 2 of the Arts subjects with History, Economics, Political Science, and Criminology, whereas group 1 contained languages such as Arabic, Chinese, French and Latin (University of Melbourne, 1959).

The universities' response indicates that the Indonesian programs in the 1950s were viewed as being linked to political and more pragmatic objectives, but it is questionable how relevant the programs were to the government's propaganda efforts, with students far more enchanted with the ancient cultures of Indonesia (see Robson, this volume). The university programs were gradually integrated more fully into the general academic programs and by the early 1960s the study of the language was gaining some momentum. Significantly, in 1962 Monash University acted autonomously, introducing Indonesian and Malay studies without government assistance or general sanction. The University of Western Australia attempted to follow suit, though it did make a request for government funding, only to be turned away with the government sighting Monash as a model.

The expansion of Indonesian and Malay programs beyond the founding three universities and into the schools in the 1960s was now a sign of the growing maturity in the country's political and cultural view of itself which was no longer related to short-term government objectives. The many barriers separating Australia from the Indonesian-Malay Archipelago for almost a century and a half were beginning to crack. However, the strident exhibition of political ideology in Indonesia during the early 1960s tempered the pace that Indonesia as a culture could be seen as a relevant influence on mainstream Australia. Unfortunately, for some Australians it also linked Indonesia to a region of instability and stoked their paranoia of the 'Near North'.

Conclusion

At the beginning of the 1950s, it was becoming increasingly apparent that Australia was somewhat of a cultural oddity in the region. As a nation, Australia was only just discovering that it had 'neighbours', so the possibility

---

44   Paul S. Thomas (Interviewer), & Zainu'ddin (Interviewee), 21 March 2007.

of such an intimate act as learning their language was unlikely to occur either quickly or in any natural fashion. This was particularly the case for a language such as Indonesian, which lay outside the language heritage of Australia's European based education system. Without government intervention, the introduction of Indonesian and Malay would have been further delayed and its teaching far more restricted in terms of the number of universities involved. This, in turn, would have delayed the introduction of the language to the secondary system, which began in 1962-63, leaving very few meaningful avenues of contact between Australians and Indonesians in the broader community.

The relative success of the programs in the 1960s in engaging Australians' interest in Indonesia, therefore, makes it difficult to evaluate the government's initiative purely from the context of its conception. Even in the fifties, there were a variety of factors at play, some solely bilateral, which sat in juxtaposition with the more imposing pressures of Australia's role in the Cold War. Additionally, the Australian Government had so little experience or capacity to implement Cold War strategies required by the Manila Pact that it is not surprising that it attempted to combine them with other initiatives that were already on the table. The government's committees on oriental languages had indicated its intent to support the teaching of Asian languages, at least at the university level. However, the need to offer something relevant to its allies that could be claimed to represent Australia's unique responsibilities allowed the government to focus on Indonesian and Malay raising it to the top of an existing list.

In summary, from the government's perspective the sponsorship of Indonesian and Malay Studies was part Cold War propaganda, part cultural diplomacy, and part education policy, though these were not necessarily of equal consideration at the time. External to the political process this may appear somewhat contradictory, but within the organic, pragmatic and opportunistic machinations of political decision making it harmonised the proposal with the government's political ideology and at the same time made it a reasonable justification of expenditure.

Whatever the motivation, the proposal was underpinned by the belief in translation as a tool of persuasion, that the Australian way of life and its values were representative of the modern democracies and could quite literally be translated to become a civilising influence in the archipelago. Menzies' efforts in presenting his message in Indonesian was symbolic of this. How exactly language teaching was to serve this purpose beyond the training of translators and interpreters, or bilingual agents of the government, was given little clarification. Fundamentally, there was faith that it would be a natural consequence of the introduction of the programs.

Perhaps unsurprisingly, students did not become Cold War warriors. Once the language programs were divorced from the political process they generally attracted students who were primarily interested in Indonesia. While students may have been reflective of their own culture and politics in terms of the manner in which it contrasted with Indonesia, the main translation that was taking place was from Indonesian into English. This was fortunate, as Indonesia was highly sensitive to external cultural influences, with Casey at one stage needing to explain that the appointment of a cultural attaché to Jakarta was not aimed at exporting Australian Culture.[45] Any flooding of translated books on Australia into Indonesia, as once had been proposed, would have been viewed with a good deal of scepticism and eroded efforts at projecting Australia's goodwill.

While little is known of Soekarno's opinion of the initiative, his Malayan counterpart, Prime Minister Tengku Abdul Rahman, visited Australia in 1959 and made the following observations:

> One hundred million people in Malaya, Indonesia, Borneo, Sarawak, Brunei, and parts of the Philippines speak Malay … they are your neighbours. Why shouldn't Australian schools teach Malay? Why teach Latin or German as an additional subject instead of Malay?[46]

The Tengku was challenging Australia's cultural affiliation. Clearly, those in the region did not see Australia as doing them a great favour by learning Indonesian/Malay; rather, it was simply considered that it should be the natural state of affairs. Even for the initiative to be effective propaganda, Australia would need to demonstrate that it was learning the language to be truly engaged with the cultures of the region and not simply a result of political manoeuvring.

By the mid-1960s the government began to believe that the programs were on a firm footing. Direct links between the government's Cold War propaganda efforts had faded and the teaching of Indonesian and Malay became situated well within an education and cultural diplomacy framework. In 1965, the Minister-in-Charge, John Gorton cited that there were over 600 students across four universities studying Indonesian/Malay and that 'the departments

---

45   Our Culture's Not an Export. *Argus*, 11 April 1956, p. 11.
46   Told: Learn Language of 100 million Neighbours. *Straits Times*, 11 November 1959, p. 1.

are well established and could now be regarded as regular part of Australian university life'. This was an early signal that the government no longer felt the need to directly sponsor the programs and in 1967 the annual grants to the three founding universities were withdrawn. Unfortunately, the confidence that the programs were on a stable foundation and would continue to grow proved over-optimistic. Student numbers in both schools and universities would fluctuate through the subsequent decades with a substantial trend downwards beginning in the post-Suharto era, ironically as Indonesia moved to its most democratic government since the proclamation of the republic (Slaughter, 2008; Hill, 2012).

The legacy of the Menzies-Casey initiative, therefore, remains mixed. The Indonesian language programs did succeed in spreading from the universities through to the primary schools to be a truly national program, Australia being the only nation outside of Indonesia to give such prominence to the language in their education system. Conversely, the general Australian views of the relationship remain political, the more than 50 years of teaching Indonesian failing to secure a cultural image of Indonesia in the popular imagination.

This leaves the contemporary programs to persuade Australians that the relationship with Indonesia, and Southeast Asia in general, is sufficiently important that it be taken beyond the political into a true cultural engagement. In part, this is a reversal of the initial notion of persuading Indonesians of the civilising influence of Australia's cultural and political system as a model Western democracy. It also requires an expansion of the translation project to an exchange and mutual understanding of national ideals.

Archives

NAA National Archives of Australia
NLA National Library of Australia
SUA Sydney University Archives

References

Aveling, H. 1998. 'Asian languages and literatures'. In *Knowing Ourselves and Others. The Humanities in Australia into the 21st Century Vol. 3*, edited by the Reference Group for the Australian Academy of the Humanities. Canberra: Commonwealth of Australia. pp. 29–39.
Bastin, J. 1957. 'Indonesian and Malayan Studies in Australia'. *Bijdragen tot de Taal-, Land- en Volkenkunde* 113 (2), pp. 201–204.
Brewster, J. & Reid, A. 1989. 'A.W. Hamilton and the origins of Indonesian studies in Australia'. In *Observing change in Asia*, edited by R. J. May & J. O'Malley. Bathurst: Crawford House. pp. 22–32.

Burns, C. 1944. 'School of Oriental Studies: part of wide federal plan'. *Argus*, September 7. p. 2.
Bussemaker, H. 1996. 'Australian Defence Cooperation 1940–41'. *Journal of the Australian War Memorial*, 29, November. Available from: http://www.awm.gov.au/journal/j29/herman.asp, accessed 12 April 2010.
Casey, R. G. 1951. 'What "Near North" means to Australia'. *Sydney Morning Herald*, September 6. p. 2.
Goldsworthy, D. 2002. *Losing the Blanket: Australia and the End of Britain's Empire*. Carlton South: Melbourne University Press.
Hill, D. T. 2012. *Indonesian Language in Australian Universities: Strategies for a Stronger Future*. Australian Learning and Teaching Council National Teaching Fellowship Final Report. Perth: Murdoch University.
Hodge, E. 1995. *Radio Wars: Truth, Propaganda and the Struggle for Radio Australia*. Melbourne: Cambridge University Press.
Hodge, E. 1992. 'Radio Australia in the Second World War'. *Australian Journal of International Affairs* 46 (1), pp. 93–108. DOI: 10.1080/10357719208445076
Jenkins, G. 1946. 'Things we must do about our neighbour'. *The Argus*, December 13. p. 2.
Patterson, J. 1949. 'Menzies urges Empire talks'. *The Argus*, November 30. p. 9.
Phelps, P. 1996. *Australia, International Diplomacy and the West New Guinea Dispute, 1949–1963*. Ph.D. thesis, University of Sydney.
Reid, A. 1981. '"Alterity" and "Reformism": the Australian frontier in Indonesian Studies'. *Archipel* 21 (1), pp. 7–18.
Robson, S. 2002. *From Malay to Indonesian: The Genesis of a National Language*. Centre for Southeast Asian Studies Working Papers, 118. Clayton: Monash Asia Institute.
Slaughter, Y. 2007. 'The rise and fall of Indonesian in Australian schools: Implications for language policy and planning'. *Australian Studies Review* 31 (3), pp. 301–322.
Sneddon, J. 2004. *The Indonesian Language: Its History and Role in Modern Society*. Kensington: University of New South Wales Press.
Sobocinska, A. 2014. *Visiting the Neighbours: Australians in Asia*. Sydney: University of New South Wales Press.
Stanley, M. 1952. 'Australians to learn Malay'. *The Straits Times*, June 29. p. 6.
University of Melbourne. 1959. *University of Melbourne Calendar 1959*. Carlton: University of Melbourne Press.
Waters, C. 1999. 'A failure of imagination: R.G. Casey and Australian plans for counter-subversion in Asia, 1954–1956'. *The Australian Journal of Politics and History*, 45 (3), pp. 347–361.
Worsely, P. 1994. *Unlocking Australia's Language Potential: Profiles of 9 key languages in Australia: Volume 5 Indonesian/Malay*. Canberra: National Languages and Literacy Institute of Australia.
Zainu'ddin, A. 1988. 'The teaching of Japanese at Melbourne University, 1919–1941'. *History of Education Review*, 17 (2), pp. 45–62.

Chapter 4

ROLLER-COASTER

The University of Melbourne Experience[1]

Charles A. Coppel

The University of Melbourne

Indonesian language has been taught continuously at the University of Melbourne for more than fifty years but the course of the program's history has been far from smooth. More than either of the other pioneering programs, it has been on a roller coaster ride, subject to tight budgetary constraints, repeated organizational restructuring, and the need to justify its continued existence in recurrent years of crisis.

Nevertheless, a close study of the Melbourne experience demonstrates features common to Indonesian language programs at all Australian universities over the last half-century. All have felt the ebb and flow of changing government education policies, initiatives and levels of funding as well as the ups and downs of the bilateral relationship between Australia and Indonesia. Their positions within their own institutions have all been at the mercy of

---

[1] The author has been a participant observer of the Indonesian language program at the University of Melbourne for much of its history. I was a student (1963–1965) and staff member in the program (1973–1987) and was Co-ordinator of Asian Studies, Faculty of Arts (October 1989 – December 1992). A good deal of this chapter is based on material in my personal archive. I have also benefited from interviews with various colleagues but responsibility for statements of fact and opinion rests with me. I am indebted to the following informants: Sander Adelaar, Syd Crawcour, Michael Ewing, Hendy Hendrata, Ariel Heryanto, Edwin Jurriens, Jamie Mackie, Julia Read, Zainu'ddin, and Ailsa Thomson Zainu'ddin.

changing university priorities, the whims of deans, and the growing subordination of academic policy to economic imperatives.

The initial design, which emphasised the integration of language and area studies programs, ensured that Melbourne had a distinctive model to offer. It was not, however, a model that was calculated to enhance student enrolments as it deterred prospective students who preferred to take the language without the area study as well as those who preferred to take the area study without the language. The nexus between language and area study became gradually more attenuated in the search for increased student numbers, but the language program continued for decades to bear the imprint of the original model. In an environment of scarce resources there was a persistent tension within the fight for survival between the need to maintain its *raison d'être* and the need to demonstrate student demand.

Origins and Foundations

In 1955 the Commonwealth Government approached the University of Melbourne, the University of Sydney and Canberra University College (then administered by the University of Melbourne but later to become part of the Australian National University) to see if they were prepared to provide teaching in Indonesian and Malayan Studies (see Thomas, this volume). Although at that time Australian universities were not funded by the Commonwealth (apart from Commonwealth scholarships), the request came with an offer to fund the new development. In initial discussions with the Director of the Commonwealth Office of Education, the Vice-Chancellor suggested 'a staff of two, a senior lecturer (European) supported by a junior (native speaker)' in the first full year.[2] The Commonwealth recognised that it was a matter for the university to decide the form of the program, but 'While the language of Indonesia might be the major study, possibly provision could be made for teaching something of the culture of the region'. Teaching was to commence in 1956 if practicable.[3]

---

2   Wm. J. Weeden to Professor G. W. Paton 24 June 1955 (University of Melbourne Archives).
3   A five-year postgraduate research program on Indonesia had already been mooted in the University of Melbourne Faculty of Arts as early as 1952. Sponsored by Professors Macmahon Ball and Max Crawford, it was to include 'an intensive study of the Malay language (with, if possible, Dutch)'. Interested parties included Herbert Feith (then doing M.A. fieldwork in Indonesia), Johannes Leyser (Law) and Joe Isaac (Economics). Faculty of Arts Minutes, 14 November 1952 (University of Melbourne Archives).

Zainu'ddin, the first 'native speaker' lecturer, started teaching Indonesian language in 1956. Initially, the subject could not be credited towards an Arts degree. It was an 'extension course' (later known as a 'continuing education subject'). He had been employed by the Indonesian Ministry of Foreign Affairs and had been in the Indonesian Embassy in Canberra. Despite his lack of academic credentials – he was concurrently enrolled at the university for his own first undergraduate degree – he created his own teaching materials which were later to form the basis for Sarumpaet and Mackie (1966). Zainu'ddin and Mackie have both informed the author that Zainu'ddin's contribution was inadequately acknowledged in the book. One of the first cohort in 1956 remembers that his class of about 15 students included a number of public servants like himself, who enrolled free of charge.[4]

Two years later the 'native-speaker' Zainu'ddin was joined by Jamie Mackie, the 'European' senior lecturer in charge of the program. Mackie, who had held a lectureship in the History Department at the University in 1955, returned fresh from working for two years with the State Planning Bureau in Jakarta as a Colombo Plan expert. It was only then, in 1959, that Indonesian Studies Part I was introduced as part of the Bachelor of Arts degree. Designed as the first of a proposed series of three subjects, it was 'divided in roughly equal proportions between Indonesian language and an "area study" of the political and economic organization, history and culture of the area'. This yoking together of language and area study was for many years a feature of the Melbourne program which distinguished it from its sister programs in Sydney and Canberra that were set up with Commonwealth funding at the same time. It also left a strong imprint on the materials used for teaching the language. Unless they already had some knowledge of the language, students were expected to attend an introductory summer course of four weeks. The stated goal was that they should reach a 'working knowledge of spoken Bahasa Indonesia' by the end of the first year. This was somewhat ambitious, because they had only three lectures (one of which was for area study) and a tutorial each week through the year.

Access to spoken Indonesian was hard to come by at that time. There were few Indonesians living or studying in Australia, and few Australians visited Indonesia. There were no Indonesian language programs on radio or television (except for Radio Australia broadcasts to Indonesia which could not readily be listened to in Melbourne) and the University did not yet have language laboratory facilities. It should be no surprise that in practice there was more

---

4   Syd Crawcour, personal communication.

emphasis on the written than the spoken language in the program. My own experience as a student several years later would confirm that the language program was more successful in enabling students to read contemporary Indonesian than to speak it.

When Indonesian Studies Part II commenced in 1960, only one of the three weekly lectures was devoted to 'more advanced study of Bahasa Indonesia and reading of Indonesian literature' while the other two concentrated on post-war Indonesian politics with its social and economic background'.[5] When I took this subject in 1965, my Indonesian language reading included Idrus's short story 'Surabaya', Sukarno's 1959 Independence Day speech (later to be contracted to the *Manifesto Politik* or Manipol), and substantial extracts from the 1945 Indonesian Constitution. Materials of this kind were supplied by the department and, in those days before photocopiers (let alone computers or even electric typewriters), they had to be laboriously typed with a manual typewriter onto waxed Roneo sheets and then duplicated on a Gestetner machine. Indonesian Studies III (in which language study was similarly subordinated to area study) was introduced in 1962 and a combined honours program commenced soon after that, with the first honours students reaching fourth year in 1966.

In the early years, Indonesian Studies enrolments were very small and grew gradually. There were only six students in the initial first year class in 1959, rising to seven in 1960, when the second year subject began with a class of two students. In 1961 there were twelve students in first year and five in second year. In 1964, when the third year subject came on stream, there was still only a total of 44 students across the three levels (of whom 29 were first year, twelve second year and three third year). The big leap forward came in 1965 when numbers more than doubled to 96 students (67 at first year, 24 at second year and five at third year) and they increased again in 1966 to 117 students (75 at first year, 30 at second year and twelve at third year).[6] That was a very exciting time to study Indonesia and Malaysia (the program was in a Department of Indonesian and Malayan Studies) and the increasing interest was a reflection of dramatic events in the region. In 1963 the former Federation of Malaya was joined with the colonies of Singapore, Sarawak and North Borneo (now Sabah) to form a new Federation of Malaysia. The Indonesian government under President Sukarno called it a neo-colonialist project and launched an armed confrontation (*Konfrontasi*) against Malaysia.

---

5   Faculty of Arts Handbook 1960.
6   Figures from a personal file of Jamie Mackie in the author's possession.

In 1965 Indonesia withdrew from the United Nations in protest against the election of Malaysia to a seat on the UN Security Council, Singapore was expelled from Malaysia and became an independent Republic, and in Indonesia the abortive 'coup attempt' on 1 October led to turmoil, massacres and the overthrow of Sukarno and inauguration of Suharto's New Order regime.

The rapid expansion of Indonesian Studies at the University of Melbourne could scarcely have come at a worse time, however. It coincided with a general financial crisis at the University and a decision by the Commonwealth Office of Education to put a cap on its funding for the program which until then had been largely financially dependent on the Commonwealth government. Meanwhile neighbouring Monash University, which had its first student intake in 1961, was growing rapidly and had more than twenty thousand students by 1967. It was teaching Indonesian and Malay and established a Centre of Southeast Asian Studies (CSEAS) in 1964. In these circumstances, the head of the Indonesian program at the University of Melbourne (Jamie Mackie) transmigrated from Parkville to Monash's Clayton Campus at the end of 1967 to become the Research Director of the CSEAS. As a result of these developments, and despite growing interest in Indonesia in Australia, enrolments at Melbourne declined. In 1967 there were 87 students across all levels and in 1968 the total fell to 63.

The distinctive integration of Indonesian language and area study which had been pioneered by Mackie at its outset remained a feature of the Indonesian Studies program at Melbourne long after his departure, but gradually and for various reasons changes were made that weakened the rationale for the nexus. Already in 1965 it was found necessary to devote the first year subject entirely to language study (with the exception of a ten-lecture survey history of Indonesia which served as an introduction to the area study to be taken with the language in later years of the course). The intensive summer school was abandoned several years later.

The Sarumpaet Decades

In 1961 J. P. (Pieter) Sarumpaet was recruited from Gadjah Mada University in Yogyakarta to take over the language program from Zainu'ddin. Sarumpaet had completed a master's degree in comparative education at the University of Exeter, and although not formally trained in linguistics had an excellent command of English and a good ear for nuances in both English and Indonesian. His Exeter thesis was later published in Indonesian (Sarumpaet, 1965). Curiously, Pieter's recruitment to Melbourne was a forerunner to other

Indonesian alumni from Exeter migrating to Australia to teach Indonesian. Monash University gained Rabin Hardjadibrata and Iman Partoredjo (who later moved to Brisbane to teach at Brisbane Grammar School and later at Griffith University), Ben Soeradinata taught at the Bendigo campus of La Trobe University and his wife Sri tutored for Sarumpaet in the Melbourne program. Having been first appointed for a period of three years, Sarumpaet returned to Indonesia in 1964 because he was unable to extend his leave of absence from his Indonesian university for a further three-year term. His place at Melbourne was taken temporarily by Supomo Surjohudojo until Supomo left to join the Indonesian program at the ANU. Mackie then advertised a lectureship with continuing tenure and Sarumpaet returned to Melbourne where he remained until his sudden death in April 1991. For nearly three decades the Indonesian language program showed the mark of his influence both in its approach and the books which the students used.

Sarumpaet believed that his students needed to have a solid grounding in Indonesian grammar and to be able to translate English texts into the 'standard and correct usage in the modern Indonesian now used in schools and universities, and by those who write and speak with care', as he put it in his introduction to *Modern Usage in Bahasa Indonesia* (Sarumpaet, 1980). More advanced students not infrequently found themselves asked to translate into Indonesian a text which could be quite difficult for them to comprehend even in English such as the abstruse and literary 'Saturday reflection' editorials in *The Age*. Not all of them relished the challenge. Sarumpaet was not alone among Indonesian 'native speaker' teachers (especially Sumatrans) in insisting that his students should avoid more colloquial forms of the language such as those found in Jakarta and other Javanese cities but he was particularly rigorous in his condemnation of what he revealingly called 'sub-standard' (rather than 'non-standard') Indonesian. His prescriptive approach to grammar and emphasis on 'good' or standard Indonesian seemed to owe much to the way in which the language had been taught in Indonesia under the influence of Balai Pustaka in the late colonial period and the Department of Education after independence. He was nevertheless responsive to 'the ongoing debates among scholars regarding standard usage' and to changes in the language as he noted them in the quality press such as *Kompas* or *Tempo*. The title of his *Modern Usage* is of course an allusion to Henry Fowler's classic *Modern English Usage* and the books have some similarities. Sarumpaet was, however, concerned with 'the needs of English-speaking students in their attempt to express themselves in good Indonesian' whereas Fowler aimed his book at 'the half-educated Englishman of literary proclivities' rather than the foreigner.

Sarumpaet participated in the Third National Congress on Bahasa Indonesia held in Jakarta in October-November 1978, and presented a paper on the teaching of Indonesian in Australia at the Fifth Congress a decade later. His traditionalist grammar and translation approach brought him into closer alignment to those who, under the auspices of the Indonesian Department of Education and Culture, were working during that period to produce the standardized Indonesian grammar (*Tata Bahasa Baku Bahasa Indonesia*) and monolingual dictionary (*Kamus Besar Bahasa Indonesia*) which were both published in 1988 to mark the sixtieth anniversary of the Youth Pledge (*Sumpah Pemuda*). He was less in tune with developments in theoretical linguistics, let alone the changing fashions in foreign language teaching methodology. It is remarkable that in his paper for the Fifth National Congress on Bahasa Indonesia in October–November 1988 he had nothing at all to say about teaching methodology for Indonesian in Australia (Sarumpaet, 1988). This is in stark contrast with the paper on the teaching of Indonesian in the United States at the same Congress (Sumarmo, 1988). Nevertheless, over the years some elements derived from other approaches (including audio-lingual exercises and structure drills) were grafted with mixed success onto the original grammar and translation approach.

Figure 1: Lecturers and tutors of the Indonesian program in the early 1980s receiving a visit from the Indonesian Educational and Cultural Attache. Left to right: Din Zainu'ddin, Syahisti Abdurrachman, Barita Gultom, Mahmud Zaki (Cultural Attache), Charles Coppel, Moh Slamet, and Pieter Sarumpaet. Early 1980s.
Photo courtesy Syahisti Abdurrachman.

Figure 2: Indonesian lecturer Zainu'ddin (left) inspecting the new language laboratory, John Medley Building, University of Melbourne, early 1970s.
Photo courtesy Ann McCarthy.

This can be illustrated by looking at the textbooks prescribed for the program, almost all of which were locally produced and mostly authored (or co-authored) by Sarumpaet himself. Dictionaries were the exception to the local production rule. Initially the program used the Indonesian-English and English-Indonesian dictionaries produced by Pino and Wittermans in Jakarta in the 1950s, replacing them with the two dictionaries published by Cornell University Press when they became available (Echols and Shadily, 1961 and 1975). The monolingual *Kamus Umum Bahasa Indonesia* (Poerwadarminta, 1961) was also added to the list of references. The *Introduction to Bahasa Indonesia* (IBI) (Sarumpaet and Mackie, 1966) was followed by the very successful *A Modern Reader in Bahasa Indonesia* (MRI) (Sarumpaet and Hendrata, 1968), which was widely prescribed for use in Victorian secondary schools and other tertiary institution Indonesian classes as well as in the Melbourne program. The MRI ran into numerous editions and was still on sale up to about 1995, four years after Sarumpaet's death. First published within the department in 1968, later editions were printed in Singapore and self-published by the authors from Sarumpaet's home address in Box Hill. The book appeared in two slim illustrated volumes, the first (with a blue cover) for beginners, and the second (with a green cover) for more advanced students. Attractively illustrated with photographs, they consisted of a series of short Indonesian texts followed by questions in Indonesian which were intended to stimulate class discussion in Indonesian. The authors aimed to reach a school and adult readership. The texts covered a wide range of topics providing a good deal of information about Indonesian life, history and culture and were graded in order of difficulty. Like the IBI, which deliberately made do with a very small vocabulary, the MRI used a relatively controlled vocabulary which was gradually extended over the course of the two volumes. Both the IBI and the MRI provided a learner's language which avoided authentic materials and gave little attention to register or cultural context in the use of the language.

In the meantime, Sarumpaet had produced another book of a quite different kind. *The Structure of Bahasa Indonesia* (SBI) (Sarumpaet, 1966) was first published by the Department, later by the author in Box Hill in 1972, and then by Sahata (Sarumpaet's own imprint) in 1977. I believe that it was first trialled in Bandung in January 1967 with an advanced class of which I was a member in a group of some 70 students of Indonesian from different parts of Australia who spent a month in Indonesia. This ambitious and imaginative exercise in in-country education for Australian students of Indonesian (perhaps the first of its kind) was organised by Sarumpaet with Arch Nelson of the University of New England. The SBI, which was used in the University of Melbourne Indonesian program for many years, consisted of a series of exercises each containing a considerable number of Indonesian phrases or sentences deploying a large and seemingly uncontrolled vocabulary. Students had to read the sentences and then transform each of them into a different Indonesian sentence structure. The structures were often quite literary in style and not very well designed for oral practice, and students complained about the burden of new vocabulary which was not found in either the IBI or the MRI. Despite this, the SBI was still being prescribed for students as a text (as was the MRI) in 1991, the year in which he died.

Another key teacher in the program was Hendy Hendrata, who was recruited by Mackie in 1965 as a part-time tutor. He had been employed as a broadcaster at Radio Australia and was completing a Bachelor of Commerce degree. Like Zainu'ddin and Sarumpaet, he had no background at all in language teaching or linguistics.[7] Before Mackie's move to Monash, he

---

7   Appointments of Indonesian teaching staff must have depended more on personal contacts than formal qualifications and previous experience. Perhaps that was inevitable at the time.

managed to attract some financial support from The Herald and Weekly Times Ltd (publishers of the daily newspapers *The Sun* and *The Herald*) which enabled Hendrata (who was by then a Commerce graduate) to be appointed as a full-time Senior Tutor in the language program from 1967 to 1969.[8] Although he then moved to a full-time Indonesian language teaching position at Scotch College and after that to a full-time lectureship in Indonesian at the Prahran College of Advanced Education, he continued to teach as a part-time tutor in the University program until about 1981. During his time as a tutor, Hendrata published *An Audio-lingual Course in Bahasa Indonesia* (Hendrata, 1969–1970) in several volumes with accompanying tapes as well as co-authoring the MRI with Sarumpaet. After the 1972 move of the program into the newly constructed John Medley Building, which contained the University's first language laboratory, he was the pioneer in using the facilities for Indonesian language. Hendrata's audio-lingual approach permitted more colloquial expression than other texts used in the program but still leaned toward formality of speech.[9] Some years after Hendrata stopped tutoring in the University, he completed a Master of Education Studies degree in teaching methodology at Monash University. Sarumpaet, an older man more set in his ways, apparently never felt the need to upgrade his qualifications in a field which was rapidly changing. He was not alone in this position; it was probably shared by most teaching staff in language departments at the University, where excellence in research rather than in teaching was seen as the path to promotion.

When Indonesian language was first taught at the University, it was one of the few languages taught solely *ab initio*.[10] Because it was not yet being taught in Victorian schools, there was no cause to provide a first year subject in the language catering for students who had already completed the language at Year 12 level. At that time also there were few students from Indonesia or Malaysia attending Australian universities and even fewer were enrolled for an Arts degree. Similarly, there was little demand for more advanced Indonesian language subjects for Australian born children of Indonesians or Malaysians resident in Australia. In the early years, students from these various backgrounds who wanted to take Indonesian at the University were

---

8   Like the earlier Commonwealth funding, this subvention was welcome but short-lived. It may have helped to save the program at a vulnerable time.
9   See Read and Reeve in this volume on the wider move to the audio-lingual approach at this time.
10 At that time a foreign language at Matriculation level was a prerequisite for entry to the Faculty of Arts.

exempted from the first year beginners' subject and allowed to enrol in the second year. Over time the numbers entering directly into the second year subject from each of these categories grew, giving rise to difficulties for both groups of students. The students moving on from the beginners' subject were now joined by an increasing number of other students with a more advanced command of spoken Indonesian. The former group had been taught with an approach that emphasised grammar and translation rather than the spoken word, and were often envious of the oral facility of the newcomers. On the other hand, the teaching staff tended to be critical of the latter group for their deficiencies in grammatical knowledge and their use of colloquial forms of the language which Sarumpaet described as 'substandard'. These students in turn felt that their oral skills were undervalued and even falling away through lack of practice. As it became more common for students to travel to Indonesia, they encountered informal usage and unfamiliar registers or dialects of the language and demanded more instruction in everyday speech. Sarumpaet was unrepentant. As he wrote in *Modern Usage* (Sarumpaet, 1980, p. vi):

> When students first visit Indonesia, they encounter local or regional varieties of the language. But if they have been taught the correct standard usage they should, within a reasonably short time, be able to understand the local and regional varieties, and be understood by most of the people they speak to. It is better for a foreign student to err on the correct or even formal side than to employ careless, incorrect or substandard usage.

In a report to the University on his 1978 study leave, he described conducting a language class at Cornell University in Indonesian:[11]

> The students noted, as I had expected they would, that somehow I spoke a rather different variant of the language to what they had been accustomed to hearing. Then followed a lively discussion, with the professor who wrote their textbooks taking part [presumably John Wolff – CAC], on the various registers in Bahasa Indonesia. I stressed that in discussions one should use the standard register, while one should attempt to understand – especially for the purposes of fieldwork – as many other registers as possible, even down to the substandard.

---

11   A copy of the report is in Charles Coppel's personal archive.

At the time of giving this class, it had been about seven years since Sarumpaet had set foot in Indonesia. He had a productive visit there later in the year and reported:

> A prolonged stay in Indonesia every 3 or 4 years is obviously a must for a teacher of the language. One could immerse oneself in the language community, observe the various changes in a fast-developing language and read the many books now being published in Indonesian.

One can glimpse here, perhaps, an acknowledgment that his own infrequent stays in Indonesia must have made him a little out of touch with those 'changes in a fast-developing language', especially in everyday speech. His *Modern Usage*, published two years later, was more a guide to the written than the spoken language. For example, for years he insisted that students should always use the word *dapat* rather than *bisa* even in speech. By 1980, when *Modern Usage* appeared, he conceded that *bisa* 'is now colloquial for *dapat*' but added 'and should be avoided in polite and formal conversation' except in certain idiomatic expressions. His reluctance to allow *bisa* may have been a reflection of a Sumatran distaste for a usage more common in Java.[12]

Changes in Organisation and Curriculum

Shortly before Mackie's departure at the end of 1967, he recruited Muhammad Slamet to teach anthropology and sociology. After some temporary appointments, the historian Pitono joined the team. When his limited tenure position was replaced by a continuing appointment in 1973, his place was taken by Charles Coppel. These 'area study' lecturers were expected to contribute to the Indonesian language teaching in addition to the areas of their own expertise. Until Slamet's retirement at the end of 1987, the core staffing in the Indonesian studies program remained the triumvirate of Sarumpaet, Slamet and Coppel. This period of fifteen years was by far the most stable in the history of the program with respect to its tenured staff, but it was far from stable in other respects. The content and structure of the program and its organizational environment was in continual flux, buffeted by the winds of economic crises, changing student demand and government policies. At several points in this history, it seemed that the survival of the program was at stake.

---

12   Sarumpaet was a particularly vigorous protagonist in the long-running debate among Indonesian language teachers about the relative merits of formal and colloquial speech, an issue closely related to debates about the use of authentic materials.

The program was first set up within a Department of Indonesian and Malayan Studies, of which Mackie was the head. When he left, he was replaced as department head not by one of the surviving members of the department (who were both Indonesians) but by Harry Simon, the head of the Department of Oriental Studies, whose field was Chinese language. This arrangement was later formalized in 1971 by a merger of the departments into a new Department of East and Southeast Asian Studies. The merger was probably necessary for the survival of the program but for the Indonesian staff the loss of autonomy and even of the word 'Indonesian' as part of the name of the department was felt as a kind of colonization, however well-intentioned it may have been. In fact it was in many respects a merely cosmetic arrangement. The Indonesian Studies program itself was largely unaffected by the merger, and it had its own secretary. The former departments occupied different floors of the west wing of the new John Medley Building. On the sixth floor Indonesian Studies students had their own small library which was to be their social centre for the next twenty years. After being moved around four different buildings in the previous decade, this was welcome stability for both staff and students. Moreover, the merger itself was explicitly subject to review and in the course of 1975 disagreements about the application of the University's statute relating to departmental governance led to a decision that the two former departments should be reconstituted.

The timing of the resurrection of the Department of Indonesian and Malayan Studies was fortuitous. Enrolments in Indonesian Studies had been fairly stable with good retention rates for several years, and the numbers were substantially higher than those in Chinese or Japanese which were taught in the former Department of Oriental Studies (now reborn as East Asian Studies). There was an average of more than 50 students in first year (although that had fallen sharply in 1975), 45 in second year and 20 in third year, about double the number enrolled in 1968. First and second year enrolments plunged further in 1976, the first year of the newly independent department, apparently in reaction to the Indonesian invasion of East Timor. In the following years the lower enrolments flowed on to the second and third year levels. It was surprising enough that the University had agreed to independence for the department in 1975. If it had been known that student demand was going to drop so dramatically, the merged department would undoubtedly have continued to exist. As it was, the University had approved the separation subject to a number of conditions. These included a requirement that there should be 'moves within the Faculty of Arts to co-operate with the other Victorian universities in the teaching of languages, notably Indonesian and Japanese'. It also foreshadowed the possibility of a School of Asian Studies 'to co-ordinate and rationalise the activities of the various departments and parts of departments which are involved in the study of different aspects of Asia'.[13]

Lacking a professorial head, the bargaining power of the newly reconstituted department was not strong. A Committee on Asian studies which had been set up by the Faculty of Arts Standing Committee of Heads of Departments in 1974 had reported that Chinese and Indian Studies should have 'particularly high priority' partly because Melbourne had strength in these areas and other Melbourne universities had little or no such strength and partly because 'the cultures and languages of both China and India have seminal importance for the understanding of Asia as a whole and have particularly high intrinsic interest'. The Committee noted the strength of Monash University in undergraduate teaching of Indonesian language and literature and in postgraduate research through the Centre of Southeast Asian Studies but concluded that the Faculty should maintain the program at least to the present level. Its stated reasons for this were the 'pioneering role' of the Melbourne program, its expertise in this area of teaching and research, the 'special nature' of the 'integrated Melbourne course', and the fact that its current retention rate was better than that at Monash which might be advantageous, if Commonwealth funds were to be provided, for 'ex-quota courses for teachers and teachers-in-training'.[14]

The department held a *selamatan* to celebrate its regained *kemerdekaan* in 1976 and almost immediately started to put in motion a series of major course changes in the hope of reversing the fall in student numbers.[15] In brief, these changes were of four kinds. First, the area study subjects were unitised and doubled in number (so that separate units were now available in history, politics. anthropology and sociology). Only two of the four units were available in any one year, but they could now be taken by students who were unwilling to take Indonesian language, either in combination as a full Indonesian area study subject or individually in combination with other Asian studies subjects or, in some cases, individually as part of a subject in the Departments of Political Science and History. Students taking Indonesian language at second and third year still had to combine it with an area study component which now

---

13   University of Melbourne Joint Committee of Council and the Professorial Board, Report and Recommendation of the Sub-Committee on the Reconstitution of the Department of East and Southeast Asian Studies (23 May 1975). Joint Committee 5/75 (9-6-75) Item No. 5. Copy in Charles Coppel personal archive.

14   Copy of committee report in Charles Coppel personal archive.

15   A *selamatan* is a Javanese ceremonial meal of thanksgiving; *kemerdekaan* means 'independence'.

consisted of one of the four new area study units. Secondly, an additional language subject (*Modern Indonesian Writers*) was introduced at third year level. This made it possible for students who had passed Indonesian at the Higher School Certificate level to complete a full major sequence of three subjects in Indonesian studies. Thirdly, the area study component of the first year subject was removed and converted into a new first year half-subject unit called Southeast Asian Studies 1, which could be combined with a new half-subject unit in Indonesian Language. Concerns had been raised that the student workload in the old first year subject was too onerous and these changes brought the Indonesian first year program into harmony with the first year program in the Department of East Asian Studies. Fourthly, the department was allowed to offer a pure honours program in Indonesian Studies where previously students could only do an honours degree in Indonesian Studies in combination with honours in another discipline or area. Honours students (who had long been taught Jawi script by Sarumpaet and were able to read some Malay manuscript materials) now had an option to take an introductory honours subject in Modern Javanese (which was given by Slamet). In collaboration with other departments, provision was also made for honours students to incorporate introductory subjects in Dutch or Arabic into their program. Enrolments had been successfully consolidated, especially through an increase in the number of honours and postgraduate students.

Another Year of Crisis

In a letter to alumni informing them that the department proposed to hold another *selamatan* early in Second Term 1982 to celebrate three *windu* (24 years) of Indonesian Studies as an Arts degree subject at the university, the department chairman (Coppel) wrote:[16]

> Despite the extent of the structural changes to our courses, we have remained true to the original concept on which the Department was founded – the combination of language and area study work is still mandatory for all students who complete a pass major or undertake honours work in Indonesian and Malayan Studies.

At the time at which I wrote this, I did not know that 1982 was to be another year of crisis for the department and the program. As far as I can now recall,

---

16   Copy of letter in Charles Coppel personal archive. A *windu* is a period of eight years in the Javanese calendar.

the *selamatan* was not held and the mood was far from celebratory. University budgets were being squeezed as part of the Fraser government's 'razor gang' economies.[17] This was exacerbated in Victoria by a state government decision to increase payroll tax without any corresponding increase in the universities' income to meet the additional tax.

The storm clouds had been gathering for about a year. In February 1981 the Universities Council chaired by Professor Dunbar had given advice to the Commonwealth Tertiary Education Commission for the 1982–84 triennium in which it observed that 'there appears to be unnecessary and costly duplication or fragmentation in areas such as Asian Studies [and] Foreign Language Studies …'[18] The Council saw benefit in the concentration of such specialist activities in a limited number of selected universities and wished to encourage universities to collaborate with one another in achieving this. In later advice in August 1981 the Universities Council observed that the Commonwealth Government had made rationalisation and consolidation the focal points of its guidelines for the tertiary education sector. The Council reiterated that it regarded Asian studies and foreign languages as typical illustrations of activities where benefits would flow from collaboration, citing the teaching of foreign languages in Victoria as a particular example. In June 1982 Professor Dunbar wrote to the university Vice-Chancellor saying that the Council wished to know what moves had been made or were in contemplation 'to reduce the range of activities offered in order to maintain the high quality of academic programs in times of reduced funding'. He drew attention to 'departments which cater for small numbers of students' and suggested that 'universities should … consider consolidating such departments into larger units and eliminating subjects or courses in little demand'. The Council also wanted to be informed of what had been done or was in contemplation with respect to collaboration 'with neighbouring institutions with a view to reducing what might appear to be unnecessary duplication of courses' once again citing Asian Studies and Foreign Languages as cases in point. Universities were being urged to cut their budgets selectively rather than across the board.

The University of Melbourne in turn applied pressure on the Faculty of Arts to cut the number of its offerings. A Committee on Student Numbers

---

17 After its re-election in October 1980, the Coalition government of Malcolm Fraser set up a committee to review Commonwealth government expenditure which was known as the 'razor gang'.

18 This and other quotations in this paragraph come from documents in the Charles Coppel personal archive.

reported to the Joint Committee on Policy late in 1981 that certain departments (of which Indonesian and Malayan Studies was one) were prima facie non-viable either because their student enrolments were too small or because their numbers had shown a marked decline over the previous eight years (or both).

The Department of Indonesian and Malayan Studies was now embattled on several fronts. It had very little bargaining power. It was the second smallest department in the Faculty of Arts, and there were three other small Asian Studies departments in the Faculty.[19] It had small enrolments, and it taught a foreign language (Indonesian). Moreover, at neighbouring Monash University there was a larger Indonesian language program headed by Professor Cyril Skinner and a much larger and highly regarded concentration of expertise on Indonesia in the CSEAS. The Arts Faculty Budgets Committee at Melbourne had already decided to make budgetary savings for 1983 by cutting the level of administrative support available to departments. In the case of the two smallest departments this meant that they could expect to have no more than one-half of a secretary each. It was plain that in such circumstances neither of these departments could maintain its independence. On 1 July 1982 the Dean of the Arts Faculty (Professor Geoffrey Blainey) wrote to each of the chairmen of the departments asking 'which department you would prefer to join with, and why'. In the following months a variety of permutations and combinations of the four departments or some of them was proposed and fought over. The outcome was a merger from 1983 of Indian and Indonesian Studies, but with the additional requirement that the new department, together with the Department of East Asian Studies, should join with other interested parties in a wider Faculty grouping, which came to be known as the School of Asian Studies.

Meanwhile, in 1982 the department also had to address the demands of the Universities Council for eliminating subjects or courses in little demand and for collaboration with Monash University. Its chairman had discussions with the Monash Arts Faculty Dean (who happened to be the Indonesian historian Professor John Legge) and with Professor Skinner. They had no desire for Monash to absorb the Melbourne Indonesian language program or for Sarumpaet, the Indonesian language specialist at Melbourne, to transfer to Monash. Nor did Coppel seek this. None of them believed that it would be practicable for Melbourne students to commute to Clayton to do Indonesian

---

19   The smallest was the Department of Indian Studies which in 1982 replaced Bengali with Hindi.

there. Coppel's concern was to find an acceptable outcome which could enable his university to demonstrate to the Universities Council that some form of collaboration between the two universities was happening. A sacrifice seemed to be demanded and it was made. Once again major changes were made to the course structure, to be phased in over the following three years. Indonesian language would still be offered at Melbourne but it was limited to a pass major for the beginners' stream and a sub-major (two subjects) for the HSC stream. The department abandoned its long held requirement that students of Indonesian language at intermediate and advanced levels should combine it with area study. All other language subjects were dropped including Modern Indonesian Writers and honours subjects like Modern Javanese (which had five students in 1982). Honours students at Melbourne would take advanced area study subjects like Indonesian Historiography, Chinese in Southeast Asia and Islam in Southeast Asia. If they wanted advanced Indonesian language subjects, they would have to transfer to Monash or take Monash subjects as complementary courses. A vestige of the old integration of language and area study nonetheless remained. For entry into honours, students must have passed the advanced level language subject, and the final honours thesis still required students to use Indonesian language materials.

Putting a brave face on it, the department pointed to significant advantages from the changes. They would concentrate language teaching into the areas where classes were largest and eliminate the honours classes which were the smallest. At the same time the mainstream language students would have a significant increase in class contact hours. The small number of contact hours in all the Indonesian language subjects, except the first year beginners' subject, had been regretted by staff and students alike for years, but it was something that they had felt unable to do anything about for budgetary reasons. The changes being introduced meant that the contact hours in the later level subjects, which were now full rather than half subjects, were doubled to four hours per week.

The newly merged Department of Indian and Indonesian Studies came into existence in 1983. The wider grouping of which it was to form part, known as the School of Asian Studies, was established in 1986 with the appointment of Professor Peter Koepping to the Baldwin Spencer Chair of Anthropology and to be Head of the School. Meanwhile, the Indian Studies staff had moved from the Old Arts Building to join their Indonesian Studies colleagues on the sixth floor of the John Medley Building and various attempts were made to integrate the two programs, but this had no implications for the Indonesian language program.

In 1987 there came a new round of pressures on the remaining Asian Studies departments to merge into a larger unit to include anthropology and possibly archaeology. Faced with this prospect, the Departments of Indian and Indonesian Studies and East Asian Studies dissolved at the end of 1987. Slamet then retired (having reached compulsory retirement age) and Coppel (together with Dipesh Chakrabarty, an Indian colleague) moved to the Department of History. At this point the fourth year area study seminars were abandoned and the fourth year Monash language program became the only way in which Melbourne students could do honours in Indonesian. Sarumpaet and part-time tutors in the Indonesian language program at Melbourne were brought together with other Asian language teachers for Chinese, Hindi, and Japanese and the anthropologists in a new Department of Asian Languages and Anthropology at the beginning of 1988. A year later, the Department of Middle Eastern Studies was dissolved and from the beginning of 1989 the Islamic Studies and Arabic language staff joined the Department of Asian Languages and Anthropology. At the beginning of 1991, the anthropologists decamped to another department and the Indonesian language program now found itself in a Department of Asian Languages.

The cumulative effect of these pressures for change was burdensome and time-consuming for the staff in the Melbourne program. Even if they had been receptive to the new approaches to language teaching that were then spreading to the teaching of Indonesian elsewhere, it was not an environment that was conducive to innovation in language teaching methodology. Students in the program now spent more hours in Indonesian language classes than ever before but there was little change either in the content or the way in which it was taught.

Struggle for Survival

On 17 April 1991, Pieter Sarumpaet, who had headed the Indonesian language program at the university for almost thirty years, suddenly died. In the last two decades of his life, he had found himself in no less than six different departments. At the time of his death, the Indonesian language program was very vulnerable. The language course offerings remained as had been foreshadowed in the 1982 rationalization: a sequence of three subjects (Beginners, Intermediate, and Advanced Indonesian) which comprised a major for those who had not passed HSC Indonesian, and a sub-major for those who had. The total number of students across all three levels had actually risen from 46 in 1988 (the year after the dissolution of the Department of Indian and Indonesian Studies) to 67 in 1991. There was also a clear increase in interest for Indonesian language (the number of students enrolled in Beginners Indonesian in 1991 was more than double the number in 1988). This improvement had been achieved despite the lack of a fourth year program in Indonesian language for those in the beginners stream or a third year program for those in the HSC stream and notwithstanding the successful introduction of an Indonesian language major at La Trobe University which had previously supplied Melbourne with complementary course enrolments in Indonesian. The increase reflected a wider surge in Indonesian language enrolments nationwide. The retention rate at Melbourne was poor, however. In 1991 there were seven students enrolled in Advanced Indonesian of whom only one was in the beginners' stream. No doubt the lack of more advanced language subjects at Melbourne contributed to this attrition, but reports that some students were applying to take Indonesian at La Trobe after completing Beginners Indonesian at Melbourne suggested that there was some dissatisfaction with the program.

At this time a struggle was taking place over the future of the Indonesian language program in the Faculty of Arts between the Budgets Committee (FBC) and the Policy Committee (FPC). In June 1990 the FBC agreed to allocate some extra funding to cover the salary of the Indonesian tutor for 1991 only and 'with the proviso that the language curriculum be reviewed with the possibility of rationalising the programme to a two-year course'. It asked the FPC for advice about the place of Indonesian in the Asian Studies program including the desirability of *reducing* the Indonesian program to a two-year sequence. In its response in July 1990, the FPC expressed its support for the *extension* of Indonesian language teaching to provide two three-year streams (for beginners and post-VCE). A later meeting of the FPC in October 1990 clarified that this had meant the addition of a fourth level of Indonesian which could form part of a combined honours degree but would not constitute a full fourth year program. It went on to state: 'The Committee considers Indonesian to be important and a priority language within the Faculty of Arts'. The battle then moved to a meeting of the Faculty's Standing Committee of Heads of Departments (SCHD) in November 1990 at which 'concern was expressed at the status and implication of such a statement', and a motion was adopted that: 'The SCHD does not consider it advisable at this time to provide additional Faculty resources for Indonesian'. At a meeting on 10 April 1991, the FBC decided to reduce funding for Indonesian by $20,000 for 1992. This meant that the current tutor (Syahisti Abdurrahman) could not be extended beyond 1991. The effect of this would have been to leave Indonesian with only

Sarumpaet in charge and $5,000 for sessional tutoring in 1992. One week later, Sarumpaet died. At a meeting on 1 May 1991, the FBC approved a replacement of Sarumpaet, and Zainu'ddin was recalled as lecturer in charge for the rest of the year. It also agreed that a limited tenure lectureship in Indonesian should be advertised as soon as possible. Thus a language which, in the view of the FPC, was 'important and a priority language within the Faculty of Arts' was to be taught by untenured staff only from 1992 onwards.

The battle within the Faculty of Arts was a reflection of a wider struggle in the university over policies and strategies for Asian studies and Asian languages. Part of this struggle revolved around the extent to which faculties like Arts were subject to academic direction by the University and to what extent they could assert autonomy. This came to a head in 1991 with the appointment of Professor Stephen FitzGerald to conduct an external review of Asian Languages and Asian Studies in the University. In her submission to the review in July 1991, the Arts Dean (Professor Marion Adams) concluded:

> Generally, the Faculty's staffing and funding policy for its teaching is to respect students' choices and try to provide for them. Any extraneous pressure on ideological or other grounds is not likely to be acceptable or to succeed. The University and government should be warned against unrealistic expectations for Asian studies.

In the case of Indonesia, she wrote, 'no more than maintenance of the current limited presence is likely to be possible'. The Dean herself came from the Department of Germanic Studies.

The approach of the Dean and the FBC made 'student choice' the determinant of academic policy. The Faculty was treated as a marketplace in which largely independent departments competed for student numbers (EFTSU). The FBC saw its role as one of rewarding activities with growing enrolments and removing resources from activities with declining enrolments. It redistributed resources in an effort to even out inequities in student staff ratios among the departments within the different discipline groupings. Increased resources enabled growing departments to diversify and expand further; reduced resources compelled declining ones to reduce their offerings further. This could create a vicious circle and a paradox: if an activity was ultimately closed down because of insufficient student demand, future generations of students would no longer have the opportunity to choose it. It was a worldview that was incompatible with any academic policymaking and made it difficult for the Faculty to respond coherently to the University's demand for strategic planning. The logic of the Faculty's position even precluded it from asking for extra recurrent funding earmarked for the development of Asian studies and languages like Indonesian.

This was in fact a period of unprecedented intervention into the tertiary education sector by the Australian government under prime minister Bob Hawke and his education minister John Dawkins. There was a series of Inquiries and Reviews to which universities had to respond quickly and their outcome would lead to the provision of funding tied to conformity with government policies rather than enrolment choices of students. Many of them bore directly or indirectly on the teaching of languages and Asian Studies. Members of staff teaching in the older established European languages saw these developments as a potential threat to their position. Many in the language departments, especially those in senior positions, were anxious that language teaching might be reduced to a service delivered by a Language Centre in which humane studies like literature, traditionally privileged in the university, would be devalued if not abandoned. Such fears surfaced in 1990 when the University prepared its submission to the Review on the Teaching of Modern Languages in Australian Higher Education (Leal, 1991). Changes in language policy and teaching had been in the air since the National Policy on Languages (Lo Bianco, 1987) and demands for the University to declare its strategies and policies now came thick and fast. The University also had to make submissions and responses to the National Inquiry into Employment and Supply of Teachers of Languages Other Than English (Nicholas 1993) and the government's Australian Language and Literacy Policy (DEET 1991).

The University was ill-prepared to respond to the many demands that were now being made of it to supply information and articulate policies and strategies. Nowhere was this more evident than in the field of Asian studies and languages. It discovered that it needed better mechanisms to coordinate Asian studies and languages, even if only at the level of collecting data about the university's own activities in the field so that it could respond quickly and accurately to demands from government and other agencies.

Under the Hawke government, Asian studies and Asian languages became a national priority. It set up an Asian Studies Council which sponsored a wide-ranging review *Asia in Australian Higher Education* conducted by Indonesian historian Professor John Ingleson (Ingleson 1989).[20] The University of Melbourne had enormous difficulty in supplying him with basic information when he sought it in 1988. The School of Asian Studies, established within the Arts

---

20 For more on the cross-currents of Australian government policymaking with regard to foreign languages and Asian languages and studies, see the chapter by Firdaus in this volume.

Faculty only two years earlier, proved inadequate to the task and was dissolved in late 1989. In its place the Faculty established an Advisory Committee on Asian Studies which reported to the FPC. At the same time Charles Coppel was appointed Faculty Coordinator of Asian Studies. At the University level, the Asian Business Centre, established in April 1989 with Professor Malcolm Smith as Director, was identified in late 1989 as the administrative unit to provide support for a University-wide program to build strengths in Asian Languages and Asian Studies and its Advisory Board took over the functions of the former Consultative Committee on Asian Studies. Charles Coppel was appointed Associate Director of the Centre, which provided him with release funding for his role as Coordinator in the Arts Faculty.

The Dawkins reforms also brought about many mergers of universities with former teachers' colleges and other tertiary institutions. One that affected the University of Melbourne directly was the 1989 merger of its Education Faculty with the Melbourne College of Advanced Education (the former Teachers' College) to form the Institute of Education. As a result the University acquired the Asian Languages in Teacher Education Project (ALITEP), a project which aimed to improve and increase the teaching of Asian languages. ALITEP paid particular attention to Chinese, Japanese and Indonesian, as these languages were taught in Victorian schools and at the University. Following the amalgamation, an earlier plan to offer undergraduate Asian language majors gave way to the existing courses in the Arts Faculty, but ALITEP staff offered complementary tutorials and language laboratory work for the rapidly growing number of Institute students taking Asian languages in their undergraduate degrees. Inspired by the National Policy on Languages (Lo Bianco 1987), they were enthusiastic about communicative approaches to language teaching in raising the level of linguistic and pedagogic competence of teachers of these languages, both pre-service and in-service. Their ideas and practice often diverged from those of teachers of Asian (and other) languages in the Faculty of Arts. Certainly Julia Soebadio Read, who was appointed as the ALITEP Project Officer for Indonesian in May 1990, found this to be the case with Sarumpaet who showed little enthusiasm for cooperation with the Institute.

She was to play an important part in the recovery of the Indonesian language program at the University, but initially her role in ALITEP seemed almost fated to provoke friction with Sarumpaet. The rationale for the complementary tutorials she gave to Bachelor of Education students of Indonesian was in part to compensate for differences in timetabling between the Institute and the Arts Faculty and student absences on teaching rounds but it 'was also designed to expose them to a more communicative approach which, as trainee teachers, they would need later on for their own teaching in schools'.[21] Furthermore, ALITEP obtained funding from the Asian Studies Council to mount intensive Asian language courses, and one of Read's first tasks was to prepare and teach an intensive Indonesian language course in the Horwood Language Centre in the summer of 1991. Although the course was primarily pitched at teachers, Sarumpaet probably saw it as further competition for his own embattled program. Another issue between the Institute and the Arts Faculty was the lack of a four-year sequence in Indonesian. From an Institute perspective, a fourth year was essential if its students were to be able to qualify for registration as teachers in the language. Within the Arts Faculty, a fourth level in Indonesian was consistent with the stance of the FPC but it was diametrically opposed to the desire of the FBC to reduce the program to only two levels. Read obtained DEET (Department of Education, Employment and Training) funding to develop a fourth year curriculum for Indonesian. Although Sarumpaet may have welcomed the possibility of the program regaining a fourth year, he would not have been happy about it being developed from outside, let alone by someone who was his junior and lacked his experience of teaching at university level.

In January 1990 the University had to respond at very short notice to a request of the Asian Studies Council for its strategies for developing Asian Studies and Asian Languages. The response drew on views that had been expressed and developed in a series of Asian Forums sponsored by the Asian Business Centre during 1989 to consider what should be done at the University to implement the Ingleson report. According to this strategies document the University had chosen to emphasise the first tier of countries identified by the Asian Studies Council (China, Japan and Indonesia) and planned to provide academic leadership in Asian Languages and Studies by ensuring that there was at least one professorial appointment to give leadership to both Asian Studies and Asian Languages in each of these areas. This came as an unwelcome surprise to the Faculty of Arts, which indeed had a Chair in Chinese under advertisement and was seeking the establishment of a Chair in Japanese but had no such plans for Indonesian.

The Faculty of Arts through its dean and powerful budgets committee was trying to resist pressures from outside the Faculty to expand what they saw as uneconomic programs in Asian languages and studies at the expense of other activities that attracted more student demand. It was for this reason that they

---

21 Julia Read, Project Report, 'Teaching of Indonesian in B.Ed. (Primary) and (Secondary), 18 December 1991.

wanted to reduce the Indonesian language program from a three-year to a two-year sequence. The Faculty's own policy committee tried unsuccessfully to meet at least some of the aspirations of those within and outside the Faculty who wanted to develop Asian studies and languages across the University. One of these was the desire to extend the Indonesian language program to a four-year sequence, but the policy committee did not have the power to determine Faculty policy. It was a slave to student enrolment choices. The University itself was less averse to formulating policy, but found it difficult to override the autonomy of its Faculties especially in a field unfamiliar to its most senior officers like Asian languages and studies. Its response was therefore to appoint an external expert (Stephen FitzGerald) to review Asian languages and studies in the University. The differences of opinion between the Faculty of Arts and those outside it like Malcolm Smith and the Institute of Education were fully exposed by the review. So were those between the Faculty's own coordinator of Asian Studies and its dean and the vulnerability of the Indonesian language program after Sarumpaet's death. It is difficult to say to what extent the prominence within the Faculty executive at this time of academics whose own interests were Europe-centric played a part in their resistance to the demands for an expansion of Asian languages and studies, since that resistance was couched in terms that argued that the demands were 'unrealistic' if students chose to enrol elsewhere.

Expansion and Contraction

It is astonishing, against this unpromising background, to realise that in the 1990s the Indonesian language program at Melbourne grew more rapidly and to a higher level than its counterparts elsewhere in Australia. The Asian Studies Association of Australia's report *Maximizing Australia's Asia Knowledge* (2002) shows that by 1997 Melbourne had the highest EFTSU enrolments in Indonesian among seven selected institutions and that this remained the case, despite falling enrolments, until 2001 (ASAA, 2002, p. 41 [Graph 3.3]). The University and even the Arts Faculty were emboldened by the rising demand to add a fourth year level to the program and to appoint extra, tenured staff including the foundation Chair of Indonesian Studies. Indeed, at its peak the staffing reached a level that had not previously been dreamed of by its most fervent supporters. The additional staff made it possible for the program to be enriched by adding more subjects. Meanwhile, the Asian economic crisis of 1997 and the later outbreaks of terrorism took the wind out of the sails of burgeoning student enrolments and the numbers declined, as they did in programs elsewhere in the country. As the enrolments fell, in due course most members of the teaching staff retired or resigned and the range of subjects contracted again.

Contrary to the conventional wisdom, it appeared in these decades as if the attractiveness of the program to students was in inverse ratio to the number of staff teaching it. The expansion in the 1990s came about despite having a small and fluctuating staff, continual administrative restructuring and inconvenient changes in the physical location of the program. The decline of the early 2000s happened despite the staffing of the program being at its highest level ever, settled within the new MIALS (Melbourne Institute of Asian Languages and Studies, later renamed Asia Institute) in the signature purpose-built Sidney Myer Asia Centre building. Then, as we shall see in the next section, the numbers rose again despite the loss of all but one of the four tenured lecturing staff.

After the death of Sarumpaet in April 1991, the staffing of the language program went through a series of rapid changes. Zainu'ddin saw through the rest of the academic year, and in 1992 Karen Kartomi (later Thomas) arrived to commence a three-year appointment as lecturer. She was assisted by Julia Read, whose project to develop a fourth year curriculum had been expanded to encompass the entire program after Sarumpaet died. Read visited Indonesian programs at the Berkeley campus of the University of California, the R.A.A.F. School of Languages and seven other Australian universities to see how the language was being taught elsewhere. She devised a curriculum that was designed to draw on what she saw as successful aspects of Indonesian programs at other Australian universities. Another Read initiative in 1991 was to develop materials for self-study based on Ian White's newly published text *Bahasa Tetanggaku* for use by students in a Self-Access Centre at the University. She adapted the exercises to make them more suitable for self-study and more relevant to tertiary students in the beginners' subject. She hoped that this adaptation of White's book for post-secondary students might itself be published but this did not eventuate for copyright reasons.

In 1992 Karen Kartomi, the newly arrived lecturer in charge, found herself in the unusual position of being presented by Read with a comprehensive plan for the redevelopment of the program. The curriculum was unusual, if not unique, in the extraordinary degree to which it addressed questions of language teaching methodology and pedagogy. Although, according to Read, many of her ideas were incorporated into the new curriculum that was actually put in place in 1992, and she was able to teach with Kartomi in the program, she herself was not in charge of it. That situation changed in the middle of 1993 when Kartomi (by then Karen Thomas) unexpectedly took maternity leave. For the second time in as many years, the lecturer in charge of the program had to be temporarily replaced at short notice. On this occasion, the replacement lecturer was Julia Read, seconded on a 0.8 basis from the Institute of Education. During 1993 she completed her master's degree in applied linguistics and was appointed to the national steering committee of the TIFL (Teaching Indonesian as a Foreign Language) Project.

By this time the academic environment for language programs at the University had changed considerably. The University had set up a School of Languages headed by Ivan Barko and the Indonesian and Arabic language programs, by then separated from the Department of Asian Languages (now renamed Department of Japanese and Chinese), were incorporated within a Department of Applied Linguistics and Languages headed by Tim McNamara. Although Barko and McNamara were sympathetic to Read's approach to teaching Indonesian, this arrangement had its problems. The language programs were peripheral to McNamara's professional interests in applied linguistics, but they were not strong enough to be reconstituted as a separate Department of Indonesian and Arabic within the School of Languages. McNamara and Barko (and the department office) were located in the Babel building, a considerable distance away from the Indonesian program in the Medley building.

Read was thus co-ordinator of the Indonesian language program in the absence of Karen Thomas. She was able to trial the TIFL materials in the beginners' class and was working for their introduction at the intermediate level. Late in 1993 she reported to McNamara that she and the tutor were keen to use the TIFL materials and activities devised by David Reeve but felt that at the University of Melbourne they needed to be integrated into a more text-based program so that by the end of an honours sequence students could read well enough to conduct research in the language. She also believed that the materials needed more cultural content content (see Read & Reeve, in this volume). Another innovation in 1994 was the use of Arnost et al. (1994) *Lancar Berbahasa Indonesia* (in which Read had had a hand) to replace the Hendrata text that was by now out of print. Unfortunately, although she rated it highly, its content was too much oriented to the New Order of President Soeharto and it was reduced to irrelevance after his fall in 1998.

Read had plenty of ideas and was enthusiastic to innovate across the whole of the program. She was, however, only a caretaker head of the program and at that stage lacked the doctorate and research profile that was by then a requirement for a tenured lectureship at the University. Thomas was expected to return in mid-1994 after her maternity leave, and Sander Adelaar arrived in February 1994 to take up a tenured position as senior lecturer in charge of the program. Meanwhile Read kept the program going and helped Adelaar to settle in, as she had done for Kartomi two years earlier. Together with Adelaar and the tutors she kept the students enthused and provided stability to the program in what was still in many ways an unstable situation.

In 1995, less than a year after returning from leave, Thomas left the program. Michael Ewing was appointed to replace her as a tenured lecturer and took up the appointment in February 1996. In August 1995 Tony Stephens (who had replaced Ivan Barko as Head of the School of Languages in mid-1994) proposed the establishment of a Chair in Indonesian Studies and the University quickly agreed. Enrolments in Indonesian had increased in recent years more than any other language at the University. Total student numbers (in EFTSU) had risen from about 17 in the crisis year of 1991 to 27 in 1993 and 50 in 1995. Unlike 1991, there was now a very high retention rate from the beginners to intermediate levels. With only 2.5 full-time staff, the student to staff ratio was blowing out, making Indonesian the School's first priority for additional staffing. The growth of student interest in Indonesian language was paralleled in other universities across Australia, increasingly from students with professionally oriented backgrounds like commerce, law and engineering. Indonesian language was also gathering strength in the schools. These changes seem to have been driven by the changing orientation of the Australian economy, continuing development of the Indonesian economy and possibly the pro-Indonesian stance of the Keating government. It is striking that Indonesian language enrolments increased at a time when film of the massacre at Santa Cruz cemetery in Dili on 12 November 1991 was repeatedly shown on Australian television. At the time when decisions were being made to expand the staffing for the program, few predicted the Asian financial crisis of 1997, let alone the instability in Indonesia that brought about the resignation of President Soeharto in May 1998.

When the Foundation Chair of Indonesian was advertised at the end of 1995, the University explained that it was 'established to provide academic leadership for the existing Indonesian language program and also to serve as a focus for other areas of study relating to Indonesia which are well-established at this university'. From the beginning of 1996 the Indonesian section would be located within the Department of Language Studies (together with Modern Greek, Arabic and Modern Hebrew) which was, in turn, part of the School of Languages within the Faculty of Arts; but applicants for the Chair were advised that these administrative arrangements might change after a review of the structure of the School of Languages in the second half of 1996. This indeed proved to be the case when Asian languages (including Indonesian) were removed from the School of Languages and placed in a new Melbourne Institute of Asian Languages and Societies (MIALS) headed by the distinguished historian of Indonesia Merle Ricklefs.

In early 1996, the Indonesian section comprised one Senior Lecturer (Adelaar), one Lecturer (Ewing) and two half-time tutors. The Foundation Professor of Indonesian (Arief Budiman) joined them in 1997 and another lecturer (Ariel Heryanto) arrived in 2000. The program had reached a staffing level of four together with a half-time tutor and, for the first time in its history, was headed by a professor. As staffing grew, so did course offerings. In 1996 Indonesian language classes were available at four different levels catering for two streams (beginners and post-VCE) over a three-year sequence. A few years later a fifth level was added, enabling a third stream (students with an Indonesian-speaking background) to do a three-year sequence, and a range of new area study enrichment subjects was introduced. By 2002 MIALS (soon to be renamed the Asia Institute) had moved with the Asialink Centre into the new custom-built Sidney Myer Asia Centre building. As a result, the staff in the Indonesian program rejoined their colleagues in the Chinese, Japanese and Arabic/Islamic Studies programs.

Although it added to the number of options available to students, the growth in staffing did not add to the coherence of the core Indonesian language program. No single person exercised authority over what should be taught and how it should be taught. The teaching staff were by and large left to their own devices, making it difficult to provide a gradual transition from one level to another. There was no overarching concept of teaching methodology. This was scarcely surprising. None of the tenured staff were appointed specifically for their expertise in language teaching. The University expected them to be productive in research but, although they were all fluent in Indonesian, none of them was oriented to this kind of applied research. The closest to it were Adelaar and Ewing, the two non-native speakers of Indonesian whose discipline was linguistics, and they did (together with Dwi Noverini Djenar) produce the second revised edition of Sneddon's *Indonesian Reference Grammar* (Sneddon 2010). Adelaar had respected Read's knowledge of and commitment to the communicative approach but he had reservations about its value, especially in the hands of teachers who were less steeped in the methodology than she was. In particular, he believed that this approach did not solve problems specific to the structure and speech pragmatics of the Indonesian language. It did not, for example, enable students to know when and why to use a passive form or give them strategies of communication.

Links with Indonesia

One problem for the program has been the difficulty of developing links with Indonesian universities and access of students to in-country study. During the Sarumpaet era, the Indonesians who taught in the program were, like him, from an older generation of long-term expatriates. After the program in Bandung in early 1967 (which was not limited to Melbourne students), Sarumpaet took no further steps to promote in-country study in Indonesia. Since his time there has been a younger generation of teachers with more recent experience of Indonesian academic life. Adelaar initiated links with the University of Indonesia. As a result, the University conferred an honorary doctorate (LittD) on Professor Anton Moeliono in 1995, and Felicia Utorodewo joined the program as a visiting lecturer and taught with Ewing in 1996. Later appointees (Budiman and Heryanto) had been academics at Satya Wacana Christian University in Salatiga, which had a long history of offering in-country experience for Australian and other foreign students. While he was at Melbourne, Heryanto tried to develop an in-country program there, but his idea of a separate program for Melbourne students did not materialise.

Melbourne students had participated in the ACICIS (Australian Consortium for In-Country Indonesian Studies) program from the late 1990s. This was curtailed by the University authorities after the Bali bombings in 2002. The University was concerned to avoid any possibility of legal responsibility for the safety of its staff or students in Indonesia when the travel advisories of the Australian Department of Foreign Affairs and Trade (DFAT) were warning Australians not to travel there. Over the next three years the Indonesia Forum (an informal network of staff at the University with shared interests in Indonesia) lobbied the University authorities to modify its duty of care and risk management policies. This met with some success in 2003 for staff and postgraduate students, but the University's aversion to risk was more entrenched in the case of in-country study for undergraduates. Sander Adelaar, who was convenor of the Indonesia Forum in 2004 and 2005, enlisted support from Indonesianists at other Victorian universities to draw attention to the problem at higher levels within several universities and to urge for a relaxation of the restrictions. In his convenor's report for 2005, Adelaar was pleased to report that Melbourne students were once more permitted to include study in Indonesia as part of their curriculum (Adelaar, 2005, p. 5).

The widespread perception in Australia that Indonesia was a dangerous destination was a problem for Indonesian language programs across the country. It was not wholly without foundation, even if its consequences for students learning Indonesian were greatly exaggerated. There were outbreaks of violence in Jakarta and other cities immediately preceding the resignation of President Soeharto, violent conflicts in certain regions such as Maluku, Central Sulawesi, and West Kalimantan, and violent reactions to challenges to Indonesian rule in East Timor, Aceh and West Papua. Of direct concern were the suicide bombings targeted at places frequented by Westerners such as those in Bali (2002 and 2005) and Jakarta (2003 and 2009) in which Australians were killed and injured. These incidents, which received prominent coverage in the Australian mass media, were a major cause of the decline in enrolments in Indonesian language programs in schools and universities across Australia in the first decade of the new century.

The Melbourne program was not immune to this decline, which it attributed to the bombings in Indonesia, the Australian media representation of the violence, the DFAT travel advisories and the University's restrictions on travel to Indonesia. Enrolments there fell steadily from their peak in the late 1990s. The total number of students fell by 44 per cent from 2002 to 2007. This was most dramatic at Level 1 (beginners), where the numbers fell from 24 to a low of 6 in 2005. Enrolments at Level 2 (which included post-VCE first year students as well as second year students continuing from Level 1) fell from 59 in 2002 to a low of 24 in 2007. The level of staffing, with 4.5 full-time lecturing staff from 2000, was already luxurious by the standards of Indonesian programs elsewhere in the country. By the middle of the decade the ratio of staff to students had reached an untenable level. The Faculty of Arts budget was in deficit and needed to take steps to cut costs. For a time, the MIALS budget was protected from economies being made in the Faculty, but once this protection was removed, the Indonesian program soon found itself with only one full-time lecturer (Ewing) left in a continuing appointment. Despite the loss of his colleagues, Ewing was able to preside over a language program with rapidly growing numbers of students.

The Melbourne Model and Curriculum Reform

These developments occurred as the University prepared to introduce its Melbourne Model, the most radical curriculum reform in the University's history. Breaking with long-established Australian traditions, this brought the University into closer alignment with the North American pattern and especially with the European Bologna model. Professional undergraduate degree programs like law and medicine gave way to postgraduate degrees, combined degrees (such as Arts and Science, Arts and Law, or Arts and Commerce) were abolished, and all of the existing undergraduate degrees were replaced by New Generation degrees. All components of the previous Bachelor of Arts degree had to be changed to fit the requirements of the New Generation Bachelor of Arts degree. The most important direct change for the Indonesian program was a reduction in the number of elective subjects available. The core Indonesian language sequence of five levels was retained, in which students had a choice of three streams (Beginners, Post-VCE and students with an Indonesian-speaking background) each offering a three-year sequence. Although combined degrees disappeared, the University replaced the concurrent Diploma in Modern Languages (DML) with the concurrent Diploma in Languages (DipLang). Both diplomas enabled students to undertake a three-year sequence in Indonesian alongside their Bachelor's degree.

The Melbourne Model had one feature that turned out to benefit the Indonesian language program and bring about a significant increase in its enrolments at a time when Indonesian enrolments continued to decline elsewhere. This was the mandatory breadth component, which required students in any of the New Generation degrees to take 75 points (or one quarter) of their course in subjects in faculties other than their home faculty. This breadth requirement attracted many students from other faculties to languages, including Indonesian. By 2007 (the year before the introduction of the Melbourne Model) total student enrolments in Indonesian had dropped to 80, their lowest level in a decade. By 2010 total enrolments had reached 126 (an increase of more than 50 per cent) and enrolments at the first and second level had doubled.

As the Melbourne Model was being devised and introduced, another challenge developed for language programs at the University. At certain levels of the University and the Arts Faculty a view was prevalent that the language programs were too expensive because of their use of small classes and staff who were expected to research as well as teach. A report was produced ('Languages at the University of Melbourne, an Options Paper, June 2008') that appears to have been informed by such views. Putting aside pedagogical factors, it focused on 'business model' options. It was widely believed that the University's agenda was to establish a Language Institute in which languages would be taught more cost effectively. This belief was reinforced because of the impact of the growing global financial crisis which seriously reduced the University's investment income precisely at the time that the new generation Melbourne Model courses were being introduced and the old ones phased out. At the same time the Faculty of Arts was seeking voluntary staff redundancies and raising the spectre of compulsory redundancies to enable it to deal with a budget deficit. Teachers of foreign languages in the Faculty of Arts protested that the Options Paper had not addressed the central educational question of how languages should best be taught and learned at the University.

To address these concerns, the Dean of the Arts Faculty invited Professor Heidi Byrnes, a foreign languages curriculum expert from Georgetown University, to conduct a review of language instruction in the School of Languages and Linguistics and the Asia Institute in early 2009. The main focus of her report was on the need for an integrated curriculum that would assure the acquisition simultaneously of language and literary-cultural content at all levels (including beginners). She wrote:

> For such a curriculum, 'proficiency' or 'communicative competence', the prevailing constructs of reference in language education, might offer insufficiently comprehensive conceptual frameworks on which to build a progression through the honours levels. Rather a textual, literacy-oriented approach might need to be espoused that gives a central role to text and genre in order to accommodate a seamless progression from the beginning to upper levels of instruction.

She was dismissive of the idea that a Language Institute with sessional staff teaching the earlier levels could achieve results that would be worthy of the University's ambitions:

> ... the big intellectual danger in the creation of Language Centers is the separation of 'language' from 'cultural content', potentially leading to a kind of instrumentalization of language teaching along with a 'communicative' and touristy-transactional down-grading of the nature of language use that should not be conducted in an academic environment.

These words might be thought to express reservations about the communicative approach, but Adelaar and Ewing both deny this. As Ewing put it to the author:

> One can be focused on literary textual skills and cultural knowledge and still take a communicative approach which emphasises active and

meaningful *use* of the language, rather than learning *about* the language and then 'applying' what you have 'learned'. Part of the problem is that in the past communicative approaches have tended to emphasise 'survival' or 'touristic' language, but I don't think they have to. Reading literature and academic works, discussing them in Indonesian and giving seminar presentations in Indonesian are all communicative activities. (Ewing, personal communication)

The legacy of the Byrnes report is a major and long-term project of Language Curriculum Reform across all the languages taught in the School of Languages and Linguistics and the Asia Institute. Its aim is to integrate language and culture across the curriculum in terms of objectives and pedagogy. Staff from all nine language programs in the School of Languages and Linguistics and the Asia Institute have been working together to establish common principles to be applied by all while at the same time recognising the important differences that exist between them due to the nature of the subject matter and the intellectual culture of each. The Language Curriculum Reform Reference Group, which included representatives from each of the language programs and the two heads of school, is now evolving into an ongoing group that will continue to facilitate joint work, cooperation and sharing of expertise between the language programs in the two schools.[22]

In the case of Indonesian, the initial rollout of six semester-length subjects in a performance-based language progression (Indonesian 1 to Indonesian 6) began in 2012. Students enter the progression at the appropriate level according to their proficiency based on an online placement test. This test was developed in conjunction with the Language Testing Research Centre at the University of Melbourne implementing a similar protocol across all languages. More advanced subjects came on stream in 2013. They are content-based, covering issues in contemporary Indonesian studies as well as literature and translation. At the advanced level subjects are meant to provide students with the experience of studying university level content in Indonesian. The advanced subjects themselves are not progressively organised and students who have completed Indonesian 6 or equivalent can take their choice of subjects.

---

22 Michael Ewing has found this continuing collaboration between colleagues across all the language programs to be one of the best outcomes of the whole process.

Conclusion

To some extent, the rise and fall of enrolments in the Melbourne Indonesian language program reflected those elsewhere. They rose rapidly in the mid-1960s, plummeted after 1975, grew strongly again in the 1990s, and fell in the early 2000s. These similarities, however, overlook periods in which Melbourne has moved against the national trend. The financial crisis at the University of Melbourne in 1965 coincided with the phasing out of Australian government funding of the program. What should have been sustained growth at that time was stifled as a result. When the next surge in interest for studying Indonesian came in the 1990s, the Melbourne program came close to extinction with low student demand and the death of its long-term lecturer-in-charge. After an initial fall of enrolments and loss of staff in the early 2000s, enrolments have risen significantly in recent years, contrary to the national decline, thanks to the introduction of the 'Melbourne Model'.

The causes of the fluctuations in student demand over more than half a century are difficult to analyse and the future demand is harder still to predict. It is clear that external circumstances (particularly political change in Indonesia) play their part, for better or for worse; so do changes in University policies. Experience in the first years of operation of the Melbourne Model led the University to water down the breadth requirement, so that from 2011 students only had to meet a minimum of 50 points (or one-sixth) of the course. In the next three years, during which the new subjects resulting from the Language Curriculum Reform were introduced, the total number of students in the Indonesian program seems to have stabilised at a level somewhat below the peak years of 2010 and 2011.

For three decades the direction of the language program at all levels was firmly set by Pieter Sarumpaet. Other staff teaching in the program (whether area study lecturers or language tutors) deferred to his authority in this field. Although this had the advantage of ensuring that a single person had oversight of the entire program, it also meant that innovation in teaching methodology was incremental at best. The trunk of the program was planted firmly in its grammar-translation roots, with some audio-lingual and pattern practice grafted on to it from the late 1960s. Sarumpaet was unresponsive, if not resistant, to the functional-notional and communicative approaches to language teaching that were increasingly and more insistently being advocated in the last decade of his life. By this time, in addition, he had lost much of the enthusiasm of his earlier years.

The first catalyst for a change in Indonesian language teaching methodology came not from within the program but from the ALITEP project in the newly formed Institute of Education which was set up to improve and increase the teaching of Asian languages in schools. Julia Read, the ALITEP Indonesian Project Officer, was an enthusiast for the communicative approach. She attempted to introduce a comprehensive curriculum for the program but never held a continuing position in the program within the Faculty of Arts that could have given her the authority to see it through. During later years when the number of staff had increased, different staff members were responsible for teaching subjects at different levels, but nobody had effective oversight of the program as a whole. In the latest period of language curriculum reform, that responsibility devolved to Michael Ewing following the departure of all his full-time colleagues.

The close nexus between language and area studies which was such a feature of the program gradually weakened until by the end of the 1980s it virtually disappeared. This movement was reversed within less than a decade when a combination of additional staff and MIALS policy led to the introduction of a range of elective subjects additional to the core language program. The emphasis in the latest Language Curriculum Reform on the integration of language and culture from the beginners' level across the entire curriculum may herald a future in which the old dichotomy is transcended.

An omission from this account of the history of the Indonesian language program is the part that has been played by non-tenured sessional tutors, usually native-speakers of Indonesian. Much of the delivery of the program has been in their hands, and their important role as teachers should be acknowledged.

The Indonesian language program at the University of Melbourne has throughout most of its history developed in isolation both from other languages taught at the University and from Indonesian programs at other universities around Australia. The Language Curriculum Reform project has decisively broken down the former isolation, but the nature of the process may incline it to look inwards within the University. The Indonesian program is already engaged in the Australia-wide ACICIS program for in-country studies. One challenge for the future is to discover in what other ways it can collaborate with its sister programs elsewhere. They too may find valuable lessons in Melbourne's roller-coaster experience.

References

Adelaar, S. 2005. 'Convenor's Report 2005'. In *Indonesia Forum Annual Report 2005*. Available at: www.indonesiaforum.unimelb.edu.au/2005-IFAR.pdf, accessed 7 Feb 2014. pp. 3–5.

Arnost, V. & Kusumastuty, N.1994. *Lancar Berbahasa Indonesia*. Melbourne: United Artists. (written in collaboration with Nani Pollard and Julia Read).

Asian Studies Association of Australia. 2002. *Maximizing Australia's Asia Knowledge: Repositioning and Renewal of a National Asset*. Bundoora: Asian Studies Association of Australia.

Department of Employment, Education and Training. 1991. *Australia's Language: The Australian Language and Literacy Policy* (Policy Information Paper and Companion Volume). Canberra: Australian Government Publishing Service.

Echols, J. M. & Shadily, H. 1961. *An Indonesian-English Dictionary*. Ithaca: Cornell University Press.

Echols, J. M. & Shadily, H. 1975. *An English-Indonesian Dictionary*. Ithaca: Cornell University Press.

Hendrata, H. 1969–1970. *An Audio-lingual Course in Bahasa Indonesia*. Melbourne: H. Hendrata.

Ingleson, J. 1989. *Asia in Australian Higher Education: Report of the Inquiry into the Teaching of Asian Studies and Languages in Higher Education*. Kensington: University of New South Wales.

Leal, R. B. 1991. *Widening our Horizons: Report of the Review of Teaching of Modern Languages in Higher Education*. Canberra: Australian Government Publishing Service.

Lo Bianco, J. 1987. *National Policy on Languages*. Canberra: Australian Government Publishing Service.

Moeliono, A. M. & Dardjowidjojo, S. (comp). 1988 *Tata Bahasa Baku Bahasa Indonesia*. Jakarta: Departemen Pendidikan dan Kebudayaan, Republik Indonesia.

Nicholas, H. R. 1993. *Languages at the Crossroads: The Report of the National Enquiry into the Employment and Supply of Teachers of Languages Other than English*. East Melbourne: National Languages and Literacy Institute of Australia.

Pino, E. & Wittermans, T. 1955. *Kamus Inggeris*. Djakarta: Wolters.

Poerwadarminta, W. J. S. 1961. *Kamus Umum Bahasa Indonesia*. Djakarta: Balai Pustaka.

Sarumpaet, J. P. 1965. *Perbandingan Pendidikan: Perantjis, Inggeris, Amerika Serikat dan Uni Sovjet*. Djakarta: Djambatan.

Sarumpaet, J P. 1966. *The Structure of Bahasa Indonesia*. Melbourne: Department of Indonesian and Malayan Studies, University of Melbourne.

Sarumpaet, J. P. 1980. *Modern Usage in Bahasa Indonesia*. Carlton: Pitman.

Sarumpaet, J. P. 1988. *Pengajaran Bahasa Indonesia di Australia* Jakarta: Kongres Bahasa Indonesia V Jakarta, 28 Okt – 2 Nov 1988.

Sarumpaet, J. P. & Hendrata, H. 1968. *A Modern Reader in Bahasa Indonesia*. Melbourne: Department of Indonesian Studies, University of Melbourne.

Sarumpaet, J. P. & Mackie, J. A. C. 1966. *Introduction to Bahasa Indonesia*. Melbourne: Melbourne University Press.

Sneddon, J. N., Adelaar, A., Djenar, D. N. & Ewing, M. 2010. *Indonesian Reference Grammar*. Sydney: Allen and Unwin 2nd revised edition.

Sumarmo, M. 1988. *Keadaan dan Perkembangan Pengajaran Bahasa dan Sastra Indonesia di Amerika Serikat*. Jakarta: Kongres Bahasa Indonesia V Jakarta, 28 Okt– 2 Nov 1988.

Tim Penyusun Kamus, Pusat Pembinaan dan Pengembangan Bahasa. 1988. *Kamus Besar Bahasa Indonesia*. Jakarta: Balai Pustaka, Departement Pendidikan dan Kebudayaan.

Chapter 5

GOYANG LIDAH!

Recipes for Teaching Indonesian

Julia Read and David Reeve

University of Melbourne; University of New South Wales

Introduction

Numbers of Indonesian language learners in Australia are very low, although Indonesia's importance to Australia is as great as ever. In fact, between 2000 and 2010, university enrolments in Indonesian dropped nationally by 40 percent, while the overall Australian undergraduate population expanded by 40 percent (Hill, 2012). It is time to look back on more than 50 years of Indonesian language teaching in Australia, to avoid the mistakes of the past, and build on the successes.

In the 50-plus years that Indonesian has been taught in Australian universities there have been marked shifts in the ways that it has been taught. The last big project in materials development for the tertiary level was the Teaching Indonesian as a Foreign Language (TIFL) Tertiary Curriculum Materials Project in 1992-1995.[1] There are some signs of a new methodological shift/emphasis in the school systems with a new emphasis on IcLL (Intercultural Language Learning), and it is high time vibrant new materials were developed for the universities.

---

[1] It was one of four projects under an umbrella project called the TIFL Project (Read, 2002, p. 4-7).

This chapter begins by mapping the shifts in teaching approaches from the first Australian texts of 1965, then re-assesses the current usefulness of materials from the TIFL project, and finally explains the lessons to be learned for the future from their fate. It was the tragedy of the TIFL Tertiary Curriculum Materials project that the materials were never properly evaluated after their creation, nor were they ever properly published. The politicians and bureaucrats who oversaw the project – and then forgot it – have all moved on, but the lecturers in universities are still teaching Indonesian language, still largely without properly designed or well-produced curriculum materials.

Overview of the First 50 Years

The story of the first 50 years of Indonesian language teaching in Australia is told here through the texts and methodologies that teachers used in the classroom, because these artefacts reveal a number of striking facts. First, the sheer number: over 60 texts were produced in Australia in the first forty years, from the late 1950s to the 1990s. This is a remarkable achievement, a great flowering of initiative and talent. Unfortunately most of them are now long forgotten, out of print, sunk without trace.

Second, waves of dominant methodologies – Indonesian teaching has passed through three clear waves: a grammar-translation phase, from 1958 to 1968 (10 years); an audio-lingual phase, from 1968 to 1988 (20 years); and a combined functional-notional and communicative phase, from 1988 to the present (30 years). Each period had its hegemonic methodology. Few writers tried to go against the trends, though some texts were hybrids, including older techniques as well. But many babies were thrown out in floods of bathwater, and wheels busily reinvented.

Third, these texts were mostly the work of individuals – rarely teams, no doubt partly from the absence of computers and email. Individual teachers produced materials for class which, as they were accumulated, turned from folders into books. But it was a shame that there was little teamwork, as individual inspiration can only go so far. From the 1990s, materials development increasingly became collaborative – a much needed change.

Fourth, Indonesian language teaching was modelled on methods that came from outside, from other language areas. As in Indonesia too, the status of internationally dominant methodologies overwhelmed local initiative. New methodologies tend to arise first in the teaching of English as a second language, then colonise the teaching of European languages, then take over

Indonesian, then come to an abrupt halt at the steep cliffs of Japanese and Chinese teaching. Grammar-translation, audio-lingual, functional-notional, communicative – all came from outside of Indonesian and outside of Indonesia. The creativity that went into texts development was nowhere matched by methodological creativity. Can we not develop a method for Indonesian that comes out of the nature of Indonesian?

Fifth, all these texts were developed by Indonesians in Australia, or by Australians. There has been no collaboration with other Indonesian-teaching countries, or (much worse) with Indonesia itself. While other languages have thrived with floods of materials from their home countries and cultural institutes – French, German, Italian, Japanese – Indonesia has had virtually no role or supporting presence in the teaching of Indonesian in Australia. Hopefully this will change in the next fifty years.

What follows is a review of the major texts and methodologies, with an emphasis on the earlier decades. These do not tell the whole story of what happened in classes, as teachers always adapted texts with their own good sense about what worked in class. There were overseas texts used as well, particularly the Wolff texts from America, but the focus here is on the wealth of Australian texts.

The three great waves of texts and methodologies took place against a background of boom-and-bust in student numbers. The first boom was from the late 1950s to the mid-1970s, followed by a dozen years of decline, reflected in low production of texts. A second boom began around 1988, with changes in government attitudes, and new materials with new methodologies. But it only lasted 10 years. From 1999 a new decline has occurred, lasting until now. Let us hope that in the future a new enthusiasm may arise, accompanied by new students and new materials, combining the best of past practice with ideas for the future.

Grammar-translation Teaching and Texts, 1950s to 1968

Indonesian teaching in Australian universities started in 1956 at the University of Melbourne (see Coppel, this volume), and in some school systems in the early 1960s. Unfortunately, we know little about what materials were used until the first Australian text was published in 1965, T.S. Lie's *Introducing Indonesian*. What happened before then? The Dark Ages? The prehistory of Indonesian language teaching? Probably teachers were frantically producing class-notes that would later become books.

Jamie Mackie has shed some light, saying in conversation that he used Pino's *Bahasa Indonesia*. He had picked it up in a bookstore when he was trying to teach himself some Indonesian. T. S. Lie's work was a strictly grammar-translation text, though that method was shortly to be superseded.

Grammar translation was such an established method of language teaching that its overthrow and banishment in the 1960s was very much the end of an era, and a shift of major importance. (Some stalwarts never accepted that the GT era was over, and indeed the decaying remnants of obsolete teaching methods can often be found festering and resentful in dark corners of university language departments). Grammar translation had been a very powerful method of language teaching; first used as the traditional method of teaching Latin and Greek in Europe, it had come to be used in teaching 'modern' languages such as French, German and English in the nineteenth century. At its best, it produced students with a fine and detailed knowledge of the workings of the formal language, and a subtle capacity to access and to translate great works of literature; hardly skills to be scorned.

The greatest problem of GT was that its most valued and practiced skills were reading and writing. It was not clear when students would listen to the language, much less speak. So it was an appropriate method for students who might never visit the country whose language they were studying, but who sought to access the riches of that society through its novels, poetry, short stories and plays, the 'languages and literatures' tradition.

There was ambivalence about the very idea of introducing Asian languages in Australia. In 1957 the Modern Language Teachers' Association had resolved in a rather non-committal way that 'there was room in Australia for teaching Asian languages'. In 1959 R. G. Casey stated that in his Department of External Affairs, out of 176 diplomatic officers, there were only two speakers of Indonesian. In 1960, however, Van Abbe, writing in *Babel*, warned against the rise of Asian languages. He stressed the intellectual rigour of a thorough study of modern European languages and their grammar. Whereas Indonesian had 'too little formal grammar to be of the kind of educational value for which I have been arguing.'[2]

Lie's 1965 text used a traditional grammar-translation format, but a hint of the change to come was Purwanto Danusugondo's *Bahasa Indonesia for Beginners*, which was highly critical of translation, and proposed instead a method based on 'productive patterns'. This latter was a transitional, hybrid

---

2   This paragraph is based on Ozolins 1993: 64, 66, 86.

text; its philosophy was opposed to grammar translation, but its contents were more traditional.

From 1965-68 six Indonesian language texts were published in Australia, mostly associated with universities in Melbourne and Sydney. From Melbourne in came J. P. Sarumpaet's *The Structure of Bahasa Indonesia*, and Sarumpaet and Mackie's *Introduction to Bahasa Indonesia* (1966). T. S. Lie came from the University of Sydney, as did H. W. Emanuels, whose course for Radio University UNSW was published as *Bahasa Indonesia Sehari-hari* (1966). The first school text was H. W. Emanuels and Vern Turner's *Indonesian for Schools*, (see Figure 2) Books 1 and 2 (1967, 1968). Vern Turner, a high school teacher and University of Sydney graduate, had been recommended by Emanuels. Purwanto came to Australia in 1963 with a fresh Masters in Linguistics from Illinois. Working with Radio Australia, the Indonesian Embassy, and teaching at UNSW convinced him that new materials were needed.

Figure 1: Vern Turner teaching at St.Mary's High School, Sydney in 1964.
National Archives of Australia, A1501, A5014/1.

Figure 2: 1967 edition of Emanuels and Turner's *Indonesian for Schools*.
Published by Science Press, Marrickville, NSW.

The core components of a typical grammar-translation lesson were the presentation of a grammatical rule, a study of lists of vocabulary, and a translation exercise. There were occasional comprehension passages. Few were conversations. Vern Turner's texts added interest to the four-square black and white look with line drawings. Their core philosophy was that '… students will learn grammatical forms which will enable them to attain fluency in speaking and writing Bahasa Indonesia'. How later teachers would laugh at such a claim!

In such texts the translation sections could be massive – sometimes more than 70 sentences sat waiting. Sentences often had a quaint, made-up feel:

> You are not allowed to climb that high mountain.
>
> It was not her desire to get married but her parents.
>
> It is her wish to have eight children when she marries.
>
> Why is your sweetheart angry at you?
>
> With whom did you go to the Hotel Samudra?
>
> Why had grandfather not yet drunk his cold coffee?

Several horses sleep under the tree.
Those crocodiles are big and fat.
Are there clouds in the sky?
The old goat died the day before yesterday.
The goat sleeps under the tree beside the horses.
What a pity! His horse died yesterday.
He died the day before yesterday.
The large snake eats the fat fowl.
Don't annoy that goat; it is sick.
Very rarely is wickedness like that not punished.
When the doctor examined the man it was clear that he was dead.
Mother was speechless to see the mouse on top of the table.
Suddenly the meow of a cat was heard from the cupboard.
Take that dead cat as far as possible away from the house!
In Australia almost every man shaves his face once day.

So much death! And startling ideas could be suggested by consecutive sentences:
Our dog is called Mimpi.
Although he is still small he can dress himself.
These practice sentences were not taken from real speech, and no one seriously believed that the students would ever say them. And there lay one of the greatest problems – the distance from speaking and listening. Possibly the best thing to say about these texts is that they were pioneering, expressly written – often at speed – to fill a void. These were a productive 3–4 years, but these grammar-translation texts were soon to be replaced by audio-lingual.

The transition from one methodology to another is usually described in terms of the attractions of one theory over another. But social and technological changes are important too. The advent of wide-bodied planes and cheaper fares in the 1960s marked the start of mass tourism; students were now much more likely to visit the countries they had studied, to want and need to talk to native speakers. For Southeast Asia, the great wave of interest generated in schools and universities was a product of involvement in the Vietnam War. The stakes were more urgent than a cultivated interest in literature. If students were to visit the countries of Southeast Asia, then they wanted to be able to discuss a range of social and political topics.

Also permitting and causing the shift to audiovisual was the relatively cheap availability of language laboratories. Here was a shift from pen and book, to mouth and machine. In the hours in the language lab, a whole class could be talking their heads off. 'Talking to a machine!' said later critics scornfully, pointing to the distance from the strains, tensions and negotiations of real-life conversations. They were right, but that later insight should not obscure what a great change was about to occur.

The Audio-lingual Years, 1968 to 1988

1968 was a threshold year, with a late grammar-translation text, Vernon Turner's *Indonesian for Schools Book Two*, and the first and most zealous of the new audio-lingual texts, *Lancar Berbahasa Indonesia* (*LBI*), from the Sydney Technical College team of Ichsan, Baker and Lane. *LBI* led the field in an eight-year burst of productivity, which saw three major state-based text series/packages (Hendrata, Victorian schools; McGarry and Soemaryono, NSW; Partorejo, Queensland) start appearing in the early 1970s. The first new university course, from Yohanni Johns of ANU, was *Langkah Baru Book One* (1975).

These were series because they developed into texts for beginners, intermediate and advanced; packages as they came with sets of tapes, slides and flashcards, and sometimes readers and guided composition texts. There were five main readers from familiar names 1968–1975: Sarumpaet and Hendrata; Yohanni Johns; Suwito Santoso and Soemaryono; J. A. Collins; and Ichsan.

1972 was a pivotal year, with a problem and a triumph. The problem was the introduction of new spelling into Indonesian (*Ejaan Yang Disempurnakan*). Publishers had to decide whether to reissue texts in the new spelling. The state-based series had established markets and jumped the hurdle, but the pioneering *LBI* failed at the jump. The triumph of 1972 was the ABC radio program *Learn Indonesian* in two series, a particular project of Bettina Gorton. The series was based on *LBI*, and 10,000 Australians bought the booklets and records to participate. Over 40 years later, it is hard to imagine anything similar occurring. In 1968 *LBI* had proclaimed itself to be unique, as 'the first textbook on Bahasa Indonesia completely geared to the aural-oral method of learning'. Its account of teaching methodology was dramatic:

> Ever since the French Revolution in 1789 set the pattern for violent and radical reform of social evils, modern man has come to the realisation that, if he did not like his particular world, he was at liberty to change it.

There was for the first time a student text and a teacher's edition, the latter containing a detailed and elaborate exposition of classroom technique. One element:

> Pattern practices aim to establish speech habits by presenting meaningful units in contexts rather than concentrating on individual sentences so often taught out of context and unrelated to normal speech behaviour.

A hint of the elaborate and prescriptive classroom practices:

> Then model the sequence four or five times from different positions in the classroom while the students turn their books face down so that they may concentrate solely on your voice. Do not allow them to follow you with their eyes around the classroom.

Here were the key elements: pattern practices; speech habits; meaningful units in context; articles with thematic titles – for example, 'An Outing', 'An Accident', 'Entertainment', 'Going Shopping'; the 20 'dialogue sentences' comprising the core of each unit; the visual aids; more realistic formats; the shift from writing and translating to imitating and transforming oral cues; native speaker recordings as models; and always the tapes to be used in the classroom and language laboratory – the golden age of the language lab.

The later text series were not as rigorous as *LBI*, the high point of orthodoxy. Those later texts followed the dominant audio-lingual methodology, but were hybrid, including several types of classroom exercises from older methodologies, syncretically adopting anything that worked in class. This was a victory of commonsense over ideology, marked in Partorejo, with his 'integrated approach', but present in others too.

These series, and over a dozen smaller texts from individual teachers or schools, deserve greater attention, but there is only room here for a few general points:

- They contained much material on Indonesian culture, through dialogues and particularly through dozens of readings (*bacaan*). Students learned a great deal about Indonesian culture in a way that has disappeared from more recent texts.
- These texts were lavish in their use of line drawings as aids for memorising dialogues, explaining vocabulary, structure and grammar points, as stimuli for conversation and composition, and

making texts lively and attractive. What a shame so much work and talent has sunk, unretrieved!

- The texts had a richness of classroom exercises, including an elaborate technique for the exploitation of dialogues, covering and uncovering the text, listening, repeating, chanting as whole-class, or by groups and individuals. There were reading passages with comprehensions, and exercises of at least seven types: substitution, transformation, fill-in, complete, matching, true/false and scrambled sentences; there were special notes and remarks, songs and games.

- These texts envisaged the task of the Australian student as learning about Indonesia, not learning how to discuss Australia in Indonesian. Several texts took the new idea of building their book around Australian visitors to Indonesia. But when Tom Johnson of the Australian Dairy Company meets business colleagues in Surabaya, they discuss the history of Majapahit rather than business (Sumaryono, Book Three, 1974).

- Although fresher elements were appearing, the old didactic high-literature tradition remained. Some of the readers had a high literature feel, with the exclusion of daily life. When daily life was covered, it was the village and its folktales. Collins' *Bunga Rampai* looked to the future, drawn from Indonesian press articles, rather serious. And Sumaryono's Book Three made much use of real-life material from magazines and newspapers, including cartoons, anecdotes, advertisements, jokes and articles. The debates on realia are 40 years old.

Thus ended the first great wave of Australian texts, 1965 to 1975, encompassing two major methodologies. Student numbers declined thereafter, eroding the publishers' market. The boom from the early 1960s to the mid 1970s was followed by a trough, with a sprinkling of new texts, mostly readers of a language and literature type, but no methodological breakthroughs.

There was little before 1988, besides the Philips record set *Bahasa Indonesia* (late 1970s), Sarumpaet's reference work *Modern Usage in Bahasa Indonesia* (1980), Lonely Planet's *Indonesian Phrasebook* (1984), and seven readers from Collins, Marian Dakeyne, Achdiat K Miharja, John Pello and Adrian Clynes. One hopeful sign was the magazine for Indonesian teachers *Pelangi* from 1985, but the editor's call for a vigorous debate on methodology met little response.

The Communicative Years, from 1988

Methodological innovation did not come until 1988, when Ian White started publishing his notional-functional text series, *Bahasa Tetanggaku*. This method had come earlier for other languages in Australia, and the 1980s saw new lively texts for Italian, German, French and Japanese. Low student demand postponed such initiatives for Indonesian, so that the new methodologies of functional-notional and communicative language teaching occurred side-by-side from around 1988.

This was a period of enthusiasm for language study at the government level, shown in the National Policy on Languages (Lo Bianco, 1987), followed by state policies and state education department initiatives, plus the vital enthusiasm of the federal Labor government for four key Asian Languages: Chinese, Indonesian, Japanese and Korean. In retrospect the lack of Hindi seems a particular oversight, but many teachers will remember, fondly and with nostalgia, the strong governmental support for Asian language study, and the lively debates within the country over Australia's 'Asian identity' and future in Asia.

The Ingleson report on Asian Languages in Higher Education (Ingleson, 1989) set ambitious targets, unfortunately never met during the boom period of 1988 to 1998, largely because universities did not commit the resources needed. Thereafter Indonesian language enrolments started a new bust.

Teachers started talking of themselves as student-centred and meeting student needs. But what had really happened was that for the first time language teachers were allowed to use the photocopiers, previously reserved for administrative staff only (as usual). Lack of access to easy methods of duplication had made teachers reliant on published texts, as they faced intoxication and addiction from the smells of spirit stencils (usually hidden in airless spaces under stairs), or permanently red and black skin and clothes from the smears of Gestetner stencils. Access to photocopiers transformed what teachers could do, as they could now select, from banks of material, what they wanted to present to the class, from what source, and in what order.

A delightfully coloured text series for schools *Ayo!* (Taylor and Sedunary, 1955) was published, based on the successful versions for Italian, German, French and Japanese, and new readers appeared from 1988: McGarry and Sumaryono; Partorejo; George Quinn; McGarry and Winarto, plus the *Ayo!* readers. But after much planning activity in education departments, reflected in the All Guidelines (Scarino et al., 1991), LOTE kits and the National Indonesian Language Curriculum Project, it was banks of material that were emphasised. The two main banks were the *Suara Siswa* materials for schools, and the TIFL Project (1992-1996) for universities, both adopting communicative methodology.

Functional-notional methodology demonstrated a shift from language form to language use. Functions were defined by asking 'what does the speaker want to do?' The answers to this question, almost always ending in '-ing', were the functions, such as 'agreeing', 'apologising', 'asking for'. A further question elicited the particular 'notions' that the function was about. The key factor in teaching and text-writing was to ask what function was needed, and then to choose between the easier and more difficult ways in which that function might be realised in real life.

This methodology has produced a single major text series in Australia, Ian J. White's *Bahasa Tetanggaku*, with three course books, including student workbooks and sets of cassettes, in 1988–1994. The functional-notional approach has taken hold in teachers' minds, in the current communicative phase, providing an alternative approach for selecting what language and structures to choose for class.

In White's texts, the contents page for each 'topic' is laid out on a grid, displaying language functions, and grammar points. One good example is the language functions for Chapter Four, on 'shopping':

>Colours
>Asking about price
>Identifying objects
>Expressing surprise and shock
>Bargaining: Offering a price
>   Refusing a price
>   Agreeing on a price
>Describing quality
>Comparing two objects
>Comparing more than two objects
>Indicating wants and needs
>Transport
>Personal language: my chores

Functional-notional ideas provided a new element in communicative developments from the late 1980s. Communicative methodology is dealt with at greater length in the second half of this article.

Moving into TIFL, within a Communicative Framework

The Brown and McKay (1991) report stated that the material available for teaching Indonesian was 'thoroughly outdated'. *Suara Siswa* and TIFL were meant to meet this problem. As part of the preparation for TIFL, a study of the earlier texts described above was undertaken in 1991, to compile an index of what already existed. This was to be treated as a resource (not throwing out the baby, not reinventing the wheel), so that the new materials would build on what existed. Unfortunately, there was not enough time or energy to send around that index to existing materials, but some of the criticisms of existing texts are given below. Apart from methodological outdatedness, it was concluded of the texts published since 1965 that:

a. The texts are too childish in orientation, to the exclusion of most of adult life.

b. There is a narrowness of emotional range, a general 'niceness' of tone, far from any of the strong emotions.

c. Those transactions that do not involve children involve tourists; there is little for the 'Asia-literate' Australian professionals who go to Indonesia to transact their business.

d. There is almost no material on Australia in the material produced in Australia, so that students may go to Indonesia well-prepared to converse about the *keris* or *Borobudur*, but unprepared to discuss their own society.

e. There is an avoidance of any sensitive social issue in Australian or Indonesian society, so that students may well be enabled to discuss all topics except those that really interest them.

f. Despite the various cuttings from newspapers, there is a great lack of real-life advertisements, printed handouts and leaflets, official forms, product labels and instructions.

g. The grammar is taught point by point rather than being related to actual use and to particular functions; there is a general tendency to have grammar divided up into little parcels, articles are the same length, with no regard as to whether any one grammar item may have dozens of uses or only a few.

h. The materials are inauthentic, written to illustrate grammar points (this does not mean that they are not useful, but they are not enough).

i. The exercises are work than can be done by students on their own, and do not lend themselves to communication.
j. There is almost no concern with register and other sociolinguistic issues; the language is pitched at no particular social situation; there is little to prepare even the casual visitor for Jakarta.
k. There is a lack of authentic writing tasks.
l. The audio material is designed for the language lab, which few teachers now wish to use as much as in the 1970s, if at all. (Reeve, 1991, p. 2)

With the methodological insights provided by communicative methodology, and a wish to overcome the problems described above, the TIFL project set to work in 1992.

TIFL: An Innovation in Indonesian Language Teaching

> I've never seen or used anything at all like the TIFL [materials], so I think – you open the workbook and you think, wow, this is fun! I mean, there's fun and humour – I think this looks interesting – look at the cartoons – look, there's some real Indonesian material! So it's the realism, I think. It's not an artificially created kind of textbook. (Jan Lingard, interviewed by the author. Read, 2002, p. 157)

The Teaching Indonesian as a Foreign Language (TIFL) Tertiary Curriculum Materials Project was set up by the Asian Studies Council (ASC) and co-ordinated by David Reeve (1992–1995). The principal Australian participants in the project team were drawn from the Sydney Consortium for Indonesian and Malay Studies (SCIMS). The TIFL tertiary curriculum materials ought to be recognised as one of the most important developments in Indonesian language teaching in recent times in Australian universities, if not the world. However, the TIFL materials are less well known than they should be, due to the incoming Howard government's refusal to honour the Keating government's original commitment to publish them.

As indicated above, the desire for improved teaching materials suitable for teaching Indonesian in universities arose from a profound sense of frustration current among Indonesianists, arising from the inadequacy of available teaching resources. The inspiration for the concept of a new focus in Indonesian language teaching came mainly from two ASC policy documents, the *National Strategy for the Study of Asia in Australia* and *Asia in Australian Higher Education*. This meant that the expected outcomes were somewhat different from those of past materials. The TIFL materials aimed to provide Indonesian language skills for Australian professionals who would visit Indonesia and work in Indonesia. Instead of being focused on Indonesia, in these materials the complex relationship between Australia and Indonesia provided much of the central focus. Whereas previously the aim had been preparation for research, these materials placed prime importance on communicative skills.

The TIFL materials comprise a huge and varied package of the most wide-ranging and comprehensive instructional materials that have ever been produced for tertiary Indonesian, surpassing the famous Cornell University materials developed by Wolff et al. in the 1980s, They were also highly innovative materials for tertiary level, because they were designed for the *communicative approach*, now the basis of the contemporary paradigm of second and foreign language teaching, but in 1992 largely unknown in foreign language departments in Australian universities.

Theoretical Underpinnings of the TIFL Materials

The basis of communicative competence theory is the understanding that there is a sociocultural dimension of language knowledge related to the communicative aspects of language (Hymes, 1970), which means that as well as phonology, vocabulary and grammar, language learners need to acquire sociolinguistic competence – for example, knowledge of appropriateness of language to sociocultural context, and of cohesion and coherence in discourse – to be able to use language to interact with other people.

Based on this theory, a body of pedagogic procedures was developed, particularly in TESOL, which has been in the vanguard of developments in language pedagogy. A focus on not just the forms of language but its functions is an outstanding characteristic of communicative language teaching in comparison with earlier language teaching. Because learners must devise strategies for relating function to form, they must be provided with ample opportunities to use the language themselves for communicative purposes. Opportunities for verbal action are thus essential.

Five innovative aspects of communicative pedagogy differ from earlier methodological approaches. The first is an emphasis on sociolinguistic appropriateness, the area formerly neglected in language pedagogy. This means learning to speak (and understand) informal as well as formal language, adjusting one's speech according to the situation and audience.

The second innovation is 'message-focus', which means that pieces of language are treated as messages rather than grammatical structures. On the level of receptive skills, message-focus is manifested in 'information transfer' exercises, where students extract information from a passage (authentic resource materials created as a means of communicating content and not for a pedagogic purpose are preferred) and use it to perform a task, for example, a reading task might be used to extract information that feeds into another task (success in the task being dependent on understanding the reading). This 'task-dependency' provides immediate feedback to the learner.

In productive practice, students are placed in positions where they will want to say something and are provided with the means to say it. Information or opinion gap activities are the pre-eminent or archetypal learning activity in communicative pedagogy, based on the rationale that where there is a genuine desire to find out something, then there exists a communicative situation, that is, one that takes the learners' attention away from practising structures (form-focus) and puts it on getting the message across (message-focus).

The third innovation of communicative pedagogy is deliberate stimulation of psycholinguistic processes. All the psycholinguistic processes used in communication begin with the speaker or listener's desire to convey or obtain a message, for example, the negotiation of meaning that occurs in face-to-face interactions. Psycholinguistics provided the insight that listening is always done for a purpose and that listeners process selectively, not attending equally to every word of a message. Unlike traditional listening comprehension exercises, in which the learner was made to focus on each word, information transfer exercises require the learner to attend only to those parts of the message relevant to a task. Meaningful tasks tap students' own situations, experiences, opinions, feelings and preferences. The tedium of older-style exercises is replaced by genuine information exchange.

Emphasis on risk-taking skills is the fourth innovation of communicative pedagogy. In the past, because of the emphasis on thoroughness and the desire to avoid errors, students were characteristically taught to read texts word by word. Communicative pedagogy recognises that this procedure not only fails to help, it positively hinders development of the important skill of understanding a message in an only partially understood context. Learners who visit a country where the target language is spoken will need this skill.

Free practice techniques are the fifth innovation. In older approaches, the emphasis was on part practice, not discourse. There was virtually no free production or preparation for it. Communicative pedagogy recognises that spoken communication is a complex skill, requiring rapid formulation of utterances simultaneously 'right' on several levels, involving far more than just the subskill of being grammatically correct. Holistic practice is thus important to allow practice of subskills in combination. The development of free practice techniques in communicative pedagogy has been a major contribution to language teaching.

All these ideas underpinned the development of the TIFL materials.

Outstanding Features of the TIFL Materials

Space permits only a brief description of the most outstanding features of the enormous body of teaching materials produced by the TIFL Project, which include 20 Introductory Themes and 14 Intermediate Themes in a two-year program – although the quantity of materials is far greater than could be used in a normal tertiary program.

(a) Group Interview Videos

A set of 102 group interview video recordings (*Video Wawancara* 1–2) is one of the original features of the TIFL materials that are still the most frequently requested item from the video materials. They were innovative in that a single native speaker interviewer interviews a group of six people. This group includes speakers from a variety of ethnic groups and regional backgrounds, including two Australian learners. Therefore, they have a variety of accents and their speech shows some regional variation. The interviewees all have distinct personalities, which adds interest.

The same questions are posed to each interviewee, with slightly different phrasing. Each member of the group replies briefly to the question put to him or her. Although their answers are different, they are structurally fairly similar to each other. Thus useful redundancy is provided to aid learning without the tedium of repetition, and students gain an appreciation of different ways of saying things. Errors made by the two learners in the group can also be observed – an original aspect. Students soon fully comprehend what's being talked about, and if a list of new vocabulary is provided and the interviews are replayed, the students can follow it all entirely.

The interviews start with survival topics – for example, food, a place to live – and go on to the level of abstractions such as ambitions and opinions. They do not contain fast speech or difficult language, especially at the beginning of the series, but they were not scripted, so they are spoken in natural conversational language, which occasionally includes colloquialisms. They are close to being authentic natural interactions, but far more accessible. They are a fresh and extremely useful learning resource, as one lecturer explained:

> There's a variety of responses, yet they are still structured enough for the students to be able to follow through. By the time they get to the sixth interviewee, the students fully comprehend what's being talked about, and when you replay them they follow it all entirely, because I jot up any new vocab on the board. They're refreshing – the personalities of the six are all different. There's the staid Bu Nur and rather withdrawn Indah, the dour Roy and the delightful Glenn. The girls love Glenn because he's such a card. Vanessa's always charming. I think the way they've been structured is excellent, so that's one of the most valuable contributions the project's made, and it can be used by any any teacher anywhere, and it can be used at any level that you want to slot it in. (Tony Pollard, interviewed by Julia Read. Read, 2002, p. 392)

(b) Scripted Dialogues

The scripted dialogues are the second main listening resource in the TIFL materials, consisting of 99 audio recordings of dialogues, created by a team of writers and spoken by native speakers. Their purpose was not only to provide listening practice, but to be the main vehicle for modelling and teaching communicative functions and sociocultural and discourse aspects of spoken Indonesian. As previously mentioned, learners must also develop strategies for relating these forms or structures to their communicative functions in real situations and real time. These scripted dialogues were the first systematic attempt in Australian materials for teaching Indonesian to adults to help learners do this – thus another highly innovative feature. The result is dialogues that are rich in sociocultural elements, and also lively, vivid and much more confronting than anything previously produced. The procedures for using them include eliciting meaning, chanting to practise prosodic features, discussing communicative functions, grammar and sociolinguistic aspects, and finally role-playing the dialogues, which the students prepare and perform in pairs.

Although not authentic in the sense of being genuine or spontaneous, the scripted dialogues are strongly *realistic* examples of discourse, exhibiting a considerable range of discourse and sociocultural elements (including moral attitudes, prejudices, superstitions, humour), unlike earlier teaching materials. Although generally brief, the scripted dialogues are rich in nuances and cultural overtones, with a vein of humorous observation of human nature, for example, they contain many examples of playful use of words. Learners always want to be able to express themselves humorously in their target language, but being humorous appropriately across cultural boundaries is notoriously difficult – yet a highly valuable ability. The dialogues even teach socioculturally appropriate oral registers, by introducing the informal register in proper context and showing how to express politeness in formal situations.

Furthermore, Australians are not just cast in the role of visitors, as in previous materials, but appear in varied roles.

For all these reasons the scripted dialogues are excellent teaching resources, and they were the materials most highly valued by students interviewed by Read. Students invariably spoke of them in positive terms, and many mentioned that they 'mined' them for idioms and language functions when they were preparing for oral presentations and oral examinations, for example:

> I love them because whenever I have to do an oral I just go through them and you can pick up all the little ways of saying things, and you can hear them [on tape] so you can hear the words and know how they're spelt and read the words and know how they're pronounced. I think they're really great.

> I think if you actually hear the tape quite a few times useful phrases do become embedded in the memory, and I presume they are sort of authentic conversations that people would have, so for that reason I think they're quite good.

> They're good. You can see the way people relate to each other and you get to know the opinions of Indonesians and that kind of thing.

(c) Vocabulary Development

The TIFL materials are remarkable for a strong emphasis on vocabulary teaching and learning, an area that was generally neglected in language pedagogy throughout the audio-lingual and for much of the communicative periods. In this the TIFL materials are extraordinary. Reeve instigated a number of innovative teaching practices, such as students themselves selecting 20 words for the class to learn each week and drilling each other at the start of each lesson; brainstorming and semantic mapping; and communicative crosswords (excellent for practising paraphrasing, an invaluable strategy for learners to acquire which is seldom specifically taught). Creative variations on a number of older techniques, such as explicit vocabulary teaching, learning to use proverbs in sentences, and dictionary exercises, were also used. Unfortunately space does not permit going into detail here about this important aspect of the TIFL materials.

(d) Communicative Activities

One of the most novel aspects of the TIFL materials is the number of communicative activities they offer, a total of 434. Table 1 reveals that the TIFL materials contain a great many communicative activities, progressing from more controlled to less controlled forms, providing holistic language practice at sequential levels of complexity. For example, contextualised drills, the simplest and most highly controlled type of communicative activity, occur at Introductory level. The second least complex activity is the survey, of which there are 36 at Introductory level and only 8 at Intermediate level. There are 25 pair-work conversations at Introductory level and 43 at Intermediate, which range from very simple exchanges and negotiations to quite sophisticated and demanding discussions. Interestingly, however, there are almost as many role-plays at Introductory as at Intermediate level (89 and 113 respectively), reflecting the range of role-play scenarios, which vary from simple to sophisticated. Communicative crosswords, which require relatively sophisticated language because they utilise descriptive words and develop the useful skill of paraphrasing when you lack specific vocabulary, occur mainly at Intermediate level.

The process involved in creating the TIFL materials was for groups of people to brainstorm ideas and develop them into communicative activities. They were then circulated for comments and trialled in universities around Australia, and any consistently disliked by students or lecturers were discarded. Thus these activities can be relied on as ones students enjoy and that 'work' from an organisational point of view. They are well thought out and carefully designed, providing a rich, wide range of message-focused and holistic speaking practice activities. Table 1 lists the TIFL communicative activities for the two-year program to give an idea of the wealth of materials available.

Table 1: Number of communicative activities in the TIFL materials, by type

Activity type	Introductory	Intermediate	Total
Barrier game		3	3
Brainstorm a topic	2		2
Communicative crossword	1	15	16
Communicative task	4		4
Contextualised drill	18		18
Exchange written messages		1	1
'Find my friend'	1		1
Group/pair/group information exchange	1		1
Group-work	2	22	24
Guessing game		3	3
Interactive lecture	1	1	2
Interview	4	10	14
Jigsaw activity	2	4	6
Pair-work activity	25	43	68
Physical response activity	5		5
Quiz	2		2
Ranking activity	2	4	6
Record an answering machine message	2	1	3
Role-play	89	113	202
Rumour game		1	1
Simulation		1	1
Story-telling game		1	1
Survey	36	8	44
Take notes (message-focus)	1		1
Team competition		1	1
Whole-class discussion		4	4
Total	**198**	**236**	**434**

(e) Sociocultural Understandings

Sociocultural aspects of the language are very important in teaching Indonesian to Australians, because of the considerable cultural gap between the two societies, and the TIFL materials were ahead of their time in offering intercultural language learning (IcLL).

Sociolinguistic discussions in English of material presented in the 'Cultural Notes' are the main way in which this is done in the TIFL materials, although there are numerous others. The Cultural Notes are a book of excerpts (in English) from various writers about Indonesian customs, differences between Indonesian and Australian culture and cross-cultural awareness. Topics covered in the materials range very widely, including sociolinguistics, etiquette, geography, history, politics, traditional customs and religions, and include far more sociocultural and sociolinguistic content than could otherwise be included in the first year of a language program, at a more complex cognitive level than if it were in the target language. Table 2 presents an analysis of the topics covered in 'Contacts and Appointments', just one of the 34 themes, demonstrating the quantity and variety of material contained in the Cultural Notes.

Table 2: Topics covered in Theme 13 of *Cultural Notes, TIFL Materials* (Contacts and Appointments)

Topics	
1.	Key value of friendliness
2.	Smiling
3.	Eye contact
4.	Chatting (importance, compulsory topics, topics to avoid)
5.	Harmony of feelings (e.g., maintenance of face, avoidance of negative behaviour, acceptable ways to be negative)
6.	Social sanctions for breaking culture rules
7.	Emotional control (importance of mastery of emotions)
8.	Casual meetings – how people behave
9.	Hospitality
10.	Meals and social visits
11.	Farewells
12.	Forms of address (e.g., use of kinship terminology)
13.	Honorific prefixes
14.	Characteristics of informal register (e.g., morphology, word order, pronunciation changes, lexis)
15.	Extremely polite formal behaviour (e.g., proper form for proper rank, indirectness, dissemination, avoidance of acts suggesting lack of self-control)
16.	Custom of asking for forgiveness for errors one might make
17.	Use of go-betweens
18.	Importance of not being judgmental
19.	Conducting polite conversation
20.	Treatment of foreigners

In the theory and practice of teaching culture in language programs, the three dominant paradigms in the past have been to present 'culture as high culture' (e.g., literature); 'culture as area studies' (i.e., knowledge about the history, geography and institutions of the target language country); and 'culture as practice' (i.e., describing cultures in terms of the values and practices that typify them).

Since the late 1990s these paradigms have been influenced by an approach called Intercultural Language Teaching (IcLT) (Lo Bianco et al., 1999). The aim of IcLT is to develop a realisation of linguistic and cultural relativity. It implies an acknowledgment and understanding of the links between language and culture as well as an understanding of how communication works across cultures. The integration of culture and language constitutes new teaching content for language teachers to introduce into their teaching practice. The three essential elements of IcLT are overt teaching of *linguaculture* – by which is meant (a) the links between language and culture; (b) teaching of the target language/culture in counterdistinction to the learners' L1; and (c) development of intercultural competence, that is, the ability to recognise where and when culture is manifest in cross-cultural encounters, and also the ability to manage an intercultural space so that all parties to the encounter are comfortable participants.

The Cultural Notes present cultural knowledge from the viewpoint of three of the four paradigms. The oldest one, 'culture as high culture', does not appear. However, 'culture as area studies' does appear in several sections, and 'culture as practice' appears in nearly every theme of the Cultural Notes. IcLT can be identified in 15 of the 20 Introductory themes. The emerging paradigm of IcLT, which is based on an expanded understanding of the nature of cross-cultural encounters and a deeper understanding of the links between language and culture, is clearly a more expanded and developed approach to teaching cultures while teaching language than the two earlier paradigms. However, this does not mean that earlier approaches no longer have value or cannot contribute to a program of teaching culture in teaching language. For example, the area studies approach, evidenced by the provision of information about the geography, history and institutions of Indonesia, obviously provides essential, though not sufficient, content knowledge related to Indonesian culture.

Table 3 displays an analysis of the Cultural Notes in terms of how often and where they embody three of these four approaches to culture in language teaching. In this the TIFL materials were well ahead of contemporary practice at the time they were created. Students spoke highly of the Cultural Notes and several who went to Indonesia took them along to refer to as a guide on their travels (Read, 2002, Section 7.3).

Table 3: Paradigms of culture in language teaching as displayed in the Cultural Notes

Location	Culture as area studies	Culture as practice	IcLT
Introduction		X	X
Theme 1		X	X
Theme 2		X	X
Theme 3		X	X
Theme 4		X	X
Theme 5	X	X	X
Theme 6		X	X
Theme 7	X		
Theme 8	X	X	X
Theme 9	X		
Theme 10		X	X
Theme 11	X	X	X
Theme 12		X	X
Theme 13		X	X
Theme 14	X	X	
Theme 15	X	X	
Theme 16	X	X	X
Theme 17	X	X	X
Theme 18	X	X	X
Theme 19	X	X	
Theme 20	X	X	

(f) Grammar Materials

Reeve felt that the need to explain grammar and usage meant that there was too much English in most Indonesian course-books. Yet the explanations were useful, and students liked to have something to refer to. His innovative solution was to combine the grammar and usage explanations into a separate reference grammar, and he arranged for Dr James Sneddon to be included in the project team as the senior linguist. The TIFL Project 'Grammar Notes' was the result. As well as the TIFL Grammar Notes, Sneddon later wrote the *Indonesian Reference Grammar* (Sneddon 1996) with a grant from the federal Department of Education through the TIFL project. It was published simultaneously in the US, UK and Australia. This book builds on the work Sneddon had done for the TIFL materials, but is a more advanced and detailed treatment. It constitutes the most complete description of Indonesian grammar targeted at learners that is available in English, and it contains clear explications of many points that learners need to know. Furthermore, unlike nearly everything that was previously available in English, it is descriptive rather than prescriptive, which represents an enormous advance on previous grammar materials for Indonesian.

The purpose of the Grammar Notes is to explain linguistic items drawn from the teaching material in language that is accessible to students. They contain no exercises for practice. They are meant to be read at home, and then discussed in class, with supporting exercises if needed. However, they can be regarded as a pedagogic grammar, rather than purely a reference grammar, because they are intended for the use of learners, and contain information that is designed to explain to English-speaking learners the appropriate way to use Indonesian. For example, the following section is quite clearly directed to inform learners about the illocutionary effects of different ways of expressing that one has lost one's watch:

9.1 ADVERSATIVE VERBS WITH AFFIX *KE-...AN*

These verbs indicate that the person involved is unpleasantly or negatively affected by the action. The sentence Jam saya hilang **'My watch is lost'** makes a neutral statement about what has happened, with no emphasis on its adverse effect on me. However the sentence Saya kehilangan jam emphasises the fact of my misfortune. The usual translation is **'I've lost my watch'** though a more literal translation would be **'I've been subjected to the loss of a watch'**. (TIFL Intermediate Grammar Notes, p. 35)

In general, the descriptions of Indonesian grammar in the Grammar Notes are designed for practical effect: they aim to help learners develop grammatical competence as a component of communicative competence. They are not included for the purpose of linguistic analysis. In other words, the approach to grammar in the TIFL materials is that grammar will be acquired naturally and inductively for the most part, with more detailed treatment for the items or entities that learners find difficult to master. The learners' attention is directed to grammar via the Grammar Notes, but grammatical items are actively taught only as needed to develop communicative competence, not for their own sake. The view was taken that grammar exercises were already plentifully available in older materials if they were needed.

Grammatical competence means knowledge of the language code, including lexical items, rules of morphology and syntax, sentence-grammar semantics and phonology. Early models of communicative competence included grammatical competence. However, Krashen's ideas subsequently contributed to a perception that formal instruction in grammar is often inefficient and of limited value to SL success. His Input Hypothesis (Krashen, 1985, pp. 2–3) amounts to a claim that if L2 learners are exposed to 'comprehensible input' and are provided with opportunities to focus on meaning and messages rather than grammatical forms and accuracy, they will be able to acquire morphology and syntax as they comprehend meaning, in much the same way as L1 learners. In other words, L2 acquisition can occur naturally; and if it does, the learner develops an implicit feeling for what is correct.

However, the concept of grammatical consciousness-raising put forward in Rutherford and Sharwood Smith (1988) rests on two characteristics of adult language learning which have been identified by a number of researchers: (1) that the provision of comprehensible input alone is not sufficient to ensure L2 grammatical accuracy; and (2) that at appropriate times some form of grammatical consciousness-raising is effective in improving such accuracy. The associated pedagogical grammar hypothesis assumes that hypothesis testing on the part of learners is an integral part of their achievement of grammatical competence, and claims that instructional strategies that draw the attention of the learner to structures will tend to result in faster language learning.

Corder (1988, pp. 129–133) suggests that learning grammar is fundamentally an inductive process, but one which can be controlled and facilitated by descriptions and explanations given at the appropriate moment and formulated in a way which is appropriate to the maturity, knowledge and sophistication of the learner. In other words, the teacher's job is to provide the learners with the right data at the right time and teach them how to learn; that is, help them develop appropriate learning strategies and means of testing their hypotheses. The old controversy about whether to provide the rule first and then the examples or vice versa is, he suggests, merely a matter of tactics, to which no categorical answer can be given. Giving a rule or description first means directing the learners' attention to the problem, or establishing a readiness for the task; giving the examples or data first means encouraging the learners to develop their own mental set of strategies for dealing with the task. This implies that they must be given the opportunity to make decisions or choices and, consequently, run the risk of making errors.

The Grammar Notes in the TIFL materials function as a grammatical consciousness-raising stimulus. The process described above is very much what can occur in an instructional program based on the TIFL materials: a mixture of (a) exposure to rules and descriptions via the Grammar Notes; (b) inductive learning based on the listening and reading exercises; and (c) focused practice if and when problems become evident. Most of the students who were interviewed spoke highly of the approach to grammar in the TIFL materials and regarded the Grammar Notes as a valuable reference, for example:

> We have a grammar book but we don't often use it. In general conversation it usually comes up, or one person asks a question that may be bothering them and the teacher elaborates on that, so you learn it as it comes up, in its relevant context – whatever we're doing at the time – so instead of having a stupid grammar lesson every Thursday we just learn it as it's relevant and needed. (S16) (Read, 2002, p. 554)

So far, this article has described the shortcomings of early teaching materials for Indonesian and some of the most successful innovative advances provided by the TIFL project. There are other aspects of the TIFL materials that have great potential but have so far been largely ignored because of perceived flaws (e.g., due to their presentation in the form of photocopies), or have not been taken up because of teachers' lack of understanding or misconceptions about how to use them. Space does not permit more details of why this occurred to be included here, but Read (2002), which is available online, analyses the TIFL materials and evaluates them from a theoretical basis (Chapter 6) and based on data in the form of classroom observations and interviews with lecturers and students (Chapter 7).

On the other hand, the TIFL materials were the first attempt in Indonesian language pedagogy to teach reading for gist. Many of the impressive total of 269 TIFL reading texts (nearly all authentic) may now be no longer in use; but the principle of reading for gist has been taken up enthusiastically, and is now widely used in Indonesian language teaching.

New Influences on Second Language Teaching

Other ideas, drawn largely from the theory and pedagogy of education, have begun to influence second language (SL) pedagogy since the TIFL materials were conceived, for example, scaffolding, task-based language teaching and project-based learning. What is common to all these is a paradigm shift from the traditional underpinning of education where learning was upheld as a result of and response to the transmission of authoritarian and coded knowledge. They legitimise learners' experiences by allowing space for learners to participate in the process of knowledge construction. The parallel with the well-known concept of interlanguage (Selinker, 1972; Richards, 1974, pp. 31–54) to describe the learner's version of the target language is obvious.

The teacher's role is not diminished in these ways of teaching, but they require teachers to use their knowledge and resources to co-produce possible and effective learning projects for and with learners. Learners set their own objectives and time-frames and plan their own study goals. They are supported to develop confidence in their ability to direct their own learning by developing awareness of their own learning preferences.

A range of learning experiences is sequenced and students develop reflective thinking upon the experiences along the provided range. Classroom activities include many types of exercises and tasks such as role-plays, simulations, project-based learning, cooperative learning, participatory activities, constructive learning, problem-solving activities, as well as group and pair work, assignments, projects, presentations, discussions, and sharing with the whole class.

The curriculum can become a collaborative effort between teachers and learners, since learners are closely involved in the decision-making process regarding the content of the curriculum and how it is taught. The activities and tasks can be linked to different perspectives on language teaching and learning and may fit more than one student learning style.

(a) Scaffolding

Scaffolding (e.g., Hammond, 2001) is based on the ideas of Vygotsky, who developed the idea of the zone of proximal development, the cognitive process in which the 'spontaneous' concepts developed by the child or learner can meet the more knowledgeable concepts of the teacher or adult in a cooperative dialogue.

Wood et al. (1976) introduced the term 'scaffolding' as a metaphor to capture the nature of support and guidance. The key feature is that teachers, through their sequencing of teaching activities and the quality of their support and guidance, are able to challenge and extend what students are able to do. By participating in such activities students are pushed beyond their current abilities and levels of understanding, and thus learning occurs and students are able to internalise new understandings.

The ideal learning context is a combination of high challenge and high support, such as can occur in conversational dialogues between the teacher and a class in the target language, for example, discussing a text, extending a discussion beyond the text to the real world in various ways, discussing aspects of language used in the text – such as alternative ways of saying things, alternative sentence structures – and so forth.

Students find such dialogues intensely stimulating and enjoyable, and they are a powerful teaching and learning activity too seldom used in language classrooms. The development of materials designed to be used in such activities, with accompanying notes for teachers on the technique, would be a most valuable addition to the pedagogy of Indonesian as a second language.

(b) Task-based Language Teaching and Project-based Learning

Within the communicative language teaching framework, task-based learning and project-based learning approaches integrate language and content learning objectives because use of language and explicit attention to language-related features (e.g., forms, vocabulary, skills) are needed at various points in the exploration of themes. Their point of departure lies in the task-chaining or continuity, in which a collection of instructionally sequenced and integrated tasks all contribute opportunities for learning and practising language.

The task-based language approach (e.g., Ellis, 2003) has become a central concept in TESOL in the Asia-Pacific region (as usual, ideas are coming into foreign language teaching from the powerhouse of TESOL, due to the continuous growth in global English).

In Nunan's (2004, p.4) definition:

> …a pedagogical task is a piece of classroom work that involves learners in comprehending, manipulating, producing or interacting in the target language while their attention is focused on mobilizing their grammatical knowledge in order to express meaning, and in which the intention is to convey meaning rather than to manipulate form. The task should also have a sense of completeness, being able to stand alone as a communicative act in its own right with a beginning, a middle and an end.

What is special about the approach is the way tasks are selected and sequenced to develop higher levels of communicative proficiency. Demands placed on students increase from one phase to the next, and skills acquired or practised in one phase are extended in succeeding steps.

An important conceptual basis is experiential learning. This takes the learner's immediate personal experience as the point of departure for the learning experience. The active involvement of the learner is therefore central to the task. It is 'learning by doing', in contrast to the traditional 'transmission' approach to education in which the learner acquires knowledge passively from the teacher.

Project-based learning (PBL) is a more elaborate and generally more fully learner-centred type of task-based learning. The earlier tasks involving controlled use of language act as a model providing students with language content to draw on when they come to produce their own language at the later stage. Bridging or motivating activities then serve as less controlled activities training part-skill communication that will then be combined into total skills of communicative activities in free-use language activities, namely full-scale projects. Activity stages include planning; gathering information through reading, listening, interviewing, and observing; group discussion of information; problem solving (e.g., task allocation); oral and written reporting; and display.

Tasks are goal-oriented because all tasks have a specific objective that must be achieved in a given time. Students will encounter holistic chunks of language that will often be beyond their current capacity. Keeping the goals in mind, students concentrate on understanding and conveying meanings so as to complete the goals successfully. Actual samples of student language, or aspects of their interactions with peers during task completion, are recorded and analysed to assess learning progress.

Because of its prominent characteristics (e.g., processing and making sense of knowledge, use of language as communication, learning a language via content, collaboration with peers and teachers, and selection and grading of tasks) PBL is a versatile approach for full integration with other language teaching approaches. It is advisable, however, that students who are used to formal and structured teaching should be introduced via a selection of preliminary activities, so as to develop receptiveness to more self-directed project work (Fried-Booth, 1987).

Although learning-centred approaches such as task-based and project-based learning were initially developed as approaches to teaching children, they have been found to be just as effective and applicable to language learning at tertiary level. The guiding principle is to teach the way people like to learn.

Conclusion

In this chapter we have employed two quite different perspectives on the TIFL project, which developed Indonesian language teaching materials for universities from 1991 to 1996. The first perspective is an exposition of why they were needed from the major planner and organiser of the development of those materials, and the second is a critique and evaluation from the scholar who conducted the most sustained examination of those materials. We have tried here to set the TIFL materials within a history of 50 years' evolution of Indonesian language teaching methods in Australia – a substantial past; and also to explore what continuing value the materials and approaches have for the future – hopefully also substantial.

We have seen how many texts and approaches have been used since the start of Indonesian teaching in the universities in the late 1950s and in the schools from the early 1960s. Such a fine creative endeavour – perhaps over 70 texts, text series, and resource banks! And also we have seen how many texts have disappeared into the rubbish bin of out-dated methodologies – so much creative endeavour no longer of use, and so many young teachers 'reinventing the wheel', with too little cumulative development of expertise and resources. We would be better off now if our development of teaching materials had been less subject to the swings and shifts of methodologies developed outside the field of Indonesian language teaching and the on/off political enthusiasm for Asian languages in Australia. No method of Indonesian language teaching has yet been developed out of the nature of the Indonesian language itself (except perhaps grammar translation, ironically, with its dry chapters based on discrete Indonesian grammar points).

We need to recapture the positive impetus that marked the teaching of Indonesian at periods in our past. It needs to be done with more enthusiasm and professionalism, because we need to teach more efficiently. It is so important for Australians to reach out to our neighbouring countries and peoples because that is how we need to grow if we are to best manage our future – because physically we are a nation isolated at the south of the globe, with Southeast Asia to the north of us; and in particular, with Indonesian spread out like a barrier between the rest of our region and us. But at present Australians do not seem to be making very good impressions on people in our region. We seem to be giving the impression that we are uncouth, ignorant and arrogant. This is not a positive development: we are not taking the right initiatives. Instead, we are just letting things slide.

In this spirit of drawing from the past to sustain a stronger future for Indonesian language teaching, we conclude with a series of recommendations:

a. A new teaching materials initiative for Indonesian language teaching at tertiary level should be mounted. It should begin with a thorough survey of the best developments in the past fifty years. It should be based on a coherent philosophy and a team approach, and include Indonesians in the planning. It should rediscover the best features of the communicative paradigm of language learning, and encompass also new developments such as those that have been mentioned briefly in this article.

b. We still need a national teaching resources bank for tertiary Indonesian, for the same reasons that we have always needed one: good teaching resources are expensive to produce, and universities cannot afford to fund their production. Lecturers are too busy to produce them because they are expected to do research and produce publications in their discipline, and (importantly) most Indonesian lecturers are required to be specialists in other disciplines than language teaching, so the materials they produce are unfortunately less effective than they could and should be.

c. Such a resource bank is largely but not completely already available in the form of the TIFL teaching resources; which have been proven to work very well, but have been almost entirely overlooked and forgotten. When they were originally planned, the importance of a teacher's manual was not considered. The materials that were produced turned out to be quite unlike the materials Indonesian lecturers were used to, and it was realised that a manual was necessary. However, the teacher's manuals were produced and distributed after the other materials, so that people did not know how to use the TIFL materials at the time they received them, put them on a shelf and quickly forgot them. Many lecturers either know nothing of them or now assume they are ancient history.

d. The TIFL materials were not only a very effective and efficient instructional program, they appealed to a very wide range of learner interests, which made them popular with students, and when the ASLPR (Australian Second Language Proficiency Ratings) test was administered to students at a number of different universities, their rankings were remarkably similar in all universities, thus suggesting that it would be possible to achieve common proficiency levels around Australia if a program like TIFL was widely used (Read, 2002, Section 7.4).

e. The materials are not conceptually out of date, but need revamping and expansion to include recent knowledge, which must be done in a collaborative way, with both Indonesians and Australians involved. Revamping and expansion should be an ongoing process.

f. We must avoid the mistakes made with the TIFL materials. The national resource bank must have a teaching manual and arrangements for publishing and distribution, be available online, and be evaluated properly in an ongoing fashion.

The expected benefit of a national resource bank would be more effective teaching and learning. A national resource bank with teaching manual(s) would also help to ensure common proficiency levels around Australian tertiary institutions.

People-to-people contacts work better when communication is effective. As a nation we need to abandon our diffidence and laziness in the areas of cultural understanding, foreign language learning and cross-cultural communication, and again make some positive, practical attempts to lift our game and achieve results. It is in our national interest to encourage issues in second-language learning that are conducive to this type of growth. In the long run, the survival of our nation and culture may depend on our ability to communicate effectively with people in our neighbourhood, which means being able to understand their languages and cultures.

References

Asian Studies Council. 1988. *A National Strategy for the Study of Asia in Australia*. Canberra: Australian Government Publishing Service.

Ingleson, J. 1989. *Asia in Australian Higher Education: Report of the Inquiry into the Teaching of Asian Studies and Languages in Higher Education*. Kensington: University of New South Wales.

Bley-Vroman, R. 1988. 'The fundamental character of foreign language learning'. In *Grammar and Second Language Learning*, edited by W. Rutherford & M. Sharwood Smith. New York: Newbury House. pp. 19–30.

Brown, C. & McKay, E. 1991. 'National Strategy for Indonesian Language Teaching and Learning'. Canberra: The Indonesian Studies Group of the Asian Studies Association of Australia.

Canale, M. & Swain, M. 1980. 'Theoretical bases of communicative approaches to second language teaching and testing'. *Applied Linguistics* 1, pp. 1–47.
Collins, J. A., editor. 1976. *Marilah Kita Membaca: A Beginner's Reader*. Carlton, Victoria: Pitman Publishing.
Collins, J. A., editor. 1977. *Bunga Rampai: A Topical Indonesian Reader*. Carlton, Victoria.: Pitman Publishing.
Collins, J. A. & Sjafei, M. 1973. *Di Kampung – Indonesian Reader*. Sydney: McGraw-Hill.
Corder, S. P. 1988. 'Pedagogic grammars'. In *Grammar and Second Language Learning*, edited by W. Rutherford & M. Sharwood Smith. New York: Newbury House. pp. 123–145.
Crozet, C. 1996. 'Teaching verbal interaction and culture in the language classroom'. *ARAL* 19 (2), pp. 37–57.
Crozet, C., Liddicoat, A. J. & Lo Bianco, J. 1999. 'Intercultural competence: from language policy to language education'. In *Striving for the Third Place*, edited by J. Lo Bianco, A. J. Liddicoat & C. Crozet. Melbourne: Languages Australia. pp. 1–20
Danosugondo, P. 1966–1971. *Bahasa Indonesia for Beginners*, Books 1 and 2. Sydney: University of Sydney.
Ellis, R. 2003. *Task-Based Language Learning and Teaching*. Oxford, UK: Oxford University Press.
Emanuels, H. W. 1966. *Bahasa Sehari-hari*. Sydney: University of Sydney.
Emanuels, H. W & Turner, V. J. 1967–1968. *Indonesian for Schools*. Books 1 and 2. Sydney: Science Press.
Fried-Booth, D. 1987. *Project Work*. Oxford, U.K.: Oxford University Press.
Hammond, J. 2001. *Scaffolding – Teaching and Learning in Language and Literacy Education*. Newtown, NSW: Primary English Teaching Association.
Hendrata, H. 1969–1970. *An Audio-Lingual Course in Bahasa Indonesia*. Melbourne: H. Hendrata
Hill, D. T. 2012. *Indonesian Language in Australian Universities: Strategies for a Stronger Future*. Australian Learning and Teaching Council National Teaching Fellowship Final Report. Perth: Murdoch University.
Hymes, D. H. 'On communicative competence'. In *Directions in Sociolinguistics: The ethnography of communication*, edited by J. Gumperz & D. H. Hymes. New York: Holt, Rinehart and Winston.
Ichsan, J, Baker, E. & Lane, M. 1968. *Lantjar Berbahasa Indonesia*. Adelaide: Rigby Ltd.
Johns, Y. 1975. *Bahasa Indonesia Book One – Langkah Baru: a new approach*. Canberra: Australian National University Press.
Johnson, K. & Johnson H. 1998. *Encyclopedic Dictionary of Applied Linguistics*. Oxford: Blackwell Publishers.
Krashen, S. D. 1985. *The Input Hypothesis: Issues and Implications*. London: Longman.
Liddicoat, A. J. & Crozet, C. 2000. *Teaching Languages, Teaching Cultures*. Melbourne: Language Australia.
Lie, T. S. 1965. *Introducing Indonesian*. Book 1. Sydney: Angus and Robertson.
Littlewood, W. T. 1984. *Foreign and Second Language Learning – Language Acquisition Research and Its Implications for the Classroom*. Cambridge: Cambridge University Press.
Lo Bianco, J. 1987. *National Policy on Languages*. Canberra: Australian Government Publishing Service.
Lo Bianco, J, Liddicoat, A. J. & Crozet, C. 1999. *Striving for the Third Place*. Melbourne: Language Australia.

McGarry, J. D. & Sumaryono. 1970, 1971, 1974. *Learn Indonesian*. Books 1–3. Chatswood, NSW: Modern Indonesian Publications.

McGarry, J. D. & Winarto, I. M. 1990. *Varia: An Early Stage Reading Book*. Chatswood, NSW: Modern Indonesian Publications.

National Indonesian Language Curriculum Project. 1993. *Suara Siswa*. Indonesian Language Teaching Materials. Carlton, Victoria: Curriculum Corporation.

Nunan, D. 2004. *Task-based Language Teaching*, Cambridge, UK: Cambridge University Press.

Ozolins, U. 1993. *The Politics of Language in Australia*. Melbourne: Cambridge University Press.

Partoredjo, I. S. c.1975. *Bahasa Indonesia Moderen – an integrated method*. Brisbane, Cranbrook Press.

Pello, J. 1980. *Bahasa Indonesia – Lihat Baca Ceritakan*. Laverton, Victoria: Lela Publications.

Pino, E. 1953. *Bahasa Indonesia the National Language of Indonesia – A Course for English-Speaking Students*. Groningen: J. Wolters, 1950; Jakarta, 1953.

Read, J. 2002. 'Innovation in Indonesian language teaching: an evaluation of the TIFL tertiary curriculum materials'. Ph.D. thesis, University of Wollongong. Available at: http://ro.uow.edu.au/theses/335/, accessed 7 July, 2015.

Reeve, D. 1991.'TIFL textbooks – a critique'. Paper presented at the Indonesia-Australia Conference on the teaching of Indonesian as a Foreign Language, Jakarta, 20–21 February 1991.

Richards, J. C. 1974. *Error Analysis: Perspectives on Second Language Acquisition*. London: Longman.

Rutherford, W. & Sharwood Smith, M. 1988. 'Consciousness Raising and Universal Grammar'. In *Grammar and Second Language Learning*, edited by W. Rutherford & M. Sharwood Smith. New York: Newbury House. pp. 107–116.

Santoso, S. & Soemaryono. 1969. *Dari Barat Sampai ke Timur: A Modern Indonesian Reader*. Sydney: Ian Novak.

Sarumpaet, J. P. 1966. *The Structure of Bahasa Indonesia*. Melbourne: Sahata Publications.

Sarumpaet, J. P. 1980. *Modern Usage in Bahasa Indonesia*. Carlton: Pitman.

Sarumpaet, J. P & Mackie, J. A. C. 1966. *Introduction to Bahasa Indonesia*. Melbourne: Melbourne University Press.

Scarino, A., Vale, D., McKay, P. & Clark, J. 1991. *Australian Language Levels (ALL) Guidelines*. Carlton, Victoria: Curriculum Corporation.

Selinker, L. 1972. 'Interlanguage'. *IRAL* 10, pp. 219–231.

Sneddon, J. 1996. *Indonesian Reference Grammar*. Sydney: Allen & Unwin.

Taylor, V. & Sedunary, M. 1991. *Ayo!* Carlton, Victoria: CIS Educational.

Turner, V. J. 1968. *Indonesian for Schools Book Two*. Sydney: Science Press.

Wesley, M. 2009. *Australian Strategy for Asian Language Proficiency – Griffith University*. Report to the Australia 2020 Summit. Griffith University.

White, I. 1988. *Bahasa Tetanggaku – A Notional-Functional Course in Bahasa Indonesia*. Course-books, Audio Recordings and Workbooks 1, 2 and 3. Melbourne: Longman.

Wood, D, Bruner, J S & Ross, G. 1976. 'The role of tutoring in problem solving'. *Journal of Child Psychology and Psychiatry* 17, pp. 89–100.

Wolff, J. U, Oetomo, D. & Fietkiewicz, D. 1986. *Beginning Indonesian Through Self-Instruction*. Books 1, 2 and 3 with audio recordings. Ithaca, N.Y.: Cornell University.

Chapter 6

EXPORTING CULTURE AND THE INDONESIAN WORLD VIEW

Hendrarto Darudoyo

La Trobe University

Introduction

Indonesia can pride itself as one of Asia's emerging cultural exporters. The nation's cultural products are well recognised in Southeast Asia and more broadly in the Malay World,[1] although the popularity of its cultural exports has not been considered as successful as other major Asian popular cultures. With a population exceeding 250 million, Indonesia is also a potential market for imported popular cultural products from China, India, Japan, South Korea, and even Australia. Indonesia is emerging as a cultural trading partner with these nations as its cultural products gradually become part of its export-oriented economy. As with the cultural exports of other major Asian economies, Indonesia primarily uses its own official language, which is a fundamental element of Indonesian culture.

This chapter discusses both government and media responses to Indonesian cultural exports with special reference to the Indonesian language. It looks into the production, export and consumption of Indonesian popular cultural products in the region particularly in the context of its relationship with

---

1   *Dangdut*, for example, has been popular for decades in Indonesia, the Malay-speaking areas of Southeast Asia and other parts of Asia. This genre of Indonesian popular music is made up of the nation's traditional music, with some influence from Indian, Malay, and even Arab music.

Australia. Addressing the correlation between Indonesian economic growth and its cultural exports, it describes the state of Asia's rising middle power and foreign interest in its national culture and language. Since the early 1980s the so-called 'cultural economy' has risen to prominence in many parts of the world (Power & Scott, 2004; Hesmondhalgh, 2013). Producing 'an enormous and ever-increasing range of outputs' (Power & Scott, 2004, p. 3), these industries 'can no longer be seen as secondary to the "real economy" where durable, "useful" goods are manufactured' (Hesmondhalgh, 2013, p. 2).

The interest in the Indonesian language in Australia, however, is primarily an Australian initiative and does not necessarily conform to a standard import-export relationship. Bambang Harymurti[2] of the Tempo Group, for example, shares a view:

> *Ekspor budaya Indonesia ke kawasan Australia menurut saya sangat ditentukan oleh pandangan penduduk Australia dan kawasan sekitarnya pada prospek masa depan Indonesia, terutama di bidang ekonomi. Jadi lebih tepat disebut "impor budaya" atau lebih spesifik lagi "impor bahasa" karena pendorongnya bukan dari Indonesia tapi di masyarakat Australia dan kawasan sekitarnya.*

> In my opinion, Indonesia's cultural exports to Australia are largely determined by Australians' interest in the future prospect of Indonesia, especially in the economic area. Consequently, it would be more appropriate to see it as a "cultural import", or even more specifically, as a "language import" because the push is not from Indonesia, rather it is from the Australian people and surrounding regions.

This chapter suggests that language as a cultural export has not been an Indonesian initiative and raises the question of whether Indonesia should take more control or be more pro-active in the manner in which this 'trade' takes place. There are other factors, however, contributing to the state of the country's cultural exports to the Australian market, which will also be discussed further in this chapter.

The first section of this chapter talks about the efforts made by the Indonesian Government to sell the nation's culture and language to foreign markets, especially to Australia. This includes some discussion about how Indonesian diplomatic missions in Australia promote the country's culture and language. The second section deals with Indonesian as *bahasa pergaulan international*, a

---

2   Harymurti, electronic communication, 3 June 2014.

language for socialisation in the international arena. The third section briefly examines coverage by Australian news organisations of Indonesia and the manner that this coverage shapes Australians' perceptions of Indonesia and the impact it has on the promotion of Indonesian culture and language. Before concluding this chapter, the fourth section takes a closer look at the prospects for the teaching of *bahasa dan budaya Indonesia* (the language and culture of Indonesia) with reference to the contribution by the business community to the promotion of the country's cultural exports.

Cultural Diplomacy

It is important to understand some concepts presented and economic terms borrowed in this chapter before further discussion about exporting Indonesian culture to Australia. The country's creative and cultural industries are discussed interchangeably.[3] These cultural industry companies supply products ranging from books, films, magazines, newspapers, radio and television programmes, and circulate them across borders. As Hesmondhalgh (2013) states, 'Cultural products increasingly circulate across national borders' (p. 2). From the economic perspective, cultural exports fall into the service-industry sector because of the significant service elements. Although exported, popular cultural products such as music and films take the form of physical goods as buyers consume the intangible benefits contained in their content. This is a marketing concept in which cultural products are treated as export commodities and they are best categorised as services rather than goods.

In marketing, it can be helpful to consider the relative importance of the physical goods and services element of a firm's offering, or in other words, which one of the two – the tangible good and the intangible service – is 'the dominant attribute' in satisfying consumer needs or wants (Rix, 2005, pp. 262–263). In the case of cultural products, consumers benefit from intangible service either as a significant element of a tangible product or in their own right. According to Rix, many products are marketed to offer what is called an 'experience' (2005, p. 263). This 'experience' is of particular importance to a service that is marketed with a physical good. *Bahasa dan budaya Indonesia* can be produced and then sold in (or sent to) Australia as physical goods but Australians purchase (or receive) their benefits as intangible services through their consumption of these cultural products. Some examples of intangible

---

3   According to Hesmondhalgh (2013, p. 23), the creative industries are 'the most often preferred alternative to cultural industries' and now used by 'many policymakers and academic analysts'.

services that come with tangible goods are Indonesian-language educational books and tapes, music compact discs (CDs) and digital video discs (DVDs).

Cultural products such as mass media content can be purposefully or accidentally exported. Some are purposefully exported to reach targeted audiences in other countries, while others are accidentally exported because content spills over national borders. Newspaper content, for example, 'is often exported anywhere there is internet access', and radio content 'is increasingly distributed by the internet through webcasting and podcasting, where the technology is available' (McKenzie, 2006, p. 304).

Indonesian mass media content is also exported to Australia by the internet. Major Indonesian-language newspapers or magazines, for example, are physically exported and distributed in Australia, and their content is exported via the internet. While radio programs such as from the country's public radio broadcaster, *Radio Republik Indonesia* (RRI), are exported by shortwave and the internet, the nation's private television stations, *Rajawali Citra Televisi Indonesia* (RCTI) and *Metro TV*, amongst others, broadcast from their Jakarta base via the internet and satellite to Australia. This is for use by expatriate Indonesians and those Australians who have or are learning Indonesian.

The export value of Indonesian cultural goods may still be insignificant in comparison to its other service-industry exports, but this is evidence of the availability of Indonesian popular cultural products in Australia. The intangible (social and cultural) benefits for both Indonesia and Australia, however, might be much greater than the economic value itself. There are a number of possible reasons why Indonesia does not export very much of its cultural product to the Australian market. The first reason is that the export of such products lack financial support from the Indonesian Government. The second reason is that, with a population of just over 24 million and low number of Australians of Indonesian cultural background, Australia is treated as a minor market by Indonesian cultural producers when compared to the huge domestic market. Additionally, Indonesian cultural products appear less attractive to the general Australian market than products from other Asian countries such as China and Japan. All these will be further discussed in this chapter.

Understandably, Indonesia's cultural and creative industries expect some sort of support from their government in relation to the export of cultural and creative products, as occurs with its main competitors. The support from the government under President Susilo Bambang Yudhoyono, as with the previous governments, was always viewed as somewhat inadequate, albeit the effort of the relevant ministries' to promote Indonesian culture and language overseas was evident.[4] It might sound tautological, but inadequate government support usually has a lot to do with the constraints on the national budget.

Three ministries are of particular relevance to the export of Indonesian-language cultural products: *Kementerian Pendidikan dan Kebudayaan* (Ministry of Education and Culture), *Kementerian Pariwisata dan Ekonomi Kreatif* (Ministry of Tourism and Creative Economy) and *Kementerian Luar Negeri* (Kemlu – Ministry of Foreign Affairs). The Ministry of Education and Culture's portfolio includes Indonesia's cultural industries and language education, while the Ministry of Tourism and Creative Economy deals with national creative industries and tourism. In the case of diplomacy, according to Killian (2012), the Ministry of Tourism and Creative Economy is in charge of the nation's cultural diplomacy, while The Ministry of Foreign Affairs is responsible for public diplomacy. Another ministry, Ministry of Trade, concentrates on economic diplomacy.[5] Taking the Ministry of Education and Culture's portfolio of Indonesian language education into consideration, this ministry may be seen as a ministry in charge of language diplomacy. These three ministries play a joint role in conducting '*diplomasi budaya*' (cultural diplomacy), on behalf of the Indonesian Government.

In Australia, Indonesian consulate generals, backed by the Indonesian Embassy in Canberra, organise cultural and economic festivals in the name of the nation within a tight budget, as allocated by the Ministry of Foreign Affairs. An Indonesian diplomat responsible for information and social cultural affairs at one of the consulate generals recalled how the office was kept waiting for the funds from the ministry allocated for a major cultural and economic event to be held in Melbourne, *Festival Indonesia* (FI).[6] Consequently, instead of making FI into a big cultural and economic event by increasing the number of sponsors, the Indonesian Consulate General in Melbourne planned a smaller, cultural-only festival, *Festival Budaya Indonesia*, utilising the support of the Victorian-based Indonesian community groups to replace the expensive 8-year old FI, which had previously been successfully organised

---

4   During Yudhoyono's presidency, the related ministries were the Ministry of Education and Culture, Ministry of Tourism and Creative Industries, and Ministry of Foreign Affairs.

5   For more discussion on Indonesia's economic diplomacy, see, for example, Killian (2012).

6   Interview with Ita Puspitasari, Consul for Information and Social Culture Affairs (Konsul Pensosbud) in Melbourne, was conducted on 19 May 2014. The financial issue combined with some managerial problems, for example, resulted in one of the biggest Indonesian cultural festivals in Australia sponsored by the Ministry of Foreign Affairs being cancelled in 2014.

by Festival Indonesia Inc. in cooperation with the Consulate in Melbourne. The idea was not to lose the cultural promotion even if the festival could not be big as it was.

It is a common practice among Indonesian diplomatic missions in Australia to cooperate with private organisers and Indonesian community groups to hold such big cultural events with the financial support from a number of parties, including Australian state or local governments. The Indonesian cultural festival in Adelaide, held annually in mid-April, has also attracted a number of sponsors, including the South Australian Government, Flinders University, the Ministry of Tourism and Creative Economy, and the Indonesian Consulate.[7]

By Australian standards, the cost to organise such a cultural festival is relatively low in Australian dollars, but it is, nevertheless, seen as a substantial investment in Jakarta, given that annual cultural festivals are held separately in two or more states. The success of this kind of cultural promotion is hard to measure. Smaller Indonesian cultural events such as music festivals or concerts, film festivals, and trade and food festivals usually attract mostly Indonesians rather than a broader Australian audience. The effectiveness of these promotional activities in generating some publicity for Indonesian culture through Australia's major news media organisations is also in doubt. The organisers are expected to present these cultural festivals as creative, attractive events to the mass media and the Australian public at large. The Consul for Information and Social Culture Affairs Puspitasari[8] at the Indonesian Consulate Melbourne thought that this kind of activity had become 'a routine that lacked innovation, creativity, or fresh ideas'.

While the diplomatic mission claims that their promotional efforts have been 'optimal', the Indonesian public do not consider the efforts to promote Indonesian culture and language by the Indonesian Government through the relevant ministries are enough to support the export of the nation's culture. The former Yudhoyono administration's claim to have had a supportive role for the country's cultural exports[9] has been denied by those involved in the cultural industries. Endy M. Bayuni,[10] senior editor of the English-language

---

7   According to Tony Hewitt, who represented the Indofest committee, they have to raise some AUD 80,000 to organise the annual cultural festival (OZIP, June 2014).
8   Puspitasari, interview, Melbourne, 19 May 2014.
9   *Pekan Produk Kreatif Indonesia* (PPKI) held in 2009, which was formerly called *Pameran Produk Budaya Indonesia* in 2007 and 2008, can be seen as part of the support shown by the Ministry for Trade during Yudhoyono's 10 year-presidency as reflected in a press release prepared by the public relations department of the Ministry.
10 Bayuni, electronic communication, 4 June 2014.

Jakarta Post compares Indonesian popular cultural product exports with those of South Korea, and concludes:

> I don't think Indonesia is doing enough to export its culture, including *bahasa Indonesia*, abroad, anywhere. I cannot recall any government policy that discusses such exports. All we hear about is exports of commodities, products and services. But we don't hear anything resembling the *Hallyu* (Korean Wave) in which the South Korean government gives full support to the campaign to export cultural products.

In his view, Indonesia has more unique cultural products to offer than South Korea due to the nation's richer cultural diversity. He suggests that Indonesia lacks a concerted campaign fully supported by the government:

> As with the experience of *Hallyu*, the exports of culture products/services would reinforce the country's overall exports, help improve the trade balance, and most important of all, raise Indonesia's prestige abroad.

What the Yudhoyono administration did in 2009, according to Bayuni, was to set up *Direktorat Jendral Ekonomi Kreatif* (Directorate General of Creative Economy) under the Ministry of Tourism and Creative Economy, but the impact of this on Indonesia's exports was minimal. Indonesian cultural producers expect this government organisation to do more to develop the national creative industry and support the export of the industry's products.

Indonesian documentary filmmaker Lexy Rambadeta[11] criticised the Indonesian Government's move in relation to cultural exports by saying that it was nothing more than a copycat of what South Korea had done:

> *Langkah (pemerintah) itu dipicu karena ekspansi budaya dan bahasa Korea ke seluruh dunia, termasuk Indonesia.*

> The (Government) move was spurred on by the expansion of the Korean culture and language across the globe, including Indonesia.

He noted:

> *Ekspor budaya dan bahasa ini sudah lama dilakukan secara parsial dan seringkali tidak resmi oleh masyarakat Indonesia. Misalnya oleh penyanyi/ pemusik, pembuat film populer, pengusaha kuliner, dan masyarakat Indonesia di Australia.*

---

11 Rambadeta, electronic communication, 6 June 2014

The export of Indonesian language and culture has actually been carried out in a piecemeal and often unofficial manner for a long time by Indonesians. For example, singers, musicians, makers of popular films, culinary entrepreneurs, and the Indonesian diaspora in Australia.

As a comparison, South Korean popular culture exports have proved to be a great success, especially in the East Asian region. Following its *shin hallyu* (the new Korean wave), this nation continued the spreading of its culture through the promotion of its tourism, fashion, and shopping (Seliger, 2013). Interestingly, this was one country applying its own cultural strategy in response to another country's cultural strategy. As was the case with Japan's response to China's domination in Asia, South Korea increased its budget for the development of cultural industries after the opening of its market for imported Japanese cultural products:

> The promotion of exports of cultural goods has been supported by the Korea Culture and Content Agency since 2012. The Ministry of Culture and Tourism and the Korean National Tourism Organization have also been active in organizing trips to Korea as part of the *shin hallyu* mass tourism. (Seliger, 2013, p. 50)

The 21st century, as mentioned by Firdaus in Chapter 1, has been dubbed 'the Asian century' and the governments in the region have become increasingly aware that 'culture is power'. After the regional financial crisis in the late 1990s, East Asian countries became more serious about the penetration of their popular culture into the region, including Southeast Asia. Japan is seen to be a dominant exporter of television drama and popular music, while:

> In terms of production and export capacity, Hong Kong and Taiwan may be said to occupy the same in-between position as the South Korean popular cultural industry. However, they occupy prominent, if not dominating, positions in the pan ethnic-Chinese segment of East Asian Popular Culture. In addition to their own domestic audiences, which still constitute the first market, television programmes, films and music from Hong Kong and Taiwan have always had a constant presence in the other locations where there are significant ethnic Chinese population, such as Singapore and Malaysia and, of course, the PRC, especially after its economic liberalization. (Chua, 2007, p. 124)

Clearly, Indonesia is in no position to challenge Japan's or even Korea's popular culture export dominance. As one of the major recipients of bilateral official development assistance from Japan, Indonesia is much less able to support the export of its popular cultural products even though these exports can actually create a huge stimulus for the development of national cultural and creative industries. This is the economic rationale for the importance of the export of the country's cultural products. Indonesia would arguably secure more from this cultural trading with Australia than simple economic gains.

Wahid Supriyadi, former Consul-General in Melbourne and former Indonesian Ambassador to United Arab Emirates who then became an advisor to the Minister of Foreign Affairs, was among those who believed that Indonesia's creative exports to Australia would help its creative economy grow. This creative economy, he noted, reached Rp104 trillion (AUD10.4 billion) in 2006 and, in just six years, it grew nearly six times the 2006 figure to around Rp600 trillion (AUD60 billion), or accounted for about 7 percent of the country's GDP (gross domestic product). The exports are likely 'to contribute to the development of the creative industries such as batik, designer fashion, handicrafts, information and communication technology, film, and advertising'.[12]

Each of these industries, however, is still in its infancy and considered small as an exporting industry. As the Executive Director of Indonesia-Australia Business Council (IABC) Vic Halim observed, designer fashion combining traditional batik with contemporary design, animations created by Indonesians for big budget Hollywood films such as *Transformers*, films screened at international film festivals, and contemporary music are among the country's creative industries that are increasingly gaining an international reputation, even if they are not yet economically significant.[13]

The Jakarta Post's Bayuni[14] also noted the importance of the country's cultural exports:

> A conscious effort to export our cultures would necessarily lead to the nation to pay more attention to the preservation, development, and improvement of our cultures, and our cultural products.

Renowned Indonesian filmmaker Garin Nugroho believes cultural exports should represent what he called 'the trilogy of a civilisation': *budaya warisan* (heritage culture), *budaya popular* (popular culture) and *budaya alternatif* (alternative culture). He warned that 'exporting only popular culture would

---

12   Supriyadi, electronic communication, 18 June 2014.
13   Halim, electronic communication, 16 June 2014.
14   Bayuni, electronic communication, 4 June 2014

mean a loss of the complete Indonesian cultural map' and said that language is essential in this cultural export.[15]

For the Australian consumption of *bahasa dan budaya Indonesia* to have an important role, he added, Indonesia needed to develop the strategy as well as the (social, educational, political and economic) functions of *bahasa dan budaya Indonesia* in Australia. In the case of Indonesian creative industries, the development of these industries would be driven by the development of creative content accompanied by both production and global market management:

> *Pada aspek manajemen produksi dan pasar global masih sangat lemah, sementara konten bukan pengolahan menjadi produk yang bersaing secara global.*
>
> Aspects of the global market and the management of production remain very weak, while the content has not been prepared as globally competitive products'.[16]

The nation's cultural goods such as Indonesian-language books, newspapers, magazines and films are not hard to find in Australian university libraries, but they are very rare in Australian public libraries, while popular cultural products from other major Asian countries are easy to find there. University libraries, however, only keep a few major Indonesian-language newspapers and magazines. Books, newspapers, magazines, radio, television programs, songs, and movies, as part of Indonesian popular culture, are of great importance to Australians interested in gaining knowledge of the country's culture or attempting to master its language.

Reading books in the Indonesian language is one way to gain knowledge of *bahasa dan budaya Indonesia*, although new books are difficult to obtain. Indonesians themselves need more books to be published each year, as the country had 'one of the lowest per capita of books published among Southeast Asian countries'[17]. According to Bayuni, Indonesians still show 'very little appreciation' towards their own literatures.

Another way of viewing Indonesian culture is through its films, which introduce the viewers to Indonesian society:

> In Indonesia, the historical stages of cinema also reflect the nation's socio-cultural and political dynamic over different periods spanning

---

15   Nugroho, interview, 12 June 2014.
16   Nugroho, interview, 12 June 2014.
17   Bayuni, electronic communication, 4 June 2014.

almost as long as film has existed as an industry – almost a hundred years. Film is not only about entertainment – this can be seen clearly in the ever-changing topics of the movies over the decades, revealing the values and preoccupation of a society at any given time. What appears on screen can also reveal the society we live in. (Nuh, 2012, p. 9)

Those involved in the country's cultural industries agree that people need to love their own cultural products first before expecting foreigners to appreciate their cultural goods such as films. Separately, cultural producers need to broaden their view, exploring the possibilities of exporting their cultural products to Australia and other places in the world, and not just focusing on marketing their products in Indonesia.

The market potential for domestic and foreign cultural products is surely substantial, but there is also relatively low appreciation by the Indonesian public towards their own culture and language:

> If we are going to export films, plays, songs, and dances then we need to develop them first at home and convince our own audience that these are worthy of their time and money.[18]

This statement is a reference to some Indonesians, who are proud of their own national culture and language only if foreigners first have an interest in them. Harymurti of the Tempo Group also talked about the relationship between the export of *bahasa dan budaya Indonesia* and national pride:

> The role of Indonesian culture and language exports is to promote the global understanding of Indonesian culture. This would lead Indonesians to the feeling of being proud (or a matter of national pride).[19]

In the short-term, according to Harymurti, the Indonesian language serves more as a language to unite the nation, while in the long-term Indonesian culture and language can gradually become the nation's key soft power resource. As an example of this, he noted, 'Balinese culture in the form of ornaments (textile designs jewelleries, etc.) has gone into the global space through Hollywood'. *Bahasa dan budaya Indonesia* can be of significance as soft power 'once Indonesia becomes a much bigger economy'.[20]

---

18 Bayuni, electronic communication, 4 June 2014.
19 Harymurti, electronic communication, 3 June 2014.
20 Harymurti, electronic communication, 3 June 2014.

Indonesians are proud of their national culture and language when it is appreciated internationally. However, the low cultural appreciation by the people, the limited budget for the industries, the poor financial support from the government, Indonesia's immediate economic prospects, plus other contributing factors such as the political relationship between Australia and Indonesia, lead to an environment not conducive to the development of Indonesian cultural exports to Australia. For the export of the country's cultural products to be of real success, more support, particularly with regard to marketing efforts, from the exporting country should be expected rather than from the importing country.

Nevertheless, the emergence of Indonesia's younger generation in national cultural production has shown some positive signs recently in the area of cultural industries. Their presence has contributed to an increase in the production of cultural goods reflecting the country's cultural revival. According to Bayuni 'I sense that there is a kind of revival of the cultures in Indonesia, as seen from the number of movies, plays, and songs produced each year. So it is an encouraging start. But we need to do a lot more.'[21]

The film industry in particular has a significant role to play. Film producers and directors have been regularly present in the annual Indonesian Film Festivals (IFF), including the ninth IFF held in Melbourne and Sydney in 2014,[22] which highlighted the work of the country's more experienced filmmakers such as Garin Nugroho, Mira Lesmana, Riri Riza, and Hanung Bramantyo. Some of these films produced or directed by Indonesians were award-winning films or they had been screened previously in international film festivals.[23] Other filmmakers that represent the Indonesian film industry regularly include Gotot Prakosa, Faozan Rizal, Nan Trivieni Achnas, and Nia Dinata (Michalik, 2009, p. 10).

---

21   Bayuni, electronic communication, 4 June 2014.
22   This event was first organised by PPIA-The University of Melbourne (the Indonesian Student Association in Australia at the University of Melbourne), but later by IFF Inc. in cooperation with PPIA (*Buset*, June 2014). It was sponsored by a number of Indonesian and Australian businesses and supported by Kemenparekraf, Kemlu, and DFAT's Australia-Indonesia Institute, as advertised on Indonesian community media.
23   As with Festival Indonesia, Indofest, and other Indonesian cultural festivals, this Indonesian Film Festival attracted extensive Indonesian community media such as Melbourne-based *Ozip* magazine and *Buset* tabloid and Sydney-based *Indomedia* and *Buletin Indo* tabloids, which are distributed in other Australian states' capitals. No local major media coverage was expected from such annual cultural events. Similarly, this happened to Indonesian cultural festivals in other countries.

This section has been about Indonesia's cultural diplomacy and its public participation in the export of the nation's culture. I have argued that if this cultural diplomacy is going to work, the current Indonesian government needs to clearly set a national culture strategy, involving all members of the public. More inter-ministerial coordination, supportive government policies for the development of national cultural and creative industries, and participation from the general public are needed. The next section will first take a closer look at recent programs by the Ministry of Education and Culture to promote the Indonesian language in the international arena, it will then look into the important role of the mass media in creating accurate perceptions of Indonesia, and finally it will discuss the prospects for the teaching of *bahasa dan budaya Indonesia* internationally.

Bahasa Pergaulan Internasional

Indonesian has a potential to become an international language, as a *bahasa pergaulan internasional* (international language of fellowship). It is a language already spoken by hundreds of millions of Indonesians, understood by people from Southeast Asian countries and currently learnt by various nationals, including Australians at both secondary and tertiary levels. According to Sneddon, 'Indonesia's population is more than 200 million, and the number speaking it is approaching 100 percent. Indonesian is thus among the languages with the highest numbers of speakers in the world'.[24]

In 2009, Ho Chi Minh City in Vietnam gave its official recognition of *bahasa Indonesia* as the second foreign language. According to the 2012 figures released by the Indonesian Ministry of Foreign Affairs, the number of native speakers of Indonesian amongst the nation's diaspora reached nearly 4.5 million, ranking Indonesian as the world's fifth largest language. In the 32nd ASEAN Inter-Parliamentary Assembly (AIPA) meeting in 2011, the Speaker of the Indonesian House of Representatives even proposed that Indonesian become one of working languages used in AIPA meetings.[25]

Unlike the successful efforts made by the South Korean Government in promoting the Korean-language through popular cultural products, the Indonesian Government has taken their own route to promote *bahasa dan budaya Indonesia* internationally. The country's education and cultural attachés are stationed at Indonesian embassies around the world, serving like an

---

24 Sneddon (2003, p. 2).
25 Cited in 'BIPA, Tingkatkan Fungsi Bahasa Indonesia Menjadi Bahasa Internasional' from *Kompas.com* (2014).

international arm of the Indonesian Government's Ministry of Education and Culture. These cultural attachés have a particular strategic role that includes the introduction, socialization and development of the nation's culture in the international arena (Ministry of Education and Culture, 2014). The embassies and the attachés, together with the country's universities, participate in educational exhibitions to promote its education and universities in regional and global markets.

The Ministry of Education and Culture's *Badan Pengembangan dan Pembinaan Bahasa* (Language Promotion and Development Board) has made the internationalisation of the Indonesian language one of its many objectives. This goal for the promotion of Indonesian onto the international stage is clearly stated in its mission. The Language Promotion and Development Board is a government institution mainly in charge of the development and preservation of Indonesian language and literature and research on these two.

The history of the language board began in 1930, when research on Indonesian language and culture was conducted by Dutch scholars under the Dutch Colonial Government. In 1947, *Instituut voor Taal en Cultuur Onderzoek* was established and, about a year later, *Balai Bahasa* was founded. Since then, this language development institution has changed name and structure a number of times before becoming *Badan Pengembangan dan Pembinaan Bahasa* in 2010. It has some 30 *Balai Bahasa* (language centres) distributed across the archipelago.[26]

Separately from the Language Promotion and Development Board's *Balai Bahasa*, in April 2008, *Balai Bahasa* Indonesia Perth Inc., a non-profit organisation, was officially launched to promote the teaching of Indonesian. Located in the Indonesian Consulate General in Perth, the mission of this *Balai Bahasa* is to provide language and cultural education (KJRI, Perth, 2014).

The spirit to internationalise Indonesian is there and, according to the Head of the Language Promotion and Development Board, Mahsun, this 'spirit can make *bahasa Indonesia* exist in the international arena and needs to be always encouraged' (Ministry of Education and Culture, 2014). For Indonesian to succeed as a language for global socialisation, it needs to be a *bahasa ilmiah*, a scientific language, Mahsun said in his speech during the closing ceremony of the tenth *Kongres Bahasa Indonesia* (Indonesian Language Conference) in 2014. More than a thousand people, ranging from Indonesian and overseas experts to students, participated in the congress which chose 'strengthening

---

26 See Badan Bahasa-Kemdikbud's website and Quinn (2012), for example, for more about the history of the Badan Bahasa.

Indonesian in the international arena' as its theme (Ministry of Education and Culture, 2014).

The ministry itself offers its own scholarship, called the Darmasiswa Scholarship as part of its current programs to overseas students. In 2012, only 750 were selected from approximately 2,400 students of different nationalities who applied for this highly competitive scholarship. These Darmasiswa recipients originating from 77 countries were enrolled in 59 tertiary institutions spreading across Indonesia. This scholarship, which was originally intended for ASEAN nationals, is a partial scholarship for overseas students interested in studying the Indonesian language, arts, music, culinary, and the nation's unique handicrafts. The Darmasiswa was first introduced in 1974 and, until 2012, nearly four thousand overseas students from a total of 97 countries had since benefited from this program (Ministry of Education and Culture, 2014). Pangesti Wiedarti, who headed the Republic of Indonesia's Darmasiswa Program taskforce stated that Indonesian was the preferred subject (65%), followed by arts and culture (30%), culinary and tourism (3%), and others (2%) (*Kompas.com*, 2013).

In 2014, five Australian students were selected for the Darmasiswa Scholarship: three by the Indonesian Embassy and two by the Indonesian Consulates General in Melbourne and Perth respectively. Each of the Darmasiswa recipients was given a return airline ticket and a monthly allowance of IDR2 million.[27] Indonesian embassies and consulates general take part in the selection process of this Darmasiswa Scholarship. Following this initial process, the documents and the names of shortlisted candidates are provided to Ministry of Education and Culture, which has the final say.[28]

The Indonesian Consulate General in Melbourne has its own various programs to promote the spreading of *bahasa dan budaya Indonesia* in Victoria by visiting schools, organising *gamelan* workshops every Monday for secondary school students, providing general information on Indonesia for students visiting the Consulate General and administering an annual consulate scholarship in cooperation with the Victorian Indonesian Language Teacher Association (VILTA) for the best student in Indonesian to participate in a workshop at the Indonesian Embassy's *Rumah Budaya* Indonesia in Canberra.[29]

In addition to these programs, this Consulate General maintains an active participation in various cultural festivals such as Pako Festival in Geelong,

---

27 KJRI-Melbourne, electronic communication, 2 June 2014.
28 Puspitasari, interview, Melbourne, 19 May 2014.
29 KJRI-Melbourne, electronic communication, 6 June 2014.

Moomba Festival, Oakleigh Music Festival, and the Wooden Boat Festival in cooperation with Indonesian ethnic groups in Victoria. Various Indonesian ethnic groups make up more than 40 Victorian-based Indonesian community groups. Among these sub-groups are West-Sumatrans, Javanese, Sundanese, Balinese, Menadonese and Buginese. The Consulate General also supported the 9th Indonesian Film Festival (IFF) by promoting what they called the 'Educational Screenings' as part of the film festival to Victorian schools, which have students learning Indonesian. They also assisted film personnel participating in the festival through official letters of support for their Australian visa applications. The tickets to this educational screening were sold out and the proceeds went to the IFF. Consul Puspitasari said that the response from the Victorian schools to this screening was 'very good'.[30]

On the Australian side, the Australian Government's Department of Foreign Affairs and Trade (DFAT) provides the Bridge Program to Australian professionals to experience aspects of Indonesian culture. Supported by the Australian Aid Program and managed by the Australia-Indonesia Institute (AII) in conjunction with the Asia Education Foundation, this project, which has a focus on intercultural understanding, has been operating since 2008 (DFAT, 2014) and it is also directed to China, Thailand and Korea. At state level, the Victorian Government has its own Hamer Scholarship specifically designed for Australian professionals to learn languages in several Asian countries, including Indonesia, Korea, Japan and China.[31]

Australians can make use of Indonesian to communicate not only with Indonesians of different ethnic groups but also with people from a number of countries in the region, where the Malay language can be understood, such as in Malaysia, Singapore, Brunei Darussalam and Timor Leste (formerly, East Timor). Indonesian is still widely spoken in Timor Leste, alongside its own languages of Tetum and Portuguese.

Bayuni[32] of the *Jakarta Post* acknowledged the potential of Indonesian to be an international language, but noted his concern that Indonesians did not take soft power more seriously:

> Indonesia can use every soft power at its disposal, including its cultural products and *bahasa Indonesia*, to live up to its new status as a rising Asian middle power, and a rising economic power. But these potentials

---

30 Puspitasari, interview, Melbourne, 19 May 2014.
31 KJRI-Melbourne, electronic communication, 2 June 2014.
32 Bayuni, electronic communication, 4 June 2014.

can only be realized if we take our own cultures, and cultural products, including *bahasa Indonesia*, more seriously.

Supriyadi noted that the Indonesian Ministry of Foreign Affairs formed the Directorate of Public Diplomacy after its restructuring in 2002. The ministry recognised 'the increasing importance of soft power as tools of diplomacy'.[33]

From the Indonesian point of view, as noted by Bayuni, 'Australia has already done its part in promoting the teaching of *bahasa Indonesia* as one of the Asian languages at schools and universities'. The question is now, whether Australian students can find some use in learning Indonesian or not. If not, students would choose other Asian languages like Chinese, Korean, Japanese, Indian and even Vietnamese, instead of Indonesian. Again, Bayuni reminded his fellow Indonesians of their low cultural appreciation and minimal efforts in the promotion of their national culture and language:

> Australia should be the obvious target for Indonesia to export *bahasa Indonesia*, but are we doing enough on our part? I doubt it. If we want others to appreciate our cultures, including our language, we need to appreciate them ourselves first.

The worrying fact is that Indonesian cultural products are increasingly commercialized at the expense of their quality. Western popular culture heavily influences the country's traditional cultural products and the increasing preference for English used by Indonesian producers for their popular film titles and song lyrics are also of particular concern.[34] This trend appears to be at odds with the Indonesian Government's (particularly, the Ministry of Education and Culture's) mission of preserving *bahasa dan budaya Indonesia*.

The Ministry of Education and Culture, which is in charge of the country's education and culture, recognized this quality problem of the national cultural goods. In terms of movies, the Indonesian Education and Cultural Minister noted that:

> Only a handful of countries have been successful in promoting their film industries worldwide, such as the USA, France, UK, India, Australia, Japan, and Hong Kong. This is mainly because they have been able to combine the provision of education and training institutions, climate for

---

33 Supriyadi, electronic communication, 18 June 2014.
34 It was not clear if (domestic or international) marketing purposes were behind the use of English for film titles and song lyrics, but some of the films presented in the 9th IFF used titles like *Something in the Way* and *What They Don't Talk About When They Talk About Love*.

creative industries, government assistance directly and indirectly, and a robust private film investment sector. (Nuh, 2012, p. 9)

Minister Nuh also notes that there was still plenty of room for his ministry 'to improve the quality of Indonesian movies':

> Identifying this potential, the Indonesian government has been working with the film community to improve public policies so that the industry can thrive in the fierce global competition. This includes strengthening educational aspects which are deeply entwined in the process. (Nuh, 2012, p. 10)

What the Directorate of Art and Film Development under the Indonesian Ministry of Education and Culture has done is to support the development of Indonesian short films. Its concern was for the quantity and quality of short-film festivals in Indonesia. The Directorate was also involved in:

> Sponsoring participation by Indonesian film makers in international festivals for short films and workshops and sponsoring the Short Film Jamboree which was launched in 2012. Other programs include giving recognition to quality films, sponsoring film production workshops around the archipelago, and developing a program to safeguard the Indonesian film archive, Sinematek. (Nuh, 2012, p. 9)

Indonesian female filmmaker Nia Dinata, however, felt that the country's movie industry faced several problems as there was no infrastructure, no government support, and no support from civil society:

> Probably only 0.001% of the foundations or non-profit organisations focus on cultural and cinematic development in Indonesia. Everything about Cinema in Indonesia is about business or profit-oriented. (Coppens, 2009, pp. 65–66)

The fact is that the country's filmmakers run their projects with relatively small budgets. In an interview, Dinata shared her experience about how she managed her film budget, which was normally less than half a million US dollars, and that she received 'very little research money' from her previous films screened at film festivals or in an international forum for film financing (Coppens, 2009, pp. 65–66). This results in a disadvantageous situation for the country's filmmakers, if they want to compete in the international markets.

This section has considered the potential of Indonesian to become a *lingua franca* in the Southeast Asian – Australian region. Indonesian cultural exports would enhance the realisation of this potential through the spreading of Indonesian-language popular cultural products, including popular press, radio and television, to other countries in the region. In fact, an examination of the role the mass media play in the export of Indonesian culture is of considerable importance. Mass media, as the term implies, can reach a large audience and is capable of creating a nation's international image through the shaping of public opinion towards their products. What happens when the Australian media presents news content, which distorts information and leads to their audience's inaccurate perception of Indonesia and, more importantly, how does this relate to the export of Indonesian culture?

Beyond Indonesia's Bali

The linguistic complexity of Indonesia as a country with one national language and hundreds of ethnic languages is the key element in its cultural uniqueness. The nation is made up of various ethnic groups that have their own cultural traditions, beside their respective ethnic languages and dialects. The Indonesian ethnic organisations and social groups in Australia reflect this diversity: Ikatan Keluarga Minang Saiyo, Sulit Air Sepakat, Punguan Batak, Paguyuban Sunda, Kawanua, Komunitas Anging Mamiri, Mahindra Bali, and many others. Members of these ethnic groups speak Indonesian, their national language, accompanying their own regional languages within their respective groups.

All these should make Indonesia appealing either to study or visit. While there is a considerable ethnic diversity across the archipelago, it is the Balinese that Australians are most familiar with. For Australian tourists, Bali is still their favourite destination.[35] However, while Bali continues to grow in popularity, the study of Indonesian in Australia continues to fall (see Hill, this volume).

As opposed to the falling Australian interest in Indonesian, according to Nyoman Riasa, Indonesian language programs at tertiary level in Indonesia have shown increasing number of enrolments from East Asian countries such as Japan, South Korea and China. He sees the problem lies with Australia, where the reporting on Indonesia in the mass media has not been conducive. Riasa, President of the Association of Indonesian Language Teachers for Foreigners (Ketua Umum APBIPA), predicts that bilateral relations between

---

35   Puspitasari, interview, Melbourne, 19 May 2014.

Indonesia and Australia will not completely recover due to political tensions in the past.[36]

It is a fact that many Australians think of Indonesia as part of Bali or believe that Bali is a country, despite Indonesia's prominent position as Australia's largest neighbour. While Indonesia, or Bali, remains as one of Australians' most popular destinations, most Australians will only learn about Indonesia through exposure to their own mass media. As their perception is mediated by the media, their knowledge of Indonesia is indirect and this may result in false impressions.

People of one culture need to have some direct contact with others of another culture. Direct experience may at least reduce negative stereotypes, if it cannot create a positive stereotype:

> When individuals have had only very limited or no contact at all with a particular culture, they commonly hold stereotypical, or broad behavioural generalisations, about that culture and its members. In the absence of direct experience stereotypes provide a set of usually negative and inaccurate guidelines that indicate what can be expected when encountering members of that culture. (Weaver and Oppermann, 2000, p. 283)

Weaver and Oppermann (2000, p. 283) also discuss tourism as 'a potent force for cross cultural understanding' because it can bring so many people 'into contact with members of other cultures'. Stereotypes, as DeVito, O'Rourke and O'Neill (2000, p. 48) highlight, distort one's 'ability to perceive other people accurately'. People often form stereotypes, positively or negatively, from newspapers, magazines, radio, and television. It is not uncommon for the mass media to 'leave whole parts of the world outside their audience's reach and report in superficial, often biased if not racist ways about foreign peoples and their cultures, often exclusively highlighting their exotic features' (Hamelink, 1995, p. 4).

The mass media can have a positive or negative impact on the number of tourist visitations. An article published by a major Australian newspaper or a program broadcast by an Australian television station may encourage or discourage Australians from visiting Bali or other parts of Indonesia.

---

36   His comments were taken from an article titled 'Penutur Asli Bahasa Indonesia Sangat Diperlukan' ('Indonesian Native Speakers Are Urgently Needed') in Ozip (May 2014). In a recent incident, the Indonesian Ambassador to Australia, Nadjib Riphat Kesoema, was recalled over a spy row, as reported by a number of Australian media. This is not the first case of an Indonesian ambassador being recalled by Jakarta due to political tension between the two countries.

Along with Australia's Department of Foreign Affairs and Trade issuing travel warnings, extensive Australian media coverage of the Bali bombing on 12 October 2002, for example, contributed to the fall of visits to Bali by Australians. Early in 2014, *The Australian* published an article about the threat of terrorist attacks in Indonesia with a provocative title 'Terror threat high in Indonesia'.[37]

The Australian media is likely to be blamed for the destabilisation of the bilateral relationship between Australia and Indonesia. After consulting numerous documents and reports for his book,[38] Indonesian journalism scholar Ross Tapsell told the *Jakarta Post* during his book launch in Jakarta that 'the Australian media was the biggest problem in the bilateral relationship'. He was also quoted as saying that 'Indonesian language in Australia has been in decline since the 1970s' and that Australia's 'educational knowledge about Indonesia is very limited'.

Extensive Australian media coverage of the 2002 bombings did not only result in the plummeting number of Australian visitors to Indonesia but also in Australian students' diminishing interest in Indonesian language. Hill and Sen (2014) wrote that 'Indonesian language enrolments have always been sensitive' to the Australian media's coverage of events taking place in Indonesia such as the 2002 and 2005 bombings. In general, Indonesian Moslems are mostly misrepresented in the Australian media and the news headlines of these media are often misleading.[39]

The following conversation between one Victorian secondary college student and his Indonesian subject teacher, for example, is relevant to this situation. The student in Lilydale once asked his teacher why he and his classmates should learn Indonesian, while 'they were bombing us'. The answer given by the teacher, who is married to an Indonesian and had lived and worked in Indonesia for many years, was that, plain and simple, the students were required to learn *bahasa dan budaya Indonesia*.[40] This illustrates confusion in regards to perceptions of Indonesian culture and language in Australia and the persistent negative images of Indonesia in the Australian mass media.

37　Brendan Nicholson, *Australian*, 2 January 2014.
38　Tapsell (2014) partly talks about the impact of the Australian news media coverage of the Bali bombings on the relations between Australia and Indonesia.
39　One of *The Bulletin*'s cover stories, for example, was entitled 'Allah's Assassins'. *Bulletin*, 5 March, 2003.
40　This conversation was taken from an article in *Ibrah* magazine published by the Indonesian Muslim Community of Victoria (IMCV) in March 2006.

It is not only the reporting of major news events that undermines the promotion of *bahasa dan budaya Indonesia* in Australia, mainstream popular programs also provide unfavourable media coverage. During May and June 2014, Seven Network ran a weekly program called 'What Really Happens in Bali' showing bad things that might happen to Australians visiting Bali. Prior to this program being broadcast on Channel 7, this television network had frequently advertised it with a statement that might mislead their audience: 'one Australian dies every nine days'. Such media coverage limits the effectiveness of any promotional efforts made by the Indonesian diplomatic missions. The Consul for Information, Social Culture Affairs Ita Puspitasari[41] described this situation like 'a race with the [Australian] media'. It means that the Consulate General had to promote Indonesia more diligently than it had done previously because of unfavourable media coverage.

It is not only negative reporting that has eroded the image of Indonesia and its culture but also the limited scope of the reporting. News organisations in Australia tend to cover more about the country's political and social issues than its economic issues. The Indonesian Ministry of Foreign Affairs, has made some efforts to gain support from the Australian media to portray a more positive image of Indonesia by inviting journalists to come to the country in what they call *Program Kunjungan Wartawan* ('Journalist Visit Program'), similar to Australia's Department of Foreign Affairs and Trade 'International [formerly, Overseas] Media Visit' program. The effectiveness of this program remains a question but, at least, there has been some support in the Australian media for Indonesia in terms of its democracy. The Indonesian elections, including the 2014 presidential elections, were reported favourably. Peter Jennings (2013), executive director of the Australian Strategic Policy Institute described former President Yudhoyono as 'strongly pro-Australian', although the general public of both countries still appear to maintain negative stereotypes about each other. The fact is that, according to Jennings, 'Australia has underinvested in Indonesia, and business has been too focused on short-term risks at the cost of long-term opportunities'.

Barry Lowe (2000) in his content analysis study of news reportage on three major Southeast Asian countries (Malaysia, Indonesia and the Philippines) by two Australian news media outlets has shown that the two media organisations put a greater emphasis on Indonesia's domestic politics and relations between Australia and Indonesia. During 1993, the *Sydney Morning Herald* (*SMH*) showed 'sustained interest in domestic Indonesian politics'. Although

---

41   Puspitasari, interview, Melbourne, 19 May 2014.

Indonesia's 'economic issues' was also one of major story categories for the country, the *SMH* printed more stories about its 'domestic politics' and 'bilateral relations with Australia' (Lowe, 2000, p. 121). Similarly, 25 years before this, Indonesia's 'economy' was also behind 'bilateral relations with Australia' and Indonesian 'domestic politics' in the *SMH* coverage of the country (Lowe, 2000, p. 123). Over the many years of the Suharto government, however, reporting was more restricted and some of the images that were created then have been difficult to shake off. This has left Australians with a dated view of Indonesian politics.

Puspitasari, the Indonesian diplomat who was formerly responsible for economic affairs and now in charge of information and social culture affairs at the Consulate General in Melbourne, acknowledged that the lack of diversity in media coverage of Indonesia was seen as a minus on the diplomatic mission's side. This lack of diversity led to the Australian publics' poor understanding of not just Indonesian culture but also its economy. Despite providing updates on Indonesian business and its economy through regular business seminars, symposiums, trade and investment clinics organised by the consulate general for local businesses, these activities have so far not attracted much Australian media attention.[42]

Indonesia's macro-economic development, current trade regulations, and recent government policies concerning foreign investment are not publicised widely in Australia. With the lack of reporting of the region's rising middle power in the Australian mass media, Australians may not become aware of the potential economic relationship Australia could pursue with Indonesia. Consequently, this has an impact on Australians' understanding of the utility of developing knowledge of Indonesian language and culture. As Indonesia gradually adopts a market liberalisation regime removing restrictions in order to attract many more foreign investments,[43] the demand for 'cultural interpreters' at large foreign corporations doing business in the country increases.[44] If Australian graduates and professionals fail to notice these opportunities, they are unlikely to see the need of gaining some knowledge of *bahasa dan budaya Indonesia*. Ultimately, economic norms also make up a nation's culture.[45]

---

42   Consulate General, Melbourne, electronic communication, 6 June 2014.
43   Australia is one of Western governments, as seen on DFAT's website (2014), that 'continues to encourage Indonesia to maintain liberalised trade and investment regimes'.
44   An example of cultural interpreters are 'practitioners of either global or international public relations' (Wilcox et al., 2003, p. 395).
45   Language, history, traditions, arts, social, political norms, and system of values are among other things that make up the culture of a nation (Watson & Hill, 2003, p. 71).

Knowledge of Indonesian is also required to utilise the Indonesian mass media for the purposes of obtaining a better understanding of the country's businesses and economy. Most business and economic news is presented in Indonesian in the country's mainstream media. This business and economic news has become increasing relevant to Australian companies because it is readily accessible on the internet (the online version of *Kompas* and *Bisnis Indonesia* newspapers, *Tempo* and *Warta Ekonomi* magazines, for example). Business news and government policy statements relevant to business are also available through online streaming of Indonesian radio stations including *RRI*'s *Voice of Indonesia* and *Radio El Shinta*. Similarly, television networks, *Metro TV*, *TVRI* and *RCTV*, for example, are available via the internet or satellite. In Australia, Indonesian-language news and features are regularly presented through Indonesian community papers such as Sydney-based *Indomedia* and *Buletin Indo* and Melbourne-based *Buset* and *Ozip*; on radio, for example, *Radio Kita* and *Southern FM*'s Indonesian program; and television, for example, *Nusantara TV*. Additionally, Indonesian programs are available on the government funded *Radio Australia*, *SBS Radio* and *SBS Television*.

The role of the Indonesian mass media is of great importance as carriers of Indonesian popular culture. The following section attempts to describe the prospects for the teaching of Indonesian language and culture, which includes the contributions from Indonesian businesses to the export of the country's cultural products.

Prospects for *Bahasa dan Budaya Indonesia* in Australia

It has been mentioned previously that the Australian general public are, for the most part, poorly informed by their media regarding Indonesia's strong economic growth and largely unaware of the opportunities for those with a knowledge of *bahasa dan budaya Indonesia*. Australians need to translate Indonesia's economic strength into opportunities they can benefit from. As the economic powerhouse of ASEAN (Association of Southeast Asian Nations), Indonesia makes up 47 percent of the region's economy, 46 percent of the total population in the region, and half of its landmass.[46]

According to Kris Sulisto (2013) of the Indonesia Australia Business Council (IABC), Indonesia has shown constant economic growth since

---

46 Facts and figures presented by Kris Sulisto, President of IABC (Indonesia Australia Business Council) in 2013.

2000 with the 2013 total GDP at USD916 billion and GDP per capita of USD3,562. It has a youthful population (70 percent under 40 years old) and a fast-growing middle class. The Indonesian Government reformed key sectors to 'create a better climate for investment' with FDI (foreign direct investment) at USD24.56 billion in 2012 and, according to the UNCTAD survey, Indonesia ranked fourth among the most popular destinations for investment. In 2012, Indonesia was the 16th largest economy in the world with 45 million consumers, 55 million skilled workers in the economy, and USD0.5 trillion-worth market opportunity in consumer services, agriculture and fisheries, resources and education. It is projected that, in 2030, Indonesia will be the 7th largest economy in the world with 135 million consumers, 113 million skilled workers needed, and USD1.8 trillion market opportunity in those sectors (Sulisto, 2013). The key to a business partnership, according to Sulisto, is 'knowing the culture' and 'finding the right local partner'.

It was stated in the Indonesia-Australia Business Partnership Group's (IA-BPG) 2012 Position Paper that 'a lack of information regarding business and trade opportunities in both markets – and even misinformation – 'was a major impediment to increased trade and investment' (IA-BPG, 2012, p. 5) and that there was 'a perception among Indonesian businesses' that Australia was 'a relatively small market and difficult to penetrate' (IA-BPG, 2012, p. 7). One of the measures to overcome impediments was 'encouraging improved mutual cultural and language understanding through compulsory inclusion in school curriculums (IA-BPG, 2012, p. 10). The IA-BPG identified education as one of 'several major business sectors of special significance to cross-border trade and investment'.[47] This Position Paper also stated that Indonesia was 'the seventh largest source of foreign students to Australian tertiary institutions', while 'the numbers of Australian students studying in Indonesia' were 'extremely low' and that the IA CEPA 'should include mechanisms for improving these levels' (IA-BPG, 2012, pp. 10–11).

In a visit by Vice President Boediono to Monash University in November 2013, he expressed the Indonesian Government's support for the Australian Government's initiatives to strengthen cooperation in areas of education and innovation and technology. These initiatives include the establishment of the

---

47   IA-BPG stands for Indonesia-Australia Business Partnership Group. It consists of the Indonesian Chamber of Commerce and Industry (KADIN Indonesia), the Australian Chamber of Commerce and Industry (ACCI), the Indonesia Australia Business Council (IABC), and the Australia Indonesia Business Council (AIBC). In October 2012, it launched a 'Position Paper on Considerations towards the Indonesia-Australia Comprehensive Economic Partnership Agreement (IA CEPA)'.

Australian Centre for Indonesian Studies and the New Colombo Plan. The latter was of particular interest, as Boediono himself was one of the (Old) Colombo Plan scholarship recipients and recalled that the experience he gained was useful for his career. He reflected that:

> Perhaps, many young Australians will have early experiences of Asia in a similar way. (Boediono, 15 November 2013)

The two governments may have their ups and downs, but the relations between the two countries' businesses and people-to-people remain steady. There is a great chance of making Indonesian a cultural bridge between the two countries. As Bayuni,[48] commented:

> If overall relations are strong, including in government-to-government, business-to-business and people-to-people, there is a chance of making *bahasa Indonesia* a cultural bridge. One sad reality in our relationship is that we are not trading with one another enough, and we don't see as many Australian investment/presence in Indonesia as should be given our geographical proximity (except the Australian tourists in Bali).

Bayuni believes that 'the potential is immense', as Indonesia and Australia 'are interacting more and more as two giant neighbours':

> Our business communities are building the economic relationship, our two governments recognize the strategic importance of this relationship, and our peoples are visiting one another, as tourists, business people, and students. Indonesia is an emerging democracy and emerging market economy, and Australia is an established democracy with strong economy. The two countries can reap benefits from having a closer relationship. And it is happening for sure, albeit not as fast as it could be.

In the view of Harymurti of the Tempo Group, the role of Indonesian as a cultural bridge between Indonesia and Australia depended on how the Australian public perceived the future of Indonesia. He considers that, 'The more prospective the Indonesia's economy is, the more important its role as cultural bridge between the two countries'.[49]

Harymurti and Bayuni shared the same view that the consumption of *bahasa dan budaya Indonesia* by the Australian public would have a better prospect in the future, while Rambadeta believed that, as long as both Australia's political

---

48   Bayuni, electronic communication, 4 June 2014.
49   Harymurti, electronic communication, 3 June 2014.

and economic interests were taken into consideration, Indonesia's neighbour to the south would be likely to have a strong cultural interest in Indonesia.

Given that Australians currently constitute the biggest Indonesian-speaking foreign community, Rambadeta[50] sees the Indonesian language as playing a role as a cultural bridge between the two nations. His prediction is that there will be more consumption of *bahasa dan budaya Indonesia* under a Jokowi government.

In the case of Indonesia's cultural diplomacy, Riasa of the Asosiasi Pengajar Bahasa Indonesia bagi Penutur Asing (Association of Teachers of Indonesian as a Foreign Language), considers that 'now is the time to strengthen Indonesia's cultural and language diplomacy before economic diplomacy can work'. In his opinion, 'if Indonesia's economy could create many job opportunities for Australians, a positive perception would automatically grow, just like the close bilateral relationship between Australia and China once the Chinese economy grew stronger'.[51]

Australia's embracing of and support for a multicultural community also creates prospects for the teachings of *bahasa dan budaya Indonesia*. The Australian public are increasingly exposed to Indonesian traditional performances, arts, and culinary offerings presented by Indonesian community and their various ethnic groups, and students at Australian universities, which enriches Australia's cultural diversity and encourages them to learn about Indonesian culture and language. The interests in learning *bahasa dan budaya Indonesia* can also come from Indonesians residing in Australia whose children are expected to learn their parents' national language and culture from school.

Both the Australian Government and the business community have stressed the benefits of a multicultural community. Addressing the Stanford Club on 5 April 2004 in Sydney, Chief Executive of Business Council of Australia Katie Lahey said that there had been studies showing that diversity is good for a country's economy:

> Studies overseas and in Australia show that social, cultural and ethnic diversity – the result of immigration and population growth – are key factors contributing to higher productivity and economic growth. In other words, population – its size, growth and diversity – plays a significant role in driving and sustaining growth. (Lahey, 2004 cited in Healey, 2005, p. 11)

---

50   Rambadeta, electronic communication, 6 June 2014.
51   His comments can be found in the Indonesian community magazine *Ozip*'s May 2014 edition.

There is a small number of Indonesians currently living in Australia. As Nia Dinata notes, Indonesia is 'probably the last nation that would send groups of people to migrate' outside the country (Coppens, 2009, p. 65). While a small number, these people can still play an important role as 'cultural ambassadors' to Australia.

The initiatives to promote *bahasa dan budaya Indonesia* in Australia are evident, but the real initiatives should come from Indonesia:

> Australians are quite an open people since they are made up almost wholly by immigrants, including now from Indonesia. So the opportunities are there for Indonesia to take the initiatives. But the real initiatives must begin at home.[52]

The future of *bahasa dan budaya Indonesia* in Australia is still promising for the following reasons: the Australian government and business have put forward their respective agendas to strengthen the link with Indonesia; recent economic ties have created new trade and investment opportunities for Australian businesses, thus opening up more career opportunities for Australian professionals and graduates; encouraging mutual cultural and language understanding has become one of the measures taken by the business communities of both countries to overcome obstacles to the bilateral trade and investment; and the potential for the Indonesian diaspora to take the role of 'cultural ambassadors' to Australia.

Conclusion

Indonesia has had some success at exporting its culture and language to its Asian neighbours. It can be said that this, in economic terms, is the country's comparative advantage, with its creative industries being a robust one, even though the products of these industries are primarily designed for domestic consumption. In the case of Australia, however, there has been comparatively little success due to the relatively small size of the market and the competition from other major Asian countries such as Japan, China and South Korea.

Nevertheless, Indonesia can only enhance its influence in Australia through the export of its popular culture products. Taking into account the potential of Indonesian to be a lingua franca of the region and Indonesia's constant economic growth, the language has become increasingly useful. As Vic Halim

---

52   Bayuni, electronic communication, 4 June 2014.

of IABC said, some products of Indonesia's creative industries are ready for global consumption due to the 'universal language' they use. These audio and visual products include designer fashion, animations, films, and music. The potential of other purposefully exported products such as Indonesian-language books and newspapers depend on the market share and the interest of the export-targeted countries for such cultural goods.

In order to compete with major Asian languages and popular cultural products, *bahasa dan budaya Indonesia* as national exports require extensive support from both countries, including the government, businesses, the mass media and the general public. The Indonesian public, however, have not seen the implementation of a clear national strategy to export the country's cultural products from their own government.

The continuing success of Indonesia's cultural and language exports to its neighbours require active involvement from the government, businesses and the mass media. This chapter views all these actors as stakeholders with a crucial interest in the business of Indonesian culture. The Indonesian Government is yet to fully support the country's domestic cultural and creative industries and it still to take a more substantial pro-active role in the promotion of the Indonesian culture and language abroad. The Australian Government is also yet to fully engage with Indonesia through an understanding of Indonesian economy and culture. Most noticeably, Indonesian businesses have yet to work cooperatively with their Australian business partners in the promotion of Indonesian culture in a similar fashion to Indonesia's competitors. Finally, the Indonesian mass media has yet to fully appreciate its role as carriers of Indonesian culture.

Indonesia's cultural influence in Australia has multifaceted purposes, which in turn creates a more politically stable relationship and encourages more fruitful economic ties. Both Indonesia and Australia will benefit from a better bilateral relationship. Australia will need to enhance its engagement with Indonesia as the economic powerhouse of ASEAN through greater public understanding of Indonesian politics, economy, culture and mass media. The Indonesian language will be critical in this process.

References

Australia-Indonesia Institute (2014). Australia-Indonesia Bridge Project. Retrieved from http://www.dfat.gov.au/aii/programs/bridge_program.html, accessed 28 May 2014.

Badan Pengembangan dan Pembinaan Bahasa (2014).Sejarah Badan Bahasa. Retrieved from http://badanbahasa.kemdikbud.go.id/lamanbahasa/sejarah, accessed 26 May 2014.

Boediono (2013). Challenges in Education Development and Innovation in Indonesia. Public Lecture, Monash University, 15 November.

Buset (2014). Memasuki Satu Dasawarsa, IFF Diharapkan Lebih Baik. Vol. 09-108 June 2014, pp. 22-23.

Chua, B.H. (2007). Conceptualizing an East Asian popular culture in K-H. Chen and B.H. Chua (Eds.), *The Inter-Asia Cultural Studies Reader*. London and New York: Routledge.

Coppens, L. (2009). Interview with Nia Dinata in Y. Michalik and L. Coppens (Eds.), *Asian Hot Shots: Indonesian Cinema*, Marburg: Schüren.

DeVito, J., O'Rourke, S., & O'Neill, L. (2000). *Human Communication*. Auckland: Pearson Education New Zealand.

DFAT (2014). Indonesia country brief. Retrieved from http://www.dfat.gov.au/geo/indonesia/indonesia_brief.html, accessed 28 May 2014.

Halim, V. (2014). Electronic communication, 16 June.

Hamelink, C. (1995). *World Communication: Disempowerment & Self-Empowerment*. London and New Jersey: Zed Books.

Hesmondhalgh, D. (2013). *The Cultural Industries*. London and Thousand Oaks (California): Sage Publications.

Hill, D.T. & Sen, K. (2014). Look who's talking: Indonesian in Australia. *The Conversation*, 10 December 2014. Retrieved from https://theconversation.com/look-whos-talking-indonesian-in-australia-35097, accessed 13 March 2015.

IA-BPG (2012). Position Paper on Considerations Towards the Indonesia-Australia Comprehensive Economic Partnership Agreement, 31 October 2012.

Ibrah (2006). Agenda Terorisme: Representasi Muslim di Media Barat. No.2, March 2006, pp. 7-12. Melbourne: Indonesian Muslim Community of Victoria (IMCV).

Jennings, P. (2013). Why we need deeper ties with Indonesia. *The Australian*, 1 October. Retrieved from https://www.theaustralian.com.au/national-affairs/opinion/why-we-need-deeper-ties-with-indonesia from www.theaustralian.com.au/national-affairs/opinion/why-we-need-deeper-ties-with-indonesia, accessed 13 March 2015.

Kemdikbud (2014). Menjadikan Bahasa Indonesia sebagai Bahasa Ilmu Pengetahuan. Retrieved from http://kemdikbud.go.id/kemdikbud/berita/1832, accessed 27 May 2014.

Kemdikbud (2014). Program Darmasiswa Kenalkan Budaya RI kepada Dunia. Retrieved from http://kemdikbud.go.id/kemdikbud/node/638, accessed 27 May 2014.

Killian, P.M.E. (2012). Paradigma dan Problematika Diplomasi Ekonomi Indonesia. *Global & Strategis* 6(2), pp.171-186.

KJRI-Perth (2014). Balai Bahasa Indonesia Perth. Retrieved from http://kjri-perth.org.au.

Kompas.com. (2013). BIPA, Tingkatkan Fungsi Bahasa Indonesia Menjadi Bahasa Internasional. Retrieved from http://edukasi.kompas.com/read/2013/10/23/1253102/BIPA, accessed 28 April 2016.

Lahey, K. (2005). Population and prosperity. Business Council of Australia, Address to the Stanford Club on 5 April 2004 in Sydney in J. Healey (Ed.), *Debating the Issues*. Thirroul (NSW): The Spinney Press.

Lowe, B. (2000). Australian News Media Constructing Asia: a case study of Malaysia, Indonesia and the Philippines in D. Kingsbury, E. Loo, and P. Payne (Eds.), *Foreign Devils and Other Journalists*. Clayton: Monash Asia Institute.

McKenzie, R. (2006). *Comparing Media from around the World*. Boston: Pearson Education.

McNair, S. (1993). *Enchantment of the World: Indonesia*. Chicago: Childrens Press.

Michalik, Y. (2009). Introduction in Y. Michalik and L. Coppens (Eds.),*Asian Hot Shots: Indonesian Cinema*, Marburg: Schüren.

Nicholson, B. (2014). Terror threat high in Indonesia. *The Australian*, 2 January 2014. Retrieved from http://www.theaustralian.com.au/news/nation/terror-threat-high-in-indonesia/story.
Nugroho, G. (2014). Electronic communication, 12 June 2014.
Nuh, M. (2012). Foreword. *A Brief Cultural History of Indonesian Cinema*. Jakarta: The Ministry of Education and Culture, Republic of Indonesia.
Ozip (2014). Penutur Asli Bahasa Indonesia Sangat Diperlukan. No.54, May 2014.
Ozip (2014). Festival Budaya Indonesia Terbaik di Australia: Indofest Adelaide. No.55, June 2014.
Power, D. & Scott, A.J. (2004). A prelude to cultural industries and the production of culture in D. Power and A.J/ Scott (Eds.), *Cultural Industries and the Production of Culture*. London and New York: Routledge.
Pusat Humas Departemen Perdagangan (2009). Pembukaan PPKI 2009: Sinergikan Budaya dan Teknologi untuk Hasilkan Produk Kreatif yang Berdaya Saing. Retrieved from http://www.kemendag.go.id/files/pdf/2009/06/26/pembukaan-ppki-2009-sinergikan-budaya-dan-teknologi-untuk-hasilkan-produk-kreati-id1, accessed 13 March 2015.
Quinn, G. (2012). Emerging from Dire Straits: Post-New Order Developments in Javanese Language and Literature in K. Foulcher, M. Moriyama and M. Budiman (Eds.), *Words in Motion: language and discourse in post-New Order Indonesia*. Singapore: NUS Press.
Riasa, N. (2014). Penutur Asli Bahasa Indonesia Sangat Diperlukan. *Ozip* (54), May 2014, p.17.
Rix, P. (2005). *Marketing: A practical approach*. North Ryde (NSW): McGraw-Hill Australia.
Robson, S. (2004). *Welcome to Indonesian: A beginner's survey of the language*. Boston and Singapore: Tuttle Publishing.
Seliger, B.J. (2013). The Opening of Popular Cultural Markets of South Korea under Economic Nationalism and International Pressure in L. Fitzsimmons and J.A. Lent, *Asian Popular Culture in Transition*, London and New York: Routledge.
Sneddon, J. (2003). *The Indonesian Language: its history and role in modern society*. Sydney: UNSW Press.
Sulisto, K. (2013). Beyond Boats, Beef and Bali. Presentation by the IABC President at the Australia-Indonesia Dialogue 24-25 June 2013. Retrieved from http://iabc.or.id/download/BeyondBoatsBeefandBali.pdf.
Tapsell, R. (2014). *By-Lines, Balibo, Bali Bombings: Australian journalists in Indonesia*. North Melbourne: Australian Scholarly Publishing.
The Jakarta Post (2015). Australians, reporting on Indonesia, 23 February.
Watson, J. & Hill, A. (2003). *Dictionary of Media and Communication Studies*. London: Arnold.
Weaver, D. & Oppermann, M. (2000). *Tourism Management*. Milton (Qld): John Wiley & Sons Australia.
Wilcox, D.L., Cameron, G.T., Ault, P.H. & Agee, W.K. (2003). *Public Relations: Strategies and Tactics*. Boston: Pearson Education.

Chapter 7

FACING THE TWENTY-FIRST CENTURY

Indonesian in Australian Universities

DAVID T. HILL

Murdoch University

Introduction

A casual observer strolling around Perth International Airport – and virtually any other international airport in Australia – on a Friday afternoon could not fail to notice the frequency with which 'Denpasar' flashes on the 'Departures' board. From Perth alone there are 74 flights a week to Bali. Crowds of Australians bearing little more than a few T-shirts and a swimming costume are ingested by rows of passing aircraft. The mood is festive, the journey familiar. The horror of the bombings of 12 October 2002 and 1 October 2005 now fading from memory, Bali is once more Australia's most popular holiday destination. So deeply is the island embedded in the West Australian psyche that some in Perth refer to it affectionately as their 'backyard'. In 2014 more than one million Australians visited Indonesia, most to Bali for at least some part of their stay (Duff, 2014).[1]

---

1   The Australian Bureau of Statistics data cited by Duff noted 1.013 million short-term resident departures to Indonesia in the financial year 2013-14.

Yet in our schools and universities enrolments in Indonesian language courses have been plummeting for decades. Australians might enjoy holidaying in Indonesia, but with every passing year fewer and fewer Australians show any interest in learning the language of our nearest and most popular neighbour. The educational curiosity that greeted Indonesian in Australian schools and universities in the second half of the twentieth century appears to have been replaced by a casual disinterest. This chapter explores the fate of Indonesian language in our universities this century, speculates on possible reasons for its decline, and posits on its future. There is always the danger that such an analysis may be either unsatisfyingly vague if too generalised or unhelpfully myopic if too detailed, so the following discussion will move between the abstract and the specific in an effort to capture a snapshot of the moving image that is Indonesian in Australian universities in the twenty-first century. The review will examine both campus-based programs and 'in-country' programs (i.e., studies of Indonesian undertaken in Indonesia), with statistics presented from an on-going research project which has been tracking the trajectory of Indonesian enrolments in Australian universities since 2000 (Hill, 2012).

Turn of the Century

Other contributions to this book by Coppel and Thomas describe the growing interest in learning Indonesian amongst Australian students from its introduction in the 1950s. By the 1990s, it was firmly established in schools and universities in every state of Australia, with Tasmania the last state to introduce Indonesian at university in 1991.[2] Interest in Indonesian appeared strong, if not as popular as Japanese or established European favourites like French. Yet in the closing years of last century there were already signs of a contraction in university enrolments in Indonesian, signalling a decline from which we are yet to recover. While enrolments had ironically been strong during the years of the authoritarian Suharto regime when many university staff and students in Indonesian studies were broadly critical of the Indonesian government (as manifested, for example, in academic studies such as those by

---

2   This chapter focuses on universities. For an excellent report on the situation in schools, see M. Kohler & P. Mahnken, (2010). *The current state of Indonesian Language Education in Australian schools*, Department of Education, Employment and Workplace Relations, Canberra. <http://www.asiaeducation.edu.au/verve/_resources/IndonesiaReport.pdf>. Indonesian was then one of the three most popular languages in Australian schools with an enrolment of about 190,000, albeit contracting by about 10,000 students annually.

Mortimer, Robison, and Foulcher, and in the establishment of publications like *Inside Indonesia*)[3] by the time of Suharto's fall in 1998 interest in the language was starting to wane.

At the beginning of this century there were around 1700 university students enrolled in Indonesian language courses around Australia. Indonesian was taught in 23 universities, covering the entire breadth of the nation.[4] Several Australian universities provided 'in-country' summer vacation language programs through partner universities in Indonesia: Sydney University through Satya Wacana University in Salatiga, and Monash University with Gadjah Mada University in Jogjakarta. In addition, interest was sufficiently strong in the first semester of 2000 for 68 students to head off from universities around Australia to study in Indonesian universities through the recently established Australian Consortium for 'In-Country' Indonesian Studies (ACICIS). This was the largest Australian cohort ever enrolled in Indonesian universities and paradoxically a figure not to be achieved again for another 15 years.[5] It was the crest of a down-turning wave.

By 2004 the financial implications of declining enrolments were becoming obvious as universities began to close their Indonesian language programs outright or to negotiate with other universities to co-teach or amalgamate operations to economise. In the six years between 2004 and 2009, autonomous Indonesian programs closed in Curtin, Charles Sturt University, University of Technology Sydney, University of Western Sydney, Queensland University of Technology, and Griffith (with the latter two forming a network with the University of Queensland to continue a joint program). By the end of the decade the University of New England was teaching what it referred to as a 'blended model' of Indonesian instruction into University of Southern Queensland and the University of Wollongong, both of which had ceased their autonomous programs. Thus, by the end of the first decade only 15

---

3   For example, Rex Mortimer (1983) *Stubborn Survivors*, CSEAS Monash, Clayton; Richard Robison (1986) *Indonesia: The Rise of Capital*, ASAA Allen and Unwin, North Sydney; and Keith Foulcher (1986) *Social Commitment in Literature and the Arts: The Indonesian 'Institute of People's Culture' 1950-1965*, CSEAS Monash, Clayton.

4   The universities were: ANU, CDU (then called Northern Territory University), Deakin, Flinders, LaTrobe, Monash, Murdoch, Melbourne, UNE, UNSW (including ADFA) UQ, USC, Sydney, Tasmania, UWA, Griffith, QUT, USQ, Wollongong, Curtin, UTS, UWS, and CSU. James Cook University has closed its Indonesian course in 1997.

5   ACICIS enrolments only surpassed 68 in first semester 2015, when 76 students enrolled for semester-length programs in both Indonesian- and English-medium.

universities were offering self-sustaining Indonesian language majors, without collaboration with another institution, while a further five retained Indonesian only under arrangements where materials and/or staffing were provided by another university.

Through 2010–11, with funding from the Commonwealth Government's Australian Learning and Teaching Council (ALTC), I endeavoured to track the enrolment trends in Indonesian language in all Australian universities from 2001 through to 2010.[6] The findings were disturbing. Over that period, enrolments in Indonesian were declining in virtually every Indonesian-teaching university in every state.[7] The national decline over that decade was 37 percent. The fall over this decade was more significant than it initially appeared, because it occurred when overall enrolments in Australian universities actually grew (by about 40%) as tertiary education became more accessible. In effect, in 2010 Indonesian attracted only about half the percentage of total university students it had drawn a decade earlier.

Table 1, which converts individual student enrolments into a standardised unit called an EFTSL,[8] provides a statistical snapshot of Indonesian over the decade 2001 to 2010.

In general terms, Indonesian's national total of 304.9 EFTSL in 2010 would equate to about 1000–1200 individual students (depending on how many subjects per year each university requires to make up a full-time load).

Statistics revealed quite substantial discrepancies in the decline across states and territories. In NSW and Queensland the decline was the greatest at 52 percent and 46 percent respectively, while in NT it was only a modest 5 percent, albeit with that sparsely populated territory accounting for a relatively small proportion of the national enrolment.

---

6   This chapter draws heavily upon David T. Hill, *Indonesian Language in Australian Universities: Strategies for a stronger future*, Australian Learning and Teaching Council National Teaching Fellowship Final Report, Murdoch University, Perth, April 2012 second edition, http://www.murdoch.edu.au/ALTC-Fellowship/_document/final_report/ALTC_NTF_Indonesian_in_Australian_Universities_FINAL_REPORT.pdf.

7   The only university to resist the decline between 2001–10 was Murdoch University, which managed a tiny increase of about 4% (see Figure 7).

8   Universities use a standardised measure to calculate their student load in a unit called an Equivalent Full Time Student Load (EFTSL), which represents the amount of load a student would have when studying full time for one year. For example, a student studying Indonesian as one of 4 subjects making up a full time load throughout a year would generate 25 percent of an EFTSL for Indonesian.

Table 1: Equivalent Full-Time Student Load (EFTSL) in Indonesian language units 2001–2010
[rounded to 1 decimal point]
(Hill, 2012, p. 21)

Year	ACT	NSW	NT	QLD	SA	TAS	VIC	WA	National Total
2001	45.0	83.1	15.3	38.7	30.9	32.3	181.5	55.1	**481.9**
2002	45.0	74.5	18.0	40.6	27.9	24.0	186.1	54.0	**470.0**
2003	36.0	63.6	14.0	38.5	40.0	27.4	176.8	58.8	**455.1**
2004	47.0	50.6	12.9	34.1	43.3	24.5	172.3	59.4	**444.0**
2005	42.0	54.7	17.0	31.0	20.5	20.6	172.6	59.8	**418.3**
2006	38.8	46.6	13.3	27.5	24.5	16.8	151.5	53.9	**372.8**
2007	34.0	46.0	16.5	24.8	24.8	16.5	149.1	45.2	**356.8**
2008	31.4	43.7	13.5	18.6	24.3	18.8	142.3	45.4	**339.1**
2009	22.9	45.0	14.6	20.5	21.9	15.8	131.4	30.3	**302.2**
2010	28.5	40.0	14.5	20.9	19.7	16.5	129.9	34.0	**304.9**
Total	371	548	150	295	278	213	1594	496	**3945.1**
% change 2001–10	-37	-52	-5	-46	-36	-49	-28	-380	**-37**

As attention focussed on this national decline, there was speculation as to the cause. Read blamed fluctuations in 'government initiatives, demographic changes, attitudes in the Australian community towards foreign language learning, events in Indonesia, attitudes in the Australian community towards Indonesia and other contributory factors specific to Indonesian, such as native speaker competition in Year 12 examinations and the popularity of Indonesia as a tourist destination' (Read, 2002, p. 64). There had been a string of crises reflecting negatively upon Indonesia. These included the undermining impact of the 1997 Asian Financial Crisis upon Indonesia's economy:

> televised images of violence and instability leading up to the resignation of former president Suharto in May 1998; negative Australian community attitudes to Indonesia's prolonged attempted integration of East Timor and particularly the very visible levels of violence against the pro-independence movement leading up to, and immediately after, the August 1999 referendum; the deaths of Australians in the Bali bombings

of 2002 and 2005, together with the bombing of the Australian Embassy (2004) and hotels (2009) in Jakarta; the trials and imprisonment of several Australian drug smugglers in Bali, most notably Schapelle Corby (2005) and the 'Bali Nine' (2006); and (drastically curtailing many educational exchanges with Indonesia) the elevated Travel Advisories issued by the DFAT.[9] (Hill, 2012, p. 25–6)

It was what Professor Tim Lindsey referred to as a 'perfect storm', a series of very public catastrophes involving Indonesia, any one of which might not have undermined interest in learning Indonesian language but which, when compounded, proved insurmountable (Fitzpatrick, 2009). As noted by Firdaus earlier in this volume, the Australian government of the day turned very little attention to strategies for reviving interest in Indonesian.

However, since the nadir captured in Table 1 and discussed at length in the 2012 Hill Report, there have been a number of very encouraging developments, giving some hope that the worst of the decline of Indonesian in Australian universities may be past.

Broader Developments

My 2012 Report made 20 recommendations: 13 directed at government and seven at universities. Most remain relevant, still awaiting adoption. Significantly, however, two – relating to the Department of Foreign Affairs and Trade travel advisory and to bipartisan support for 'in-country' study – have, in effect, come to pass. The lowering of the DFAT travel advisory for Indonesia, from 'reconsider your need to travel' (Level 3) to 'exercise a high degree of caution' (Level 2) in mid-2012 had a noticeable impact upon educational institutions' willingness to permit student travel to Indonesia. The elevated travel advisory that had been in place since the first Bali bombing had made it problematic for universities (and virtually impossible for schools) to approve student travel to Indonesia.[10]

---

9   On Australian media coverage of the Schapelle Corby case, for example, see Krishna Sen, (2006). 'The trials of Schapelle Corby', *Australian Journal of Anthropology* 17 (1): 72–76.

10 There are four levels in the DFAT Travel Advice: Level 1 – Exercise normal safety precautions; Level 2 – Exercise a high degree of caution; Level 3 – Reconsider your need to travel; Level 4 – Do not travel. See <http://www.smartraveller.gov.au/travel-advice-explained.html>, sighted 4 November 2014. Although some private schools did visit Indonesia despite the DFAT advice, government schools found it virtually impossible to get permission to travel there while the elevated advisory was in place.

The Rudd and Gillard Labor Governments had also stimulated public discussion about the value for the country of encouraging Australian students both to study Asian languages and to study in Asia. This was particularly evident during the public consultations and discussion leading up to the publication in October 2012 of the government's *Australia in the Asian Century* White Paper, compiled under the direction of Ken Henry.[11] To support Australian students seeking to study in Asian universities, in early 2013 the Labor Government launched a scholarship scheme entitled 'AsiaBound', with funding for outbound students provided via their home institutions.

Indonesian enrolment statistics for 2011-2012 gave some cause for optimism, with a 10 percent increase in EFTSL enrolments in Australian universities over just those couple of years. There was some hope that, having reached its low point in 2009, Indonesian was regaining popularity and enrolments were starting to rebound. The key stimulus was the National Asian Languages and Studies in Schools Program (NALSSP), under which the Labor Government had provided $62.15 million over four years (2008–9 to 2011–2) to support the learning of Asian languages and studies in Australian schools. Such explicit funding and policy emphasis was crucial to support languages, as school principals often found the competing demands of different subjects for both funds and a place in a crowded timetable hard to accommodate. While these funds were targeted explicitly at schools, some funding was provided to particular universities to train prospective schoolteachers of Asian languages, including Indonesian.[12] This injection of funding enabled a small number of universities to boost their enrolment significantly over those years.

Closer inspection of individual university data for 2011–12 reveals just how dependent growth was upon the NALSSP effect. One university managed to turn a 27 percent decrease over the period 2001–10 into a 24 percent increase over 2010–12 because of a single NALSSP-funded program for school teachers. Another university turned a 40 percent decline

---

11 The Abbott Government rapidly archived the White Paper, abandoned any discussion of its recommendations, and even the term 'Asian Century' fell immediately into disuse. The document remains accessible at: <http://pandora.nla.gov.au/col/c12842>, sighted 4 November 2014.

12 In addition to funding languages, some funds were provided to universities to train teachers in Asian studies so they could use Asian examples in their everyday teaching, thus providing a broader context for the learning of languages. See Ross Tapsell, 'Across the curriculum: access to Asian languages isn't everything', *The Conversation*, 1 November 2012, <http://theconversation.com/across-the-curriculum-access-to-asian-languages-isnt-everything-10427>.

during 2001–10 into growth of more than 200 percent between 2010 and 2012, with 'the spike in 2012 enrolments in Indonesian ... precisely due to the NALSSP funded ... Indonesian initiative' (personal communication, 28 August 2013).[13] Sadly, claiming the short-lived program had failed to demonstrate immediate results in schools, the government ceased NALSSP in 2012, despite protests from analysts that substantive returns would only become apparent after a decade of consolidated investment. The NALSSP effect quickly waned, in the absence of any specifically designated funding to support or promote the study of Indonesian on Australian university campuses.

The incoming Abbott government abandoned any discussion of their predecessor's White Paper. Yet it was noteworthy that the Asiabound concept of funding Australian students to study in Asia was, in effect, adopted by Foreign Minister Julie Bishop as a 'signature policy', albeit expanded and re-branded as the New Colombo Plan (NCP). This policy was given high-profile promotion by a front-line Minister of Foreign Affairs. A dedicated NCP Secretariat was established within the Department of Foreign Affairs and Trade to oversee the program on the basis that the NCP was an arm of foreign policy as much as it was of education. These strategies provided a significant fillip to the promotion of outbound student mobility to Asia. With Indonesia designated by Minister Bishop as one of the four pilot countries for the initial year of the NCP in 2014, considerable attention focussed on increasing the flow of Australian students to Indonesia under the flagship NCP.

Ignoring for a moment the tussle over terminology and branding – Labor's Asiabound or the Coalition's New Colombo Plan – outbound student mobility to Asia had achieved a demonstrably high level of bipartisan commitment, with study in Asia and study there of an Asian language now firmly accepted as benefitting Australian society. That is, both sides of politics were publicly and vocally committed to the goal of increasing the study of Asian languages by providing financial incentives for Australians to study in Asia (with specific scholarship loadings for the study of languages). It is a rare example of bi-partisanship in national politics, suggesting a considerable victory for those long arguing for the importance of such a policy.

This was nowhere more evident than in the fortuitous overlap in funding programs in 2014, which was both the final year of funding for the AsiaBound

---

13   I discuss the 2011–12 situation in more detail in 'Language as 'soft power' in bilateral relations: The case of Indonesian language in Australia', *Asia Pacific Journal of Education*, 36:3, September 2016, http://dx.doi.org/ 10.1080/02188791.2014.940033.

program, as well as the pilot year of funding for the New Colombo Plan. As a result, there appeared more government funds released to support outbound mobility to Asia in 2014 than ever before. The rather hasty nature of the dispersal, however, had the effect that some universities were not able to award the number of travel grants they were allocated and consequently may have returned some funds to the Commonwealth unspent. Staff from one university, for example, recounted to me with considerable disappointment that, when they took the initiative to offer some 100 grants to encourage undergraduates to study in Asia, only 10 applications were forthcoming! In the 2014 round of the New Colombo Plan mobility grants, the largest number of mobility project grants were allocated for studies in Indonesia.[14]

In a further effort to demonstrate the importance the Coalition placed on the Australian-Indonesian relationship, after meeting in October 2013 with Indonesian President Susilo Bambang Yudhoyono, Prime Minister Tony Abbott announced $15 million over five years to establish an Australia Indonesia Centre (AIC). Based at Monash University, this new entity involves the CSIRO and the universities of ANU, Melbourne, Sydney, along with several Indonesian partner universities.[15] The AIC espouses the goals of 'understanding, relationships and research', but appears to see no particular role in supporting or promoting Indonesian language teaching. Nonetheless, the establishment of such a well-funded Centre may raise the profile of Indonesian studies in Australia, and by implication, accentuate the value of Indonesian language studies.

Coalition policy did not extend to supporting endangered Indonesian language programs. Despite the 2012 Henry White Paper promoting the importance of Asian languages, in 2013 both La Trobe and UNSW announced the intention to cease Indonesian teaching. In the case of La Trobe the public response and support from various interest groups convinced the university administration to step back from the brink, with La Trobe retaining a reasonably healthy Indonesian language program with several staff. Unfortunately, in 2013 UNSW ceased teaching Indonesian.[16]

---

14   Over Tranche 1 and 2, a total of 72 mobility projects were funded of which 23 were for Indonesia, 22 for Japan, 15 for Singapore and 12 for Hongkong. See <http://www.dfat.gov.au/new-colombo-plan/summary-tranche-one-offers.html> and <http://www.dfat.gov.au/new-colombo-plan/summary-tranche-two-offers.html>, sighted 21 January 2015.

15   See <http://australiaindonesiacentre.org/>.

16   Indonesian is still offered at the Australian Defence Force Academy campus of UNSW in Canberra, but no longer at the main Sydney campus.

Indonesian Trends

With the cessation of the NALSSP, the absence of any comparable program to support Asian language acquisition in schools, and with the government's focus on outbound mobility through the NCP, several predictable outcomes occurred. As Table 2 illustrates, growth peaked in 2012 only to return by 2014 to virtually the same point nationally as in 2009. That is, in 2014 there were 302.5 EFTSL, which was almost identical to 2009's 302.2 EFTSL.

Represented in chart form, Figure 1 shows the downward trend is stark.

Table 2: Indonesian language EFTSLs 2001–2014
[rounded to 1 decimal point]

Year	ACT	NSW	NT	QLD	SA	TAS	VIC	WA	National Total
2001	45.0	83.1	15.3	38.7	30.9	32.3	181.5	55.1	481.9
2002	45.0	74.5	18.0	40.6	27.9	24.0	186.1	54.0	470.0
2003	36.0	63.6	14.0	38.5	40.0	27.4	176.8	58.8	455.1
2004	47.0	50.6	12.9	34.1	43.3	24.5	172.3	59.4	444.0
2005	42.0	54.7	17.0	31.0	20.5	20.6	172.6	59.8	418.3
2006	38.8	46.6	13.3	27.5	24.5	16.8	151.5	53.9	372.8
2007	34.0	46.0	16.5	24.8	24.8	16.5	149.1	45.2	356.8
2008	31.4	43.7	13.5	18.6	24.3	18.8	142.3	45.4	339.1
2009	22.9	45.0	14.6	20.5	21.9	15.8	131.4	30.3	302.2
2010	28.5	40.0	14.5	20.9	19.7	16.5	129.9	34.0	304.9
2011	26.9	42.1	24.0	21.4	19.6	12.1	120.7	32.7	301.2
2012	21.3	50.3	23.5	24.8	20.0	10.4	146.8	39.9	337.9
2013	31.8	50.9	23.8	21.9	14.4	6.8	126.0	34.0	308.5
2014	32.5	38.9	18.8	24.6	14.0	8.5	133.0	33.0	302.5
Total	483	730	240	388	346	251	2120	636	5195.0
% change 2001–14	-28	-53	23	-36	-55	-74	-27	-40	-37

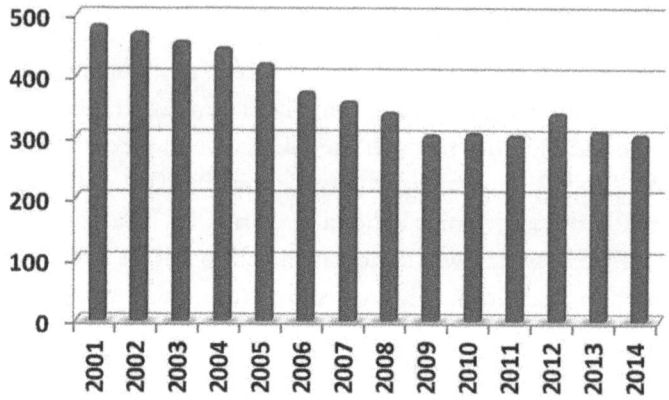

Figure 1: Australian National EFTSLs 2001–2014

As Table 3 illustrates, the brief gain in 2011–2012 was soon lost. If we look at the 2001–14 perspective, while enrolments were no longer going down, they had definitely flattened in the years since 2009. Focussing on 2010–14, what is revealing is the variation between states. In some, the fall has been quite significant; in others enrolments are virtually flat; while in still others enrolments are noticeably buoyant. Queensland's growth of 18 percent is definitely cause for optimism. Northern Territory has gone up by an impressive 29 percent (albeit from a very low base). The ACT is also up markedly. But the majority of states, particularly those with the largest share of enrolments, are either flat or falling. Noteworthy is the dramatic drop in Tasmania where load has halved in just four years.

Table 3: Indonesian language EFTSL by state: 2010–2014 [rounded to 1 decimal point]

	ACT	NSW	NT	QLD	SA	TAS	VIC	WA	National Total
2010	28.5	40.0	14.5	20.9	19.7	16.5	129.9	34.0	304.9
2011	26.9	42.1	24.0	21.4	19.6	12.1	120.7	32.7	301.2
2012	21.3	50.3	23.5	24.8	20.0	10.4	146.8	39.9	337.9
2013	31.8	50.9	23.8	21.9	14.4	6.8	126.0	34.0	308.5
2014	32.5	38.9	18.8	24.6	14.0	8.5	133.0	33.0	302.5
Total	141	222	105	114	88	54	656	174	1555
% change 2010–14	14	-3	29	18	-29	-49	2	-3	-1

Further disaggregating the statistics reveals significant variations between different types of universities or university groupings. Indonesian is strongest in the Group of Eight (Go8) universities, all of which – except for UNSW since 2013 – offer Indonesian (with the University of Adelaide doing so by longstanding arrangement with Flinders). The Go8 account for just under half of Australia's Indonesian language enrolments (about 140 out of 300 EFTSL).

Four of the seven members of the Innovative Research Universities (IRU) network offer Indonesian.[17] IRU enrolments continue to fall, albeit after a brief plateau in 2008–9, with this category of universities now accounting for a little under 50 EFTSL.

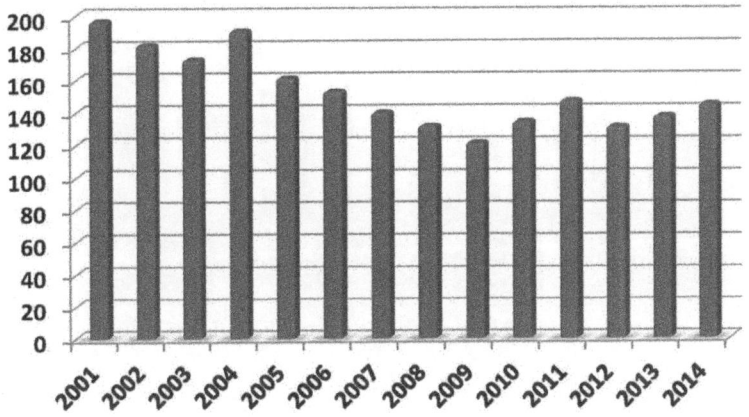

Figure 2: Group of 8 Indonesian EFTSLs 2001–2014

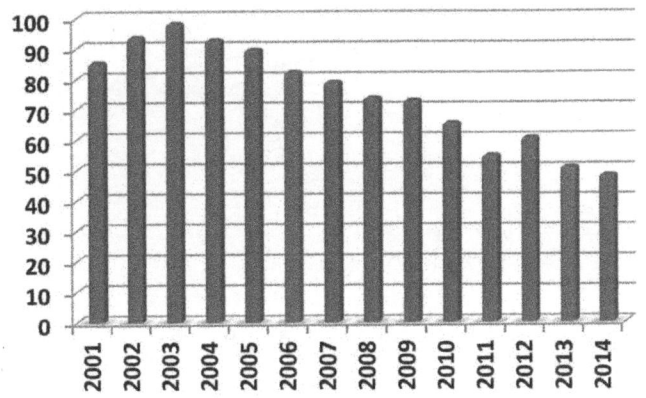

Figure 3: Innovative Research Universities EFTSLs 2001–2014

---

17   Of the IRUs LaTrobe, Flinders, Murdoch and CDU offer Indonesian.

Those universities included in the Regional Universities Network (RUN) tend to be small non-metropolitan institutions.[18] Interestingly, again, as Figure 4 illustrates, their Indonesian load is going up, compared with 2011, partly due to the stimulus of past NALSSP funding and strong emphasis on in-country study (to which we will return in due course).

The line in Figure 5 tries to capture the national trend this century in a single image.

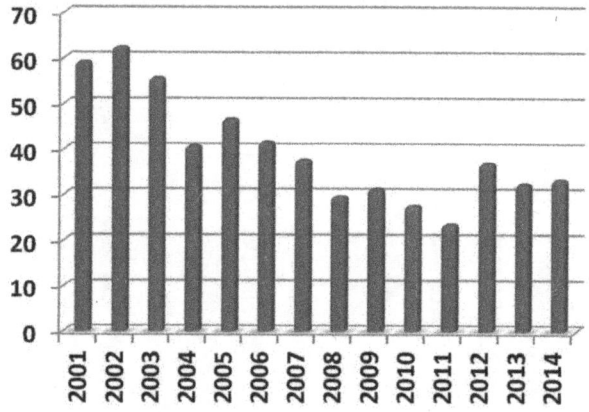

Figure 4: Regional Universities Network EFTSL 2001–2014

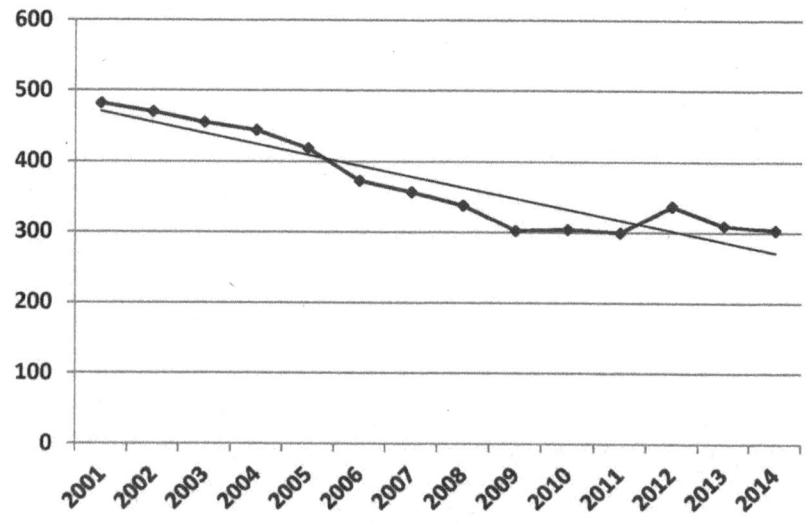

Figure 5: Indonesian EFTSL, Australia 2001–2014

---

18 The three RUN universities that offer Indonesian either autonomously or by collaboration are UNE, USC and USQ.

It is even more alarming to project this trend forward, for it throws up the spectre of Indonesian disappearing from our universities by 2031 (see Figure 6). It is not my contention that Indonesian will disappear. As I have observed above, it is relatively healthy in the Go8 and some of the RUNs. But trends this century are cause for alarm. Indonesian is contracting, and contracting dramatically. Students are not enrolling, despite numerous statements from government (and business) emphasising the value of acquiring an Asian language. As university Indonesian departments wither, Indonesian-teaching staff are being laid off, and those who leave the profession are not being replaced. Now commonly university administrators regard an Indonesian program as unable to pay its way, as they increasingly factor Indonesian out of their future subject profiles.

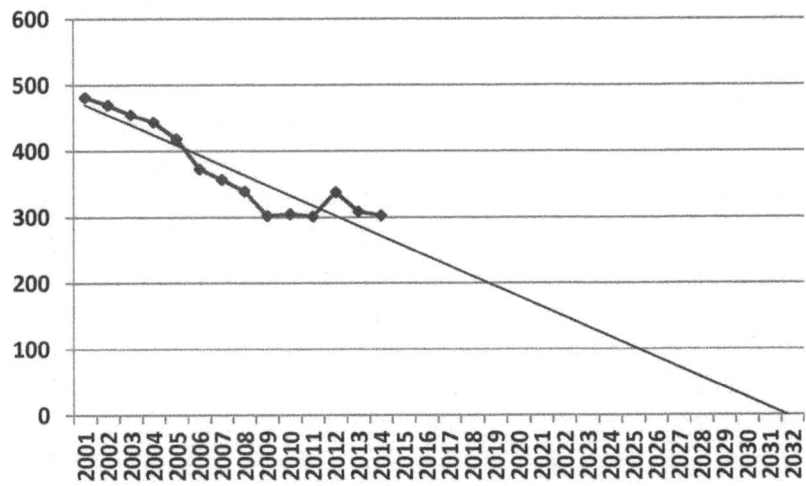

Figure 6: Future Projections (EFTSL) Australia 2001–???

Cause for Optimism?

Given such projections, is there any cause for optimism? Indeed, there have been a couple of hopeful developments.

Firstly, two universities have made major changes in the structure of their degrees, consequently stimulating Indonesian uptake. Both the University of Melbourne and the University of Western Australia reduced the number of their Bachelors degrees and required students from all disciplines to take at least one subject designated as 'breadth' to provide variety to their degrees. In this process, these universities defined languages as fulfilling the 'breadth' requirement, and noticed significant increases in their first year enrolments in Indonesian (along with all other languages).[19] Evidence from both these institutions demonstrated that when degree structures were relaxed, with students required to experiment with a breadth unit in a new area, and when languages were classified as breadth, languages proved to be attractive. In the case of UWA, renewed interest in Indonesian commenced even before the new degree structure, with a targeted promotion exercise in 2009 during which an Indonesian-speaking UWA graduate undertook incursions into schools in the university's feeder zone to promote the benefits of Indonesian to prospective students.

By contrast, when Murdoch University went through a similar simplification in the range of Bachelors degree in 2013 and required all students to take breadth subjects, it crucially did **not** categorise language units as breadth. Instead, it constructed new cross-disciplinary breadth units. Having to include the newly designed 'breadth' units alongside their discipline majors, students found they actually had less space to include a language. Regrettably, language enrolments declined (as Figure 7 over leaf illustrates).

It should be noted that both documented successes in open degree structures were Group of Eight universities offering a wide suite of languages. Evidence suggests that the more languages a university teaches, the more inclined the institution will be to encourage language learning. Languages flourish in institutions that offer a range of languages. In such universities there is a both a consciousness of the contribution linguistic skills make to a rounded education, and the consequent view that the loss of one language from a campus weakens all languages offered. However, the challenge for those universities that have stimulated interest in Indonesian through breadth requirements will be to sustain the upswing, as it appears enrolments in Indonesian peaked several years into the new degrees only to decline once more.

Recent government support for Indonesian (and Asian) language acquisition has focussed primarily on in-country study – that is, studying a language in the country where that language is used. Both AsiaBound and the NCP provide additional scholarship payments to assist students studying in Asia to learn a language while there. This stimulus builds on a slender history of Australians studying in Indonesia. The first regular in-country Indonesian study program for Australians was pioneered by Dr George Quinn who arranged for 37 Australian students to do a vacation Indonesian course in January 1974 at Satya Wacana Christian University in Salatiga in partnership

---

19 On the UWA case, see Bernard Lane (2013) 'More take tough tongues', *The Australian*, April 24, <http://www.theaustralian.com.au/higher-education/more-take-tough-tongues/story-e6frgcjx-1226627358627>, sighted 16 January 2015.

with the University of Sydney. Participation in this annual month-long course peaked to well above a hundred students in the early 1980s.

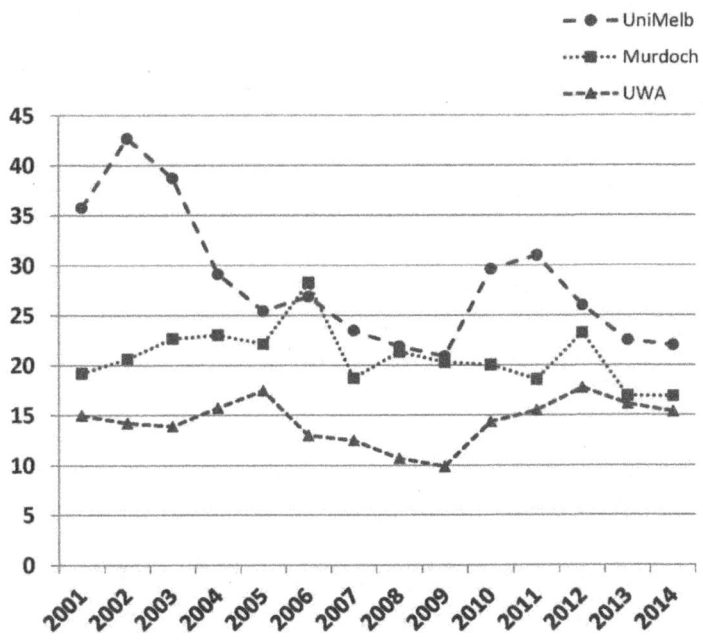

Figure 7: Comparison of EFTSL at University of Melbourne, University of Western Australia and Murdoch University (Indonesian was included as a breadth subject at University of Melbourne in 2008 and UWA in 2012. Indonesian was **not** categorised as 'breadth' unit at Murdoch in 2013. However, in June 2015, after the text of this article had gone to press, Murdoch University reversed its previous position and decided to include Indonesian language in the breadth units. It is too early to assess the impact this will have on enrolments)

Over subsequent decades similar vacation programs were arranged by the ANU (which inherited the link with Satya Wacana), Deakin (which alternates annually between universities in Padang and Malang), Monash (with Gadjah Mada University) and various other universities. Currently the largest such vacation program is run by the Regional Universities Indonesian Language Initiative (RUILI) – a collaboration between UNE, USC, CDU and UTas – delivered at Mataram University in Lombok, with a planned expansion to Nusa Cendana University in Kupang.[20]

---

20   I would like to thank Dr Richard Curtis of USC for providing information on RUILI (telephone conversation, 19 November 2014). RUILI's in-country program is discussed in detail as a case study in Joanne Winter, *Collaborative models for the*

The lowering of the DFAT travel advisory in 2012 has coincided with an upswing in the number of Australian university students undertaking Indonesian language studies in-country. After more than a decade of very slow growth, rebuilding after the decimation which followed the 2002 Bali bombing, in-country enrolments now constitute a significant proportion of total Indonesian language load in Australian universities. Two specific cases illustrate.

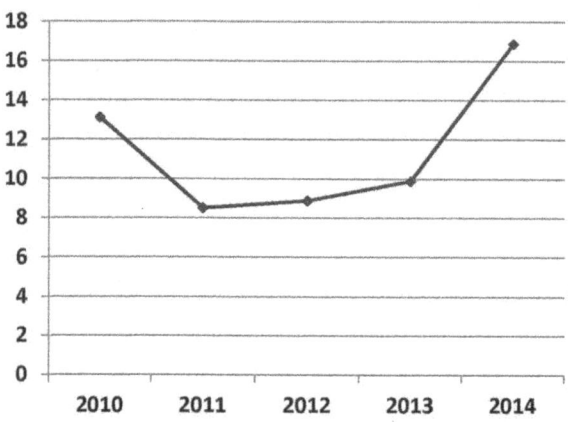

Figure 8: RUILI Language Program EFTSL 2010–2014

RUILI was established in 2007 to develop common curriculum materials to be shared between the four participating universities. From this emerged the concept of co-convening an in-country language program using these materials during the end-of-year university vacation. While focussed on students from the four RUILI universities, participation is open to other students. Participants generally cross-enrol in a subject code at a RUILI university, to where the EFTSL load flows. RUILI has developed the teaching materials and supported the program by inviting a key Mataram University staff member to undertake his PhD in Indonesian language teaching at USC. The growing popularity of the RUILI vacation program is illustrated in Figure 8, which shows the EFTSL doubling from just over 8 in 2011 to around 17 in 2014. The dramatic increase between 2013 and 2014 suggests strong potential.

If RUILI focuses on vacation language programs, the other in-country consortium has a broader brief. The Australian Consortium for 'In-Country'

---

provision of languages in Australian universities, DASSH/CASR, n.p. February 2009 pp. 82–93, <http://www.murdoch.edu.au/ALTC-Fellowship/_document/Resources/Collaborative-models-for-the-provision-of-languages-in-Australian-universities>, sighted 11 November 2014.

Indonesian Studies (ACICIS) was established by Murdoch University in 1994 to facilitate the placement of Australian undergraduate students into Indonesian universities, for semester-length programs. The consortium has since expanded to include 22 Australian universities together with the School of Oriental and African Studies at the University of London, and Leiden University in the Netherlands. ACICIS primarily places foreign (mainly Australian) students into pre-existing Indonesian university semester courses, liaising with the host universities to accommodate international learners. In addition, ACICIS collaborates with Atma Jaya University in Jakarta to offer various six-week professional practicum programs during January–February each year, and has developed a suite of tailored study programs of varying lengths for university students, school students and teaching staff.[21] Whereas ACICIS initially offered only Indonesian-language semesters, it now promotes a growing suite of study programs taught in English.

ACICIS' primary innovation was to break away from the conventional model of 'in-country' study as primarily a language study excursion to Indonesia, usually undertaken in an 'enclave', alongside other Australian students. Instead, ACICIS endeavoured to integrate Australians into Indonesian universities, studying alongside Indonesian nationals, in such a way as to be credited into a variety of Australian home university degrees. As the consortium operates collectively, ACICIS offers the same opportunities to all member universities irrespective of their size or academic ranking.

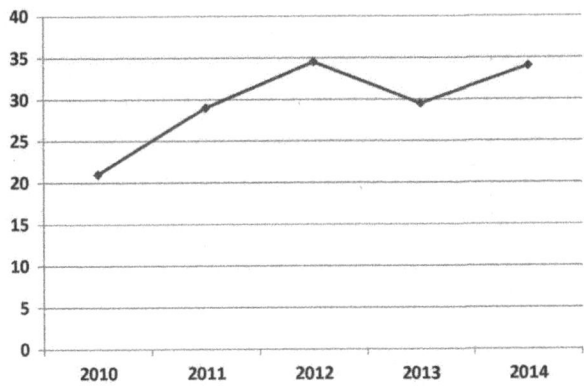

Figure 9: ACICIS Semester Language Programs EFTSL 2010–2014

---

21 Details of ACICIS study programs are at: <http://www.acicis.edu.au/programs/>, sighted 1 April 2015. In the interests of full disclosure, I am the Founder and former Director of ACICIS.

Figure 9 illustrates the rise in students studying Indonesian in Indonesia through the ACICIS program during the period 2010–14 (excluding those studying English-medium courses). Enrolments expanded from about 20 to 35 EFTSL. If the RUILI and ACICIS loads are combined, growth in in-country language studies increases from about 35 to over 50 EFTSL in just those four years (see Figure 10).

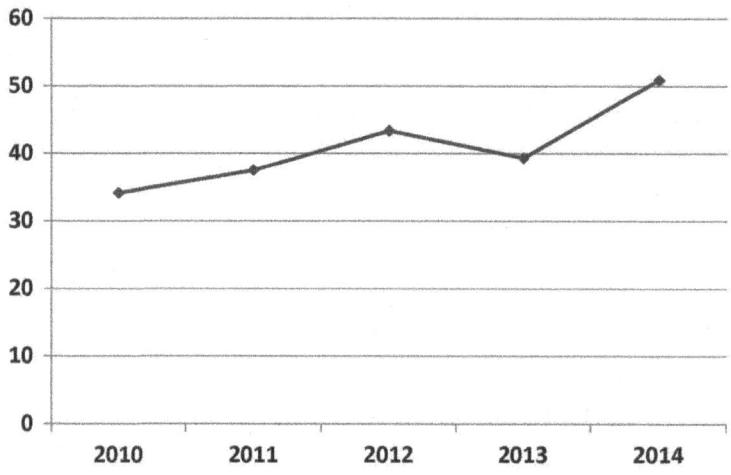

Figure 10: ACICIS and RUILI In-Country Language Programs EFTSL 2010–2014

There is no doubt that in-country study has been stimulated by bipartisan government support for outbound mobility to Indonesia, through AsiaBound and the New Colombo Plan. The consequence, however, has been a noticeable shift away from the status quo in Indonesian language learning in Australian universities. As a percentage of Indonesian's total of about 300 EFTSL in both 2010 and 2014, the proportion actually studying in-country (through RUILI and ACICIS) has increased from about 11 percent in 2010 to 17 percent in 2014 (see Figure 11).

In other words, about one in five of those Australian university students learning Indonesian language are actually studying not in an Australian classroom but in Indonesia. If the various smaller short-language programs administered by individual universities (such as the ANU program at Salatiga and the Deakin program in Padang and Malang) were included in these statistics, in-country learning would definitely exceed 20 percent.[22]

---

22   The Deakin University in-country program generates approximately 10 EFTSL each year (telephone conversation with Alistair Welsh, Malang, 14 November 2014).

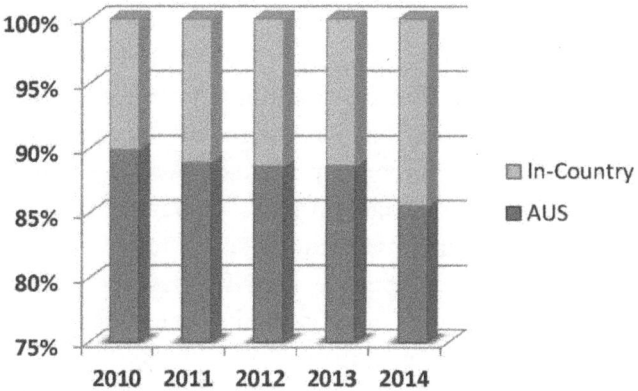

Figure 11: ACICIS and RUILI In-Country Language Programs EFTSL 2010–2014 as a percentage of all Indonesian language EFTSL in Australian universities.

Such evidence suggests that, when encouraged and supported to study Indonesian in Indonesia for credit back to their Australian degrees, students will grasp the opportunity in ever-increasing numbers. It is vital, therefore, that universities encourage and facilitate such opportunities. In-country study opportunities have been particularly beneficial for advanced proficiency students who are increasingly finding that universities have cut advanced level classes with low enrolments. An in-country intensive course, for example, can provide a valuable replacement for a fourth year unit for some students.

More broadly, interest in studying in Indonesia – whether in Indonesian-medium or English-medium programs – is increasing, if ACICIS provides an example. In the first half of 2015, which was the 40th semester of its operations and its 20th anniversary year, ACICIS hosted the largest number of Australian students ever. Enrolments in ACICIS' Indonesian semester programs had peaked with 68 students participating in the first semester of the 2000 academic year, with numbers during the calendar years 1999–2000 the strongest over the consortium's initial decade. It was not until Semester 1 of 2015 when 76 students enrolled for an ACICIS semester in Indonesia that numbers exceeded the previous record set in Semester 1, 2000. In recent years, these ACICIS enrolments are spread across not just Indonesian-language programs, but include English-medium study programs, such as International Relations (at Parahyangan University) and Islamic Business, Law and Society (at the Islamic University of Indonesia, Jogjakarta). These are targeted at participants with no Indonesian language skills, though Indonesian can be studied as one of the subjects. This provision and promotion of discipline-based study programs taught in English may be stimulating a broader awareness amongst Australian undergraduates of the benefits of a study experience in Indonesia.

While statistics indicate that interest in studying in Indonesia is strengthening, a corollary may be that the traditional forms of language learning in Australian classrooms may be increasingly less appealing to students as 'on the ground' experience in-country becomes more accessible. The immediacy of such in-country language learning is an obvious appeal. Yet, not all students find in-country language studies suited to their learning style or personal circumstances. Furthermore, the NCP has an explicit bias against participants over 28 years of age, which limits benefits for such mature-age students (including, for example, in-service teachers).[23] In this context, the maintenance of Australia's Indonesian language skills base will continue to require strong Indonesian language programs in conventional 'on campus' and 'external' modes at Australian universities. In-country programs will undoubtedly grow in popularity, but are likely nonetheless to remain supplementary to, rather than a complete replacement for, Australia-based language learning.

The Unfolding Context

The teaching of Indonesian does not exist in a social, political or economic vacuum in Australia. Government policies – or the lack of them – have a profound impact. Just as the AsiaBound and NCP policies have stimulated enrolments in in-country studies, so too has the cessation of the NALSSP (and its predecessor, the National Asian Languages and Studies in Australian Schools program) undermined language growth.

Despite rhetorical flourishes, in recent years Australian governments of both persuasions have displayed a growing reluctance to fund universities – and the teaching of languages within them. While there have been considerable benefits from NCP funding, there is also an inherent message to students that 'if you want to study an Asian language, we will pay you to go to that country and study it there'. In the absence of direct funding to support the conventional teaching modes, enrolments in Indonesian are likely to continue to decline.

---

23   NCP 2015 guidelines, for example, specify that: 'At least 90 per cent of the Students participating in any given Mobility Project must be aged 18 to 28 inclusive at the commencement of the Mobility Project'. <http://www.dfat.gov.au/new-colombo-plan/mobility-program-guidelines-2015.html#eligibility>, sighted 19 November 2014.

Nonetheless, as the chapter in this volume by Firdaus illustrates, some developments in Australian higher education have the capacity to support Indonesian language teaching and learning, at least tangentially. In 2011, the Languages and Cultures Network in Australian Universities (LCNAU)[24] was established with funding from the Australian Government's Office of Learning and Teaching (OLT, superseding the previous Australian Learning and Teaching Council). The network is driven mainly out of Melbourne University but is national in scope. While there is currently very little participation in LCNAU by Indonesianists, it offers considerable potential for collective action and lobbying on issues of mutual concern for all languages.

As an example, LCNAU, again with OLT funding, is establishing the 'University Languages Portal Australia' (ULPA).[25] ULPA will be a single online location with information for students on availability of all languages, whether indigenous or global, taught across all delivery methods and durations in all Australian universities. The portal can provide key information to aide student choice through a 'one stop shop'.

Although the success of inter-university language collaborations is mixed, there have been some noteworthy initiatives. RUILI is a case in point. In addition, the University of New England provides Indonesian language materials and coordination, using a 'blended model', to other universities such as Wollongong and USQ by agreement. Griffith University (GU), Queensland University of Technology (QUT) and The University of Queensland (UQ) formed the Brisbane Universities Language Alliance (BULA),[26] to provide access for all their students to the suite of languages available in the BULA universities, with the units credited back to the home degree. The Innovative Research Universities (IRU) have established an Asian Languages Network, with the aim of collaborating (in a yet to be determined manner) in the offering of Asian languages within the IRU network.

It has been observed elsewhere that the Indonesian government has provided minimal support for the teaching of its language abroad.[27] There has certainly been nothing to compare with the investment in language teaching provided by entities such as the Japan Foundation, the Korea Foundation or the Confucius Institutes, both internationally and in Australia. Since 1976 the Indonesian government has provided a growing number of in-country

---

24 See Languages and Cultures Network for Australian Universities <http://www.lcnau.org/>
25 See University Languages Portal Australia <www.ulpa.edu.au>
26 See Brisbane Universities Language Alliance <https://www.bula.edu.au/>
27 For a longer discussion, see Hill 2014. See also Darudoyo in this volume.

Darmasiswa scholarships.[28] However, since the studies undertaken on the *Darmasiswa* scholarships are generally not credited by Australian universities, students may view this as less appealing than alternative 'in-country' opportunities for which academic credit is obtained.

Additionally, a combination of local community initiatives with modest investment by local Indonesian diplomatic representations has supported the establishment of several Indonesian Language Centres, known as *Balai Bahasa Indonesia*. The concept was initiated in Perth in 2007, with the BBI Perth being launched the following year. The solidity of the venture was secured when the BBI Perth gained a grant of more than $300,000 from NALSSP in 2011–13 to support Indonesian language teaching in schools. Driven largely by the initiative of founder Karen Bailey and a core of dedicated volunteers, the BBIP currently runs community classes in Indonesian language, an annual Indonesian Film Festival, a Language Assistant Program for schools, and study tours to Indonesia.

The concept next took root in Canberra in 2009 when Dr George Quinn was approached by the Indonesian Embassy to set up the *Balai Bahasa Indonesia (ACT)*, which was formally launched by the Indonesian Minister of Education in 2011.[29] The BBI (ACT) has convened two major Indonesian language conference (known as ASILE), poetry readings and dinners, and undertakes occasional language activities in schools. A *Balai Bahasa Indonesia* for Victoria and Tasmania has also been established, with encouragement from the local consulate. In addition, the Education and Cultural Attaché in the Indonesian Embassy, Canberra, Professor Ronny Rachman Noor, has initiated discussions with at least one Australian university regarding the establishment of a 'House of Culture' (*Rumah Budaya*), with various nodes in other locations. While details remain limited, the implication is that this initiative would include some Indonesian government support.

Conclusion

The first 15 years of the twenty-first century have been a period of backsliding for Indonesian in Australian universities. Enrolments have fallen steeply, at best managing only a modest levelling off in recent years. There have been some successful government strategies to reverse the flow, injecting specific funding like NALSSP and the NCP. But history suggests such government

---

28 See Darmasiswa Indonesian Scholarship http://darmasiswa.kemdikbud.go.id/darmasiswa/.
29 See Balai Bahasa Indonesia (ACT), <https://bbiact.wordpress.com/>

programs will be short-lived, as too will be their beneficial effect. Some individual universities have devised innovative degree structures to stimulate language learning, with favourable outcomes, at least in the immediate term. Evidence indicates that degree structures and choices by university administrations can, if supportive, turn a decline around.

If one took an optimistic stance upon the future, it is possible to identify 'green shoots', new initiatives, emerging with the potential to revitalise the teaching and learning of Indonesian by Australians. Firstly, increased mobility of larger numbers of young (and not-so-young) Australian students to Indonesia is creating an expanding citizenry with a direct personal – and often profound – experience of living in Indonesian society, and a deep commitment to bilateral understanding and Indonesian language skills. Thousands of alumni of the various 'in-country' programs are working their way into influential roles in Australian society, government and business, bringing fresh expectations of future engagement with Indonesia.

In addition, the practices and technologies of teaching are also being rapidly transformed in ways we can barely imagine. Australian classrooms are already linked instantly with Indonesian classrooms as students work jointly on common tasks, transcending geographical divides. Future technologies will enable seamless instantaneous interaction and shared learning. Modes of learning not yet invented may emerge to provide opportunities for tomorrow's students to learn languages in ways their current teachers cannot conceive. Tomorrow's learners may approach the challenge of mastering a new language with very different expectations of the learning process than do the current generation. To take advantage of these transformations, we need to be training the next generation of Indonesian language teachers to lead such innovations.

Institutionally, the economic constraints which lead today's universities to shut down 'languages of lesser demand' may be rendered obsolete by global teaching strategies, operating on very different models of financial viability. New approaches by universities may mean that a single student, anywhere, could enrol to learn a language, interacting globally with other learners across institutions and countries, with teaching support provided from an entirely different location again. All facilitated and credited by their university, at a viable price.

Such possibilities are not, in themselves, panacea, for if such next-generation pedagogy is to become a reality to support the learning of Indonesian by Australians, then the educators and administrators over coming decades must be encouraged to innovate and collaborate, without intimidation but with incentives and inducements to experiment. Indonesian-language teaching staff must be encouraged – and funded – to take a lead in such discoveries.

When reflecting upon the changes experienced this century in the teaching of Indonesian language in Australia, individual bright spots in select universities and innovative pedagogies enabled by technological change could provide some slender basis for optimism, in the face of the broad national decline identified above. Yet, without government facilitation and intervention – from either the Australian or the Indonesian government, or preferably both – in concert with dedicated teaching staff in universities across the country, funded and supported to innovate and experiment, the trend line points to Indonesian language expiring in ever more universities over the coming decades as Indonesian language learners in Australia diminish in number. If the evidence from the past 15 years is any indication, without dramatic and systemic intervention, the language of our nearest neighbour faces a bleak and uncertain future in its second half century in Australian universities.

Acknowledgments

Support for this research has been provided by the Australian Government Office for Learning and Teaching. However, the views in this publication are those of the author alone, and do not necessarily reflect the views of the Australian Government Office for Learning and Teaching. An earlier version of this paper was presented at the ASILE Conference, Bali, on 30 September 2014. I wish to thank Ms Janelle May for her research assistance with this study, and to all those colleagues who have kindly provided data, comments or criticism.

References

Duff, E. 2014. 'Indonesia prepares to welcome millionth Aussie tourist for the year', 9 November 2014. Available from: <https://www.smh.com.au/national/indonesia-prepares-to-welcome-millionth-aussie-tourist-for-the-year-20141108-11iuv4.html>, accessed 10 November 2014.
Fitzpatrick, S. 2009. 'Asia focus fails test of reality' *The Australian*, 24 June 2009.
Hill, D. T. 2012. *Indonesian Language in Australian Universities: Strategies for a stronger future*, Australian Learning and Teaching Council National Teaching Fellowship Final Report, Murdoch University, Perth, April 2012 second edition. Available from: http://www.murdoch.edu.au/ALTC-Fellowship/_document/final_report/ALTC_NTF_Indonesian_in_Australian_Universities_FINAL_REPORT.pdf
Hill, D. T. 2014. 'Language as 'soft power' in bilateral relations: The case of Indonesian language in Australia', *Asia Pacific Journal of Education*, 36:3, September 2016, pp.364-378 http://dx.doi.org/ 10.1080/02188791.2014.940033.
Read, J. 2002. 'Innovation in Indonesian language teaching: an evaluation of the TIFL tertiary curriculum materials'. Ph.D. thesis, University of Wollongong, Australia.

Section II

Reflections

1. NEW HORIZONS

Getting to Know the Neighbours

JAN LINGARD

University of Sydney

It was only twenty years after Indonesian independence was gained that I began my own Indonesian journey. I knew nothing about Indonesia in 1969, but was intrigued by what I learnt in an adult education course called 'Our Northern Neighbours', which I took because I needed respite from the job of mothering four small children and because I was not sure who those neighbours were. To my surprise I discovered that such a fascinating and different culture was here, right on our doorstep and I was ignorant about it. I made up my mind that I would visit one day, and determined to learn the language. My first course was a couple of hours a week at Sydney Technical College using the textbook *Lancar Berbahasa Indonesia*, by Ichsan, Baker and Lane – very behaviourist and lots of drills. I can still rattle off some of the responses. I recall that at the time ABC Radio also had an Indonesian course, complete with booklet and a 45-rpm record for home practice. I conscientiously tuned in every week. I might add that at the time, my friends could not understand my interest – invasion theories were prevalent – and used to joke that I was learning Indonesian so I could say, 'take me to your leader'.

It was when my family moved to Canberra in 1973 that I had the opportunity to convert my hitherto very interesting hobby into something more serious. Gough Whitlam introduced free tertiary education, giving me the opportunity to go to university for the first time and to change my life. There, waiting for me was the ANU with its wonderful Faculty of Asian Studies, so I enrolled as a mature age student, majoring in Indonesian and Asian Civilisations.

The sixties and the early seventies were the heyday of tertiary study of Indonesian – with students flocking to university courses in numbers that are now just a fond memory in light of today's dire situation. At ANU we had the services of some of the first Javanese scholars who came to Australia to gain their PhDs and then stayed on to become lecturers. These were Soepomo, Soewito-Santoso, and Soebardi – who enthralled us with tales of his experiences during the Revolution. The driving force behind the first year course in my day was language teacher extraordinaire, Yohanni Johns from the Minangkabau region of Sumatra. She had just completed the first of her language textbooks designed for tertiary study. This, if I am not mistaken, was the first such text in Australia, so a great contribution to Indonesian studies in this country. I recall my visit to Bukit Tinggi in later years and hearing Indonesian spoken there just as I had learned it in *Bahasa Indonesia*, by Yohanni Johns. The ANU course was comprehensive, not only offering language, but literature, classical Malay texts, a touch of politics and economics, and if you did Honours, opportunities to study Reading Dutch, Old Javanese or Arabic.

When I completed my course and an Honours year I was delighted to be offered a job as a tutor, and so I crossed over and became a colleague of my former teachers. By the time I left ANU after teaching there for 13 years I could almost recite *Bahasa Indonesia* word for word, and when I meet former students even today, we sometimes act out some of the dialogues. They, like I, am grateful for the grounding it gave us in *Bahasa Indonesia yang baik dan benar*, (good, correct Indonesian) that we could use as a basis for acquiring the other varieties of the language.

I moved back to Sydney in 1991 and was fortunate to get a position at the University of Sydney, first as a tutor then eventually as a lecturer. I joined Marcus Susanto and Jon Soemarjono in the language teaching program, initially using materials created by Marcus. After he retired and I became responsible for the program, we joined the consortium of universities using the TIFL materials – an interesting experience for me. I can say that I was never wedded to any one particular methodology – but had an eclectic approach and used anything that worked, from a variety of methods and materials.

One of the highlights of my 11 years at Sydney University was when one of my students, after taking the ACICIS program at UGM in Yogyakarta during the 1998 economic and political meltdown in Indonesia, was inspired to form the OzIndo Project. She rode a bicycle round Australia to raise money to provide relief for some of the impoverished people and to raise awareness about Indonesia and ordinary Indonesian people in general. She asked me to join the crew as a support person, which I did. This was an amazing experience as we travelled some 17,000 km and visited hundreds of towns. We were astonished to find kids learning Indonesian in all sorts of schools, large and small, all around the country. As we addressed community groups, churches and service clubs we often encountered a great lack of knowledge about

Indonesia and plenty of fear of the unknown, but in most cases a genuine hunger for information. One of the crew was a young Indonesian man. He was a wonderful ambassador for his country and the first Indonesian most of these country people had ever met. Their generosity to our cause was outstanding

The great reward for me, as I am sure it must be for any teacher, has been watching the progress of students and seeing them take their Indonesian experience into their lives in some way: in their professions, their personal lives – specially if they married Indonesians, or just in maintaining an ongoing interest.

I count myself lucky to have found my new horizons through my knowledge of Indonesia – its language, its culture and its people. I can go there, and despite differences in ethnicity, gender and age, I can feel at home and engage in conversation with anybody. What could be more satisfying than to go and ride in a horse and cart (in Lombok), stop in a little village and haggle fiercely and happily for some basket ware, then get talking to the vendor, be invited in for a cup of tea and a chat about our grandchildren, and then try to refuse offers of more goods as gifts 'for friendship', goods more valuable than those I had just bought.

I do not know why Indonesian and Australians get on so well at the people to people level – but they do, if they have the chance to engage meaningfully with each other, and have done since they first got together back in the forties. It is sad that it seems there will be fewer Australians having the opportunity to gain the understanding and knowledge of Indonesia that have so much enriched my life, because of the parlous state of Indonesian language study in this country.

2. INDONESIAN AT SYDNEY UNIVERSITY IN THE EARLY 1960S[1]

Stuart Robson

Monash University

The following remarks are based mainly on reminiscences from the time when I personally participated in the development of Indonesian language and studies at the University of Sydney in the early 1960s.

Teaching had begun in 1958, two years before I enrolled in 1960. The subject was called 'Indonesian and Malayan Studies', and was a second and third year subject. The first generation of students included Glenda Adams (1939–2007), who went on to write novels, and Toni Barrett, who later wrote a PhD on Old Javanese inscriptions at the School of Oriental and African Studies (SOAS) in London. Japanese and Chinese were already being taught in the Department of Oriental Studies, under Professor A. R. 'Bertie' Davis (M.A. Cambridge).[2]

The first appointment in the Department of Indonesian and Malayan Studies was Dr F. H. van Naerssen (1904–1974),[3] known as Kees to his friends. He came from an old Indies family and had grown up in Klaten (Central Java), so he had a strong affinity with Java and had the almost 'mystical' air of a silver-haired sage. He had taken a doctorate on Old Javanese epigraphy at the University of Leiden in 1941, immediately before this was closed during the German occupation; after the war he spent some time in Kalimantan observing the Dayaks, and then got a job teaching sociology at Wageningen Agricultural College.

But his lectures always brought him back to the inscriptions, and in no time he would be rambling on about 'those palmy days of Majapahit' (his little joke) or Ken Angrok's outrageous deeds – things that meant very little to a bunch

---

1 First published in *RIMA: Review of Indonesian and Malaysian Affairs*, 42 (1) (2008): 185–189. Republished with permission.
2 Founded in 1922, with Professor A.L. Sadler.
3 See the obituary for him written by Peter Worsley, in *RIMA* 10 (1) (1976), pp. 33–8.

of Australian students at that time, especially in view of his broken English and the need to ask one of the students for help translating from the Dutch ('Ria, how say you?'). However, somehow he managed to convey an image of early Java that was highly attractive, probably because of its remoteness and romance. The very mention of Old Javanese or palm-leaf manuscripts was enough to send the imagination racing. He smoked four cigarettes per lecture hour, and took coffee in the morning and tea in the afternoon, not to mention a half-hour nap after lunch: ten minutes to get there, ten minutes there, and ten minutes to get back. Then he would be available again.

For the language side, the first appointment was Dr A. H. Hill (1913-1961),[4] who before the war had taught science in Malaya, had done some Malay under R. O. Winstedt at SOAS, and in 1938 joined the Federated Malay States Volunteer Force. He saw action against the Japanese in Malaya and after the British surrender managed to escape. After the war he became an Inspector of Schools in Pahang. This explains why his idea of language was the Malay of Malaya – or perhaps the British idea of it, as in 'Dear soda piggy' [= Dia sudah pergi]. It was said that Indonesian would also be taught, but with some regret, as Indonesian was not a proper language, just Malay gone wrong. After all, it had a lot of Dutch mixed in it, and scarcely possessed a literature, a prerequisite for respectability. Dr Hill's scholarly work consisted of an annotated translation of the *Hikayat Abdullah* (1955), a romanisation and English translation of the *Hikayat Raja-raja Pasai* (1960), and some articles, all published in the *Journal of the Royal Asiatic Society* (JMBRAS). He was killed in a plane crash on 24 January 1961, somewhere outside Bandung.

This ushered in the 'emergency year', so called as there was no one to teach language, so Van Naerssen managed to find a Dutchman called Fischer, who was thought to know some Indonesian. He was told to read the *Tjerita dari Blora* with second year students. This was a risky undertaking, and there was some debate about the difference between *dibawa ke randjang* and *di bawah krandjang*.[5]

As language textbooks we had E. Pino's *Bahasa Indonesia for English-speaking Students* (1954) (Vol. 1), and S. van der Molen's *Bahasa Indonesia, An elementary textbook of the Indonesian language … adapted for the use of English-speaking students* (second edition, 1952) – which still had a strong whiff of the Dutch

---

4   Obituary in *Journal of the Malaysian Branch of the Royal Asiatic Society* 35(1) (1962). Hill also wrote a book about his experiences in Malaya, *Diversion in Malaya* (1948). Thanks to Russell Jones for this information.

5   Probably this relates to the sentence 'Bunda membawa daku ke ranjang', on page 12 of the Hasta Mitra edition (1994).

'Maleis' of the colonial period. The dictionary was E. Pino and T. Witterman's *Kamus Inggeris* (two volumes, second edition, 1955); for some odd reason the English-Indonesian volume is much bigger than the Indonesian-English one.

But rescue was at hand, with the appointment of Russell Jones, who arrived from London on 24 August 1961, after a five-week voyage aboard the *Johan van Oldenbarnevelt* (20,000 tons). Russell would stay till 20 June 1965, and in that time taught Malay with energy and a solid background knowledge obtained in the civil service in Malaya, followed by academic study at SOAS.

This was an exciting time, when Australia was just waking up to the existence of Asia. Some enterprising people went forth and discovered Indonesia. They returned full of enthusiasm and told of their experiences, meeting the Indonesians and exploring a new culture. The newspapers were full of reports about the West Irian crisis, when Indonesia demanded that this remnant of the East Indies be surrendered by the Dutch and become part of Indonesia. Visiting Java for the first time at the end of 1963 and early 1964, the scenes of poverty and filth in Jakarta, and the dire straits of the farmers in the countryside, made a deep impression on a boy from humdrum Chatswood. Not only was the economy in meltdown, but trouble was clearly brewing, with Soekarno's fierce campaign to *Ganjang Malaysia* ('Crush Malaysia!'; NB old spelling), and truck-loads of troops cruising the streets. The British Embassy had recently been burnt.

At this point special mention has to be made of the role of Indonesian students in Australia at that time. Some had come under the Colombo Plan to study, and there was a group at Sydney University studying English. The names Eddy Harjono (from Muntilan) and Soemarjono (from Wates) come to mind. They were eagerly sought out by students of Indonesian, and this formed the basis for friendships that lasted – proof that person-to-person relationships can be more powerful and valuable than governmental or official ones. This is how we are sometimes accepted into Indonesian society, as 'family', and treasure the things we have learned from such relationships.

Two more appointments in this period are worth mentioning. The number of students was large, requiring more staff. Mr H. W. Emanuels, of Surinam Javanese background and with training in law, arrived from Europe where he had collaborated with Prof. A. Teeuw on the bibliography *A Critical Survey of Studies on Malay and Bahasa Indonesia* that appeared in 1961. He taught Indonesian in a precise and pleasant manner and was well liked. He was the first to allude to the 'object construction' in grammar, and was keen on correct translation. His critical edition of the *Undang-undang Malaka* was at an advanced stage. He died suddenly in September 1966 in tragic circumstances.

Another arrival was Drs T. S. Lee (Lie Tjwan Sioe), who had a degree from Universitas Indonesia. He was the first to produce a textbook for Australian secondary students, *Introducing Indonesian* (Book I, 1965).

From the previous discussion certain trends can be traced. The courses were in the beginning divided equally between 'language' and 'studies'. There were several reasons for this. Firstly, in those days Asian components had not yet been included in 'mainstream' departments, so history and sociology of Indonesia had to be given as well as language. These would supply some of the background needed for language and might fill the void to some extent. Secondly, there was a perception that Indonesian was not a 'heavy' subject in the same sense as Japanese or Chinese, with their vast and venerable literatures and indigenous scholarly traditions. One lecturer in Japanese jokingly referred to Indonesian and Malayan Studies as 'Jungle and Swamp Studies'. There was not enough time for language study under these arrangement, and the standard was desperately low – after two years we could still not hold a conversation in Indonesian. This was of course long before the appearance of the language laboratory. Malay and Malaya finally disappeared from the menu.

But there was an Honours level, where we could go deeper into other things: there was an introduction to Javanese (*Damar Wulan*), and Old Javanese (*Adiparwa*). Mr Lee, a gentleman who had retired from the Indian Civil Service, discussed the Sanskrit loanwords in Indonesian, and Russell Jones gave some elementary Dutch for reading purposes, as well as an introduction to the Jawi script. The Honours group for 1962 consisted of four: Peter Worsley, Harry Aveling, George Miller and Stuart Robson. All would make a contribution to the study in the course of their careers.

The question of academic lineage is important. Because of Van Naerssen's influence, it was natural to look to Leiden. At that time Leiden was felt to be the 'Mecca' of Indonesian studies. So it was also only natural for first Peter and Louise Worsley in 1964, and then Stuart and Rosemary Robson in 1965, to pack their bags and board a ship for the Netherlands, planning to seek out the scholars in the fabled city of Leiden, and with the intention of returning home with the treasures won there for the benefit of Indonesian studies in Australia. But it would take some time for that to bear fruit …

3. THE '60S, THE STUDENT AND PAK EMANUELS

An Indonesian Adventure

Ron Witton

Freelance Translator and Interpreter

It was in February 1962 that I started a Bachelor of Arts degree at the University of Sydney. I was 18 and had just completed my Leaving Certificate at North Sydney Boys High School. In those days it was assumed that students who completed their studies at the school would go on to university. It was a selective state high school and virtually all of us completed our final – fifth – year, and were awarded a Commonwealth Government University Scholarship. The scholarship paid for the minimal fees charged for university study.

In truth, I had absolutely no idea what I wanted to do with my life. I only knew that after high school one went to 'uni', and so off I went. At school I had done well in languages, which in those days meant German and French. The fact that my parents had been pre-war German-Jewish refugees had of course helped me with my language studies, and I achieved honours in German and French. Our language learning at school was, in retrospect, a dull mechanical process that in no way brought the languages to life. Indeed, the teaching methods somewhat reflected the way such subjects as mathematics were taught, given that learning a language was predominantly a written exercise where marks were deducted for errors.

Having no life goals, I was not sure what to study at university. I therefore chose subjects in which I had done well at school. Hence I enrolled in German, French and, because I happened to have fluked a reasonable pass in Economics in the Leaving Certificate, I also took Economics (although in fact I had no real interest in the subject). University was, for me (and I suspect many of my fellow students) something one just did, and in many ways it resembled a continuation of high school.

The '60s, the Student and Pak Emanuels

Figure 1: Albert Kwee in the Fisher Library in 1962.
Photo Ron Witton.

A few weeks into the first term at university, a significant event occurred that was to change my life. One day I was studying in the former Fisher Library, located at the southern end of the Arts Quadrangle. That was the time when we actually borrowed books and sometimes even read them; there being no such thing as the internet and Wikipedia. I happened to be sitting next to an Asian student and we got talking. It turned out he was Indonesian and, who knows why, he began to teach me a bit of Indonesian. I was truly amazed. Here was a language with no conjugations and no declensions! What's more, it was an Asian language that had no tones and was written in Latin script! The student, Albert Kwee (see Figure 1), and I began to meet regularly and I found fairly soon that I could construct simple sentences and felt more at ease speaking it than I ever did with French during the five years I had studied it at high school.

I then found out that the University of Sydney was actually teaching this language. I went with a sense of wonder to the Department of Indonesian and Malayan Studies, and soon after amended my enrolment at the university registry. I enrolled in Indonesian and Malayan Studies, thus taking four subjects, the maximum number allowed in first year. The next day I attended my first lecture and began formal learning in a language I had only just discovered.

By the end of my first lecture I was enchanted by the language. In retrospect, I realise that my enthralment was due to the energetic, entertaining and absolutely engrossing style of the lecturer, Mr Hedwig Emanuels, whom we quickly learnt to call 'Pak Emanuels'. He was a dapper gentleman with a neat moustache and the dark skin of a Javanese. However, as he often reminded us, he hailed from Suriname, former Dutch Guiana, on the northeast coast of South America. His Javanese forebears had been brought there as indentured labourers by the Dutch, in the same way that Indonesians, mainly Javanese, worked as indentured labourers in the British colony of Queensland and the French colony of New Caledonia. Pak Emanuels told us that he had been adopted by a Dutch family, which explained how he had acquired a Dutch name. He had academic expertise in Indonesian linguistics. His Indonesian was precisely articulated and was usually accompanied by an engaging smile and a twinkle in his eye, which endeared him to all of us. As one can see from the photo (Figure 2), he was amazingly adept at 'chalk and talk'.

With clarity and precision, he drew circles around the prefixes and suffixes that modify an Indonesian root word so that, in a most regular manner, one can produce a great variety of meanings. Thus from a two-syllable root word, one can generally create a verb (whether intransitive or transitive, or both, and if transitive, whether active or passive). Add a different prefix and/or suffix, and a variety of nouns can be produced, often including gerunds. Many of us had done three years of Latin and this proved to be invaluable in understanding grammar. But for those who did not have such a background, Pak Emanuels, with his coloured chalk circling and highlighting prefixes and suffices, could explain all.

What was most amazing, however, was that all this learning was done while reading, from the very first day, a story in Indonesian. There were no abstract grammar lessons as such. Everything was learnt in the context of reading an Indonesian story and analysing each word as it appeared. I can still remember our first story, about a dull fellow called 'Dul Kampret' ('Abdul the Bat').

The '60s, the Student and Pak Emanuels

Figure 2: A picture of Pak Emanuels taken surreptitiously in class by the author ca 1962.
Photo Ron Witton.

Often we would spend a whole class on just one or two sentences, exploring all the aspects of language demonstrated. As a result, language was learnt *in context* and allowed for many diversions into the fascinating by-ways of culture, history and social context that words and phrases reveal about Indonesian society and history. Before long we were made aware of the richness and diversity of a country to our north, of which many of us had had no prior understanding. In addition, we were soon reading, still in the pre-1972 Indonesian spelling, classic novels such as *Semasa Ketjil di Kampung* by Muhamad Radjab, and famous short stories, such as those by Idrus in his collection *Dari Ave Maria ke Djalan Lain Ke Roma*.

I cannot stress how important it was that Pak Emanuels taught us, through his entertaining and innovative style, to understand the whole grammatical structure of the language from the very beginning. Many of us went on to become teachers of Indonesian and his idiosyncratic approach informed our teaching styles. As a result of his dedication and charisma, student numbers of this fledgling department grew exponentially, and indeed began to threaten the traditional empires of French and German! An article in the Sydney Press, entitled 'Indonesian: the up and coming-language' (*The Sun-Herald*, 4 August 1963) began with the words 'A rush to learn Indonesian has begun in Sydney' and the article was accompanied by a photo of Pak Emanuels with three of us in one of his classes (Figure 3).

Figure 3: Report of the exponential growth in Indonesian studies.
The Sun-Herald, 4 August 1963, pg. 48.

The article reported how Pak Emanuels was assisting in the development of a curriculum in Indonesian for the NSW Department of Education and worked closely with the Sydney Teachers' College. As a result, there was within a decade an exponential growth in the number of Indonesian language teachers in NSW schools and, as the article reports, the beginning of a long-running controversy about the role of Asian languages in Australia's school curricula and the threat they posed to the long-held dominant role of French and German.

Pak Emanuels encouraged us to speak the language as much as we could. There were many Indonesians on campus, often recipients of Colombo Plan scholarships, and he helped create situations where we could practise our language skills outside the classroom. Occasionally there were weekend intensives that Indonesian students would attend (see Figure 4), helping us with our language fluency.

The '60s, the Student and Pak Emanuels

Figure 4: Weekend intensive in the early 60s:
Left to right: Evelyn Erikson (now Diradji), Andres Perendi, Franke Hutabarat (an Indonesian student who helped us, now deceased), Pak Emanuels, [unknown student], and Jill Cridland (now Sutanto).
Courtesy of Ron Witton.

By the end of first year I could not wait to see the fabulous country I had learnt so much about. In December 1962 I set off (by boat), armed with the addresses of many of the families of Indonesian students who had become my friends in Sydney.

Disembarking at Tanjung Priok, Jakarta's port, in December 1962 remains one of the most vivid memories of my life. Hearing Indonesian being spoken, and being enveloped in the swirling sights, sounds, tastes and smells of colourful Indonesian life was an experience like no other.

For the next three months, I travelled through Java, Bali, Sumatra, Penang, the Malay Peninsula, Singapore and Kalimantan. In Palembang (a city in Sumatra) I was 'adopted' by Bambang Utoyo, a former Indonesian Army Chief of Staff, and his wife, Ibu Siti, who were both Scrabble addicts like my parents. The Utoyo family later moved back to Jakarta and have remained my 'second' family to this day. In later years they also became good friends with my parents, who also visited Indonesia. The Utoyo children are like my second set of siblings, and I still stay with them and their families whenever I visit Indonesia.

After three months of deep immersion in Indonesian life and language, during which I can still remember vivid dreams in which I spoke Indonesian and re-lived my daily experiences, I travelled back to Australia through 'West Irian' and witnessed the last days of the transition of that territory from post-Dutch UN administration to Indonesian control.

I returned to Australia with my language skills finely honed – a tribute to the thorough grounding that Pak Emanuels, with his chalk and blackboard, had given me – and a deep affection for Indonesia that has lasted my whole life.

At the end of second year I travelled to Noumea, New Caledonia, where there is a small but vibrant Javanese population (they were brought there last century as migrant labour). I lived in an Indonesian restaurant run by the family of an Indonesian student at the University of Sydney. My friend's father was also the *dalang* (puppeteer) of the local *wayang* group. This connection gave me further practice in speaking Indonesian.

This second period of immersion in Indonesian family life, albeit in a French-speaking colony, meant that Indonesian had become almost a second language to me. On my return to Sydney to begin my third year of studies, I was asked to help tutor first year students.

The Indonesian Consulate in Sydney was most supportive of Indonesian studies, particularly Pak Ali Marsaban, the Indonesian Cultural Attaché, who donated many books and other material to the department.

One of the most memorable experiences of our time at university was that at lunchtime once a week we would sing Indonesian songs with Kris Biantoro, who later became one of Indonesia's most famous singers and film stars. At the time he was an assistant to Pak Ali Marsaban at the Indonesian Consulate. Kris' lively, exuberant and entertaining personality meant that, before long, we had overcome our somewhat repressed Western reserve and would sing our hearts out at these lunchtime gatherings.

Many of us were immersed in the wonderful world that Indonesian students were creating for themselves in Sydney. In this they were often assisted by the networks nurtured by the Australian-Indonesian Association. Many members of this venerable Association had been involved in the struggle for Indonesian Independence that had occurred a little over a decade before. Some of them had been involved in the events in Sydney, when Dutch ships were prevented from leaving Sydney Harbour – events that were vividly portrayed in Joris Ivens' film *Indonesia Calling*, a film that became very familiar to us as we studied about the Indonesian revolution and Australia's support for that struggle.

Figure 5: Two covers from Kris Biantoro's many very popular cassettes. After he returned from Australia he became a national entertainment figure.
Courtesy of Biantoro family.

Figure 6: In 1964 the Australia-Indonesia Association held its fourth annual symposium on Australian-Indonesian relations in Sydney. The Indonesian Ambassador, Brigadier-General Suadi Suromihardo, who gave the keynote address, is seen here with Mr A Seymour Shaw, President of the Australia-Indonesia Association, A Badjabir, an Indonesian student, and Ronald Witton, then President of the University of Sydney Indonesian Study Group.
National Archives Australia A1501, A5032/2.

We also had occasional contact with the Indonesian Embassy in Canberra, and with Brigadier-General Suadi Suromihardo, the ambassador, who had fought against the Dutch in the revolution.

At the end of my third year, I again travelled to Indonesia to collect material for my honours thesis on the speeches of President Sukarno. I was able to hear him give one of his electrifying speeches at Senayan Stadium (now called the Gelora Bung Karno Stadium) and even managed to have breakfast with him at the Jakarta Presidential Palace. He asked about Indonesian studies in Australia and even made me prove that Kris Biantoro was teaching us by having me sing an Indonesian song. He then gave me a book of his speeches, which he inscribed to me, providing invaluable material for my honours thesis.

By this time, early 1965, there was increasing political tension among Indonesia's political parties, and particularly the very strong Indonesian Communist Party, the Army and resurgent Islam. I witnessed many political demonstrations and events.

At the end of 1965 I graduated with honours in Indonesian and Malayan Studies and then completed a Masters Degree in the Department before travelling to Cornell for my doctoral studies. The thorough grounding in the Indonesian and Malaysian languages I received in the Department has stood me in good stead for the rest of my life and I continue to work as an Indonesian interpreter and an Indonesian and Malaysian language translator.

The friendships the Australian students who studied Indonesian at Sydney University and the Indonesian students who helped them with their language, continued for more than fifty years. Albert Kwee, who taught me my first Indonesian words at that chance meeting in 1962, was best man at my wedding, as was I at his. He married an Australian and lived in Sydney. Until his recent death, I enjoyed meeting him from time to time to reminisce. Kris Biantoro, who returned to Indonesia and became a mega-star there, also remained a good friend until his death in 2013. There were also marriages, many of which have lasted for over fifty years, including Jill Cridland who married John Sutanto, and Evelyn Erikson who married Kamaludin Diradji. Most Colombo Plan students returned home and many later went on to hold influential positions in Indonesia.

A group of us who studied Indonesian at the University of Sydney in the 1960s have recently begun to meet again on a regular basis. For all of us, our Indonesian studies had been a pivotal experience in orienting our lives towards Indonesia and Asia generally. In 2014, having heard of the sad demise of Kris Biantoro, we took the opportunity to send a photo of us holding books by Kris, to his family in Jakarta (Figure 7).

The '60s, the Student and Pak Emanuels

It is my belief that Pak Emanuels' sudden and tragic death in 1966 contributed to the end an era of rapid Indonesian language expansion that had laid the basis for Indonesian studies in Sydney and beyond. These days of course there are language labs, DVDs and all manner of electronic teaching aids. While one cannot deny their helpfulness in assisting language learning, I remain convinced that the inspirational, enthusiastic and, above-all, logical approach developed by Pak Emanuels, together with access to students from Indonesia who were also studying at the university, is what is required to inspire and motivate students. I for one will remain eternally grateful that I was one of Pak Emanuels' students.

Figure 7: 50 years on: a reunion of students from Sydney University Indonesian and Malayan Studies students in 2014.
Standing (left to right): Julia McAdam/Herjandono, Margaret Malhas (nee Brierley), Ron Witton, Andres Perendi, Jill Sutanto (nee Cridland), Paul Cohen.
Seated (left to right): Toni Pollard, Ruth Holmes, Anne McCarthy.

Courtesy of Ron Witton

4. WEBS AND RAINBOWS

Accomplished Language Teaching and *Pelangi* Magazine Bridging Indonesia with Australia

Lesley Harbon

University of Technology Sydney

A key concept within the current thinking among contemporary intercultural languages education scholars is that when we are teaching a language we are actually teaching culture, and that teachers and resources mediate the learning of that culture (Buttjes & Byram, 1991; Harbon, 2007; Moran, 2001). Looking back over my forty (plus) year involvement with the learning and teaching of Indonesian in Australia, I have seen evidence that language teachers and the learning resources they provide for their learners, do, in fact, mediate in the learning of cultural knowledge.

I myself am a product of an education system that has allowed me to come into contact with accomplished Indonesian teachers and engaging Indonesian language and culture learning materials. I have learned Indonesian language, and I have learned about the cultures in Indonesia, alongside very accomplished (in my opinion) language teachers both at school and at university. So inspired by their teaching was I that decided to learn the craft of Indonesian teaching myself.

Over the past 20 years I have taught alongside wonderful Indonesian teacher colleagues, observed others from afar, collaborated with native-speaker and non-native speaker Indonesian teachers, comical and serious ones, young and not so young ones. I have learned from resources and materials that had me translate from one language into the other, and which gave me insights into ways of living of Indonesian people. I have engaged with photographs in textbooks that allowed me to escape into another world. I have been involved in the publication of *Pelangi* magazine in the eighties and nineties, and more recently an intercultural textbook series, *Dari Kami Ke Kita* (Morgan, Kohler & Harbon, 2011). I believe I have led an enriched life because of all my culture learning. I have learned about 'other', but I have more importantly perhaps, learned a lot about 'self'.

My reflections in the following paragraphs allow me to indulge in an introspection of my own narrative, to reflect on accomplished Indonesian language teaching, to reflect on teacher preparation programs, to recall names of teachers who have impacted generations of learners of Indonesian in Australia, and to recount the story of *Pelangi* magazine, a particular resource that may be considered to have impacted a generation of Indonesian language teachers and their students in Australia and beyond.

I have chosen two metaphors to explain and make sense of my reflections adding a very personal flavour to this volume. The first is the image of a web. The way I see it, the Indonesian language teacher network over the past 40 years is woven together in a web, and Indonesian language teaching has managed to connect people across Australia and beyond. Like a web encasing all who encounter it, so it has been, it seems, with the connecting of Indonesianists. The lines of connection, I believe, are woven between teachers and resources, creating clear connections, bonding strongly to keep us connected. With social media now, this is even more the case.

The second metaphor I adopt to bring my reflections together is the image of the rainbow. The pelangi/rainbow metaphor was adopted by a group of us at University of Southern Queensland in the mid-1980s as we designed and published an Indonesian language learning resource, *Pelangi* magazine, continuing over 15 years. Like the web, the rainbow also has a sense of joining people and places. *Pelangi* magazine, too, played its role in bonding the Indonesianist network together.

My own story with Indonesian began in the early 1970s. I learned my first Indonesian at Galston High School in Sydney's Hills District as a student in Year 7. Our class experienced 'taster' courses of Latin, French and German, and Donna Wood, our Indonesian teacher, brought the language alive. There were other Indonesian teachers who like Donna had either trained at Sydney Teachers College, or who were teaching Indonesian at this time, from the early-mid 1970s. I recall names such as Geoff Woollams, Peter Reynolds, Louise Robert-Smith, Leonie Wittman, Cheryl Taylor, Jane Jacobs and Wendy Gray. I was being caught up in these first strands of the 'web'.

As an undergraduate in Indonesian classes at the University of Sydney between 1978 and 1980, I was being taught by teachers who had taught my teacher. I enrolled in language classes (and then later *Introductory Javanese*) with Jon Sumaryono, I elected to study Malay literature with T. S. Lie. I explored the history of the archipelago with Peter Worsley. I grappled with grammar and translation in the classes taught by Boy Joseph. I dabbled in some introductory Minang classes with Marcus Susanto. Modern Indonesian literature came alive with George Quinn and David Reeve. My own contemporaries were Jennie Brown, Cathy Watt, Sarah Moeda, Pat Skinner, Amanda Gibson, Libby Gill, Rosemary Guyatt, Ros Levitus, Sue Jackson, Katrina Hoffman, Lynne Fisher, Kerrie Murphy and Lynne Laguida. I stood in awe of others who studied there: Adrian Vickers, Ratih Hardjono, Wendy Robinson, Alex Murphy and Melissa Gould-Drakely.

My key memories of life in the Indonesian and Malayan Studies Department for those three years were not just what and who I could see, but what I could hear and smell. Who could forget Pak Sumaryono's hearty laugh, or the *selop* sound of Pak Li's slippers clapping along those corridors? Who could forget the aromas of the various professors' pipes and *kretek* cigarettes? As for inspirational teaching, it would be hard to beat Tony Day and Jennifer Lindsay's idea to blend Javanese wayang performance with Norman Hetherington's Mr Squiggle-style puppet characters in a unit of study about the arts in Indonesia. I still keep the memorabilia surrounding W. S. Rendra's visit to our hallowed halls at that time. These strands of the web were glistening and mystical (Lindy Norris, this volume, calls them 'heady days') and were nothing like I had ever experienced before.

Perplexed by the question of how to continue an involvement with Indonesian after graduation, I, like many others at the time, progressed to a one-year Graduate Diploma in Secondary Education at Sydney Teachers College, and trained as an Indonesian teacher. In 1981 there were only a small number of us in Miriam Albert's Indonesian Curriculum class: a small class compared to the more than fifty in French and German, but a much larger group than my current pre-service Indonesian teacher group in the same program nearly thirty years later, where often there is only one pre-service Indonesian teacher in the whole group of fifty. I qualified as an Indonesian teacher, not knowing how this career path would enrich my life as I moved out through higher and wider strands of the web.

My first teaching position was Indonesian teacher at Tennant Creek High School in the Northern Territory in 1982. The Northern Territory Teaching Service and the Department of Education had established Indonesian at a number of schools in the Northern Territory at that time, especially at primary schools. The reality was that Northern Territorians were travelling more to Bali and Jakarta than to Sydney, Canberra or Melbourne and were keen for their children to learn Indonesian. The Indonesian teachers in Alice Springs, Tennant Creek, Katherine and Darwin rarely gathered together to meet and share due to the isolation of each town. However, from 1982 to the end of 1984, we met 'virtually' via a cutting edge technology called 'teleconferencing'. The NT Languages Curriculum Officer, Vince Phelan, funded and supported us all in our isolation. I had now, it seems, found a place to locate myself in another area of the spider's web.

While in Tennant Creek, I received a letter of invitation from Abe Kelabora, in Melbourne, inviting me to be a founding member of the *Indonesian Cultural and Educational Institute* (ICEI). The ICEI was established in order to promote the teaching and learning of Indonesian. It was intended, among other things, to support teachers and assist with access to teaching resources. Sadly, as I lived in the Northern Territory, there was no possibility of me attending meetings in Melbourne, but at least this part of the web was spinning out to collect me in its grasp, out in the Northern Territory's 'never-never'. At an ICEI Conference in Melbourne in the mid-1980s however, I met Indonesian teachers from other states and territories, including Lindy Norris, Umi Quor, Phil Mahnken and Kathy Kiting, and we learned much from each other as we faced common problems.

From teaching at secondary level in the Northern Territory, I took hold of the web and moved interstate. I accepted a position at the Darling Downs Institute of Advanced Education (now the University of Southern Queensland) in Toowoomba. I taught Indonesian alongside Junedi Ichsan. The parts of the web were all inter-connected: Pak Ichsan was not only the author of an Indonesian textbook I had used at school, *Lantjar Berbahasa Indonesia*, but also my Indonesian teacher at an adult learning class at Macquarie University in my final year of school in 1977. My Masters level research higher degree thesis during this time examined the notion of motivation among the adult learners of Indonesian who were enrolled in our Associate Diploma in Asian Studies program (Harbon, 1990; 1991).

Colleague Indonesianists at USQ Toowoomba included Peter Wicks (also an authority on the writings of Singapore writers such as Catherine Lim), Adrian Allen (also a geographer whose vision it was to establish the Japanese Garden which sits behind the USQ campus), Philip Kitley (an Indonesianist of long standing, who moved to Jakarta for a period as Cultural Attaché at the Australian Embassy before returning to academia), and Allan Bruce (a visual arts lecturer and a strong advocate for Southeast Asian visual arts education).

It was the strong support that Ichsan and I received from our Asian Studies colleagues that assisted us in creating *Pelangi* magazine (see Figure 1), an Indonesian teaching and learning resource that supported Indonesian teaching and learning in Australian education institutions over a 15-year period. The web was now wider and stronger. *Pelangi* was published for a period of 15 years between 1985 and 1999. Darling Downs Institute Press published *Pelangi* between 1985 and 1989 and the University of Southern Queensland Press continued between 1990 and 1999. *Pelangi*'s predecessor was *Warna*

Sari, created by Pak Dede Sujatna in Western Australia years earlier. *Pelangi* took over where *Warna Sari* had left off.

The magazine was published as *Pelangi Rainbow* for 14 issues between 1985 and 1988. The name changed to *Pelangi: Australia's Cultural Magazine on Indonesia and Southeast Asia* from 1989 to 1992 for 16 issues. Then from 1993 to 1999 for the final 28 issues, the name changed again to *Pelangi: An Educational Magazine About Indonesia*. In total there were 58 issues published. Subscribers to *Pelangi* were mainly secondary school teachers of Indonesian across Australia's states and territories. Junedi Ichsan was the General Editor between 1985 and 1986, shifting to the role of Editorial Advisor in 1987. I began as Executive Editor from 1985, then became General Editor from 1987 to 1989, and Editor from 1989 to 1999.

The first Editorial Advisory Board included Peter Wicks, Adrian Allen, Philip Kitley and Allan Bruce. Ross Steele joined the Board between 1986 and 1988. Wenny Dahlan joined the Board after 1990; Richard Gehrmann and David Williams joined after 1995. Between 1998 and 1999, the Editorial Advisory Board comprised Philip Kitley, David Williams, Julia Read, Linda Hibbs, Gerard Ross and Yacinta Kurniasih. We were joined by Henny Supolo Sitepu as Consultant Editor in Jakarta from 1994. Desmawati Radjab from Universitas Negeri Padang was our native-speaker proof-reader from 1998 to 1999.

Pelangi, with its underlying metaphorical image of a bridge between the cultures and the source of the 'pot of gold', published the writing of many authors over the 15-year period. It included travelogues, short stories, interviews, descriptive narratives, case studies, research, in-country program reviews, book reviews, recipes and jokes among other things. I interviewed the famous I Wayan Gandra (Balinese gamelan), Peter Mares (radio's *Asia Pacific* program), the author Umar Kayam, and a particular highlight for me was the opportunity to interview W.S Rendra on one of his visits to Canberra. The Australian Foreign Minister at the time, Gareth Evans, wrote the foreword for our 50th issue. Among the notable contributors were Harry Aveling, Sujit Mudjirno, Allan Bruce, George Quinn, Bryce Alcock, Toni Pollard, Julia Read, Les Brooking, June Ross and Dede Sujatna. *Pelangi* can even pride itself on publishing the earlier writing of Dewi Anggraeni and Ikrar Nusa Bakti.

As an added focus for primary school learners of Indonesian, reflecting my own move into teaching Indonesian at primary level, was the addition of *Pelcil (Pelangi Kecil)*, a pull-out section of each edition of the magazine where teachers in early childhood education could construct their own small early reader. The storylines and simple language and culture notions worked well in primary school language programs.

Figure 1: Cover from the first issue of *Pelangi* magazine Volume 1, number 1 1986.

Wenny Dahlan, daughter of the Canberra-based Indonesian writer, Achdiat Karta Mihardja, whose novels were in the curriculum I had studied at The University of Sydney as an undergraduate at the end of the 1970s, was soon recruited to replace both Ichsan and I after our respective moves away from USQ: Ichsan to Northern Territory University (now Charles Darwin University), and me to Parkes in the Central West of New South Wales. The web where I was now located took on other foci and meaning.

This next interstate move saw me progress into primary school Indonesian teaching. I became Indonesian teacher at Parkes Public School for a six-year period between 1990 and 1995. The children who began learning Indonesian in Year 1 with me in 1990 graduated from primary school at the end of 1995, having experienced an Indonesian language learning program of close to 200 hours, which by no means gave them any level of real spoken or written proficiency, rather an awareness that different people from different parts of the world speak in a different code and one of them is Indonesian.

My time at Parkes Public School allowed me to take over the weaving of different parts of the web. Because of *Pelangi* magazine, Parkes became known as a centre for the learning and teaching of Indonesian language and culture. We received visits from the Sydney Consul General of the Republic of Indonesia, we visited the Indonesian Embassy in Canberra. We linked with Yolanda Albina's program at Daramalan College in Canberra and her Computer Assisted Language Learning which was clearly motivating learners there.

Parkes was a hub for a series of visits by Indonesian exchange students. Families in the town hosted Rotary and Lions exchange students from Indonesia, and my own family hosted a 17 year old AFS Exchange student from Kudus Central Java for a year in 1992. As well as studying Year 11 and assisting with various *Pelangi* tasks, Adim Dwi Putranti became an engaging assistant teacher for the Indonesian program at Parkes Public School. She called herself the '*kamus berjalan*'. Interestingly the web has extended as far as Kudus, Central Java now, where Adim has opened *Pelita Nusantara* bilingual playgroup, with much of her curriculum built upon what she learned about early childhood education in Australia.

The web was expanding even in the Central West of New South Wales. Indonesian language programs sprang up at Bogan Gate under the direction of Indonesian teacher Lynn Britt, at Red Bend College Forbes with Indonesian teacher Dawn Phipps, and with Gae Golsby in Young. The web we had woven in Bogan Gate and Parkes stretched out to enlist the assistance of Russell Darnley and Tina Pentes of Asia Field Study Centres, and we took a student and parent study tour to Bali in 1994 from Parkes and Bogan Gate.

The web's outreach connected with Indonesian-focused activity at Charles Sturt University, Bathurst. My work with Julia Robertson, Bob Hill and Noel Thomas involved Indonesian teacher re-training. How curious now that the web had spun me closer to eventually meeting David T. Hill OAM, Bob Hill's brother from Murdoch University in Perth.

In the mid-1990s I moved to take up the position of Lecturer in Primary Languages in the Faculty of Education at The University of Tasmania. I reflect that the web continued to be strongly woven during that time. Indonesian teacher education in the Faculty of Education at The University of Tasmania between 1996 and 2002 remained chiefly in the Bachelor of Education (Early Childhood and Primary) degree program on the Launceston campus. Within the structure of the four year degree, there was the opportunity for pre-service primary teachers to elect either a beginner or continuers Indonesian language course. This is where I came across Faculty of Arts lecturers Phil Mahnken (initially in Launceston, before his move to the Sunshine Coast), Ismet Fanany (also in Launceston, before his move to Deakin University), Pam Allen (from the Hobart campus), and later Barbara Hatley (Launceston campus). Pam's inspired teaching and curriculum offerings meant that as many as 15 pre-service teachers in each year cohort came through with an Indonesian language expertise, and these graduates were able to contribute to staffing the Primary Languages policy implemented in Tasmanian schools at the time. These young teachers were to receive outstanding support from stalwarts such as Phil Mahnken, Pam Allen, Umi Quor, Kaye Wilson, and later Julie Browett and Greg Ashman. The accomplished Indonesian teachers in Tasmania at the time included Jo McGee, Umi Quor, Vicki Brumby, Ingrid Coleman, Vicki Fischmann, Vicki Hales, Jan Paine – to name just a few.

Ismet Fanany's relationship with the State University of Padang in West Sumatra Indonesia, meant that he had a well-established in-country Indonesian language intensive course in Padang. I was able to build on this for language teacher education, offering a similar program with an in-school teaching component after winning an Australia-Indonesia Institute Grant which led to me coordinating the Australia Indonesia Rural Areas Exchange Scheme (AIRAES) program in 1998 and 1999. The AIRAES participants that year still keep in touch with me and with each other: many among the Australian group, the wonderful Declan, Gary, Rod, Steve, Jaclyn, Lamanda, Angela, Hayley, Suzanna and Belinda, are still engaging with Indonesia. Every now and then I receive emails from many of the Indonesia group too, including Afrianto Daud who has undertaken postgraduate study in Australia since that time. My research work with Professor Atmazaki at Universitas Negeri Padang still continues.

I jointly offered, with University of Tasmania academics, Michele McGill and Mary Fearnley-Sander respectively, two further 'short term international experiences' (STIE) in Tasmania before I moved to The University of Sydney in 2002. In-country professional development programs are enrichment experiences for pre-service teachers, and they are now included (at least for Asian languages) in the Commonwealth government's Endeavour Language Teacher Fellowships programs.

Well entrenched in the 'web', I continued in my role with the preparation of more Indonesian language teachers through the first decade of this century. As well, I have accompanied my pre-service Indonesian teachers to the early childhood classroom of Veronica Carnell, daughter of Steven and Esther Dharmanto, whom I had met during our undergraduate years at Universitas Kristen Satya Wacana in Salatiga, Central Java, the venue of Sydney University's In-Country Indonesian Language Program, where Sydney students fast-tracked their degree by studying in-country, essentially a predecessor to ACICIS.

A report, *The Current State of Indonesian Language Education in Australian Schools* (Kohler & Mahnken, 2010), tells the grim story of a declining amount of Indonesian language education programs across Australia (see also chapters by Firdaus and Hill, this volume), and the picture is not much better for Indonesian language teacher preparation programs at this current time. Harbon, Fielding, Moloney, Kohler, Gearon, Dashwood and Scrimgeour (2012) mention this as they lamented the challenges for preparing language teachers in Australia at present. Yet although I have seen the decrease in numbers of pre-service secondary Indonesian teacher enrolments in the past ten years, I still believe that the beginning Indonesian teachers are clearly committed to becoming accomplished teachers.

The Endeavour Language Teacher Fellowships have provided support to Indonesian teachers over the past 10 years. However, even more support is needed to keep the cycle of teaching and learning going. Teacher re-training is one way that some state systems have coped with teacher supply issues, but when that combines with teacher retirement or teacher career direction changes, re-training cannot provide a total solution. Sadly we have to concede that there is a political side to Indonesian language teaching and learning here (see Firdaus, this volume, for a longer discussion about policy and politics impacting studies of Indonesian in Australia).

Indonesian language teacher educators around Australia – Michelle Kohler, Anne Marie Morgan, Ilian Yang, Greg Ashman and Lindy Norris notable names among them, continue to provide quality pre-service learning experiences for pre-service primary and secondary Indonesian language teachers. The web, it seems, has stretched far and wide and the rainbow has connected people, places and high quality, authentic learning materials such as *Pelangi* magazine.

In these paragraphs I have only just captured one small part of how extensive and broad sweeping the webs and rainbows actually are. In the days before the world wide web phenomenon, *Pelangi* magazine filled a gap for much-needed, authentic teaching and learning resources. Even in the far-from-ideal current context, I believe that accomplished Indonesian teachers and their cutting-edge and authentic materials are still 'making a difference' with their inspired teaching. With Bali, Boats, Bombs and Beef continually paraded on our television and social media screens, I can only emphasise once more of the importance of the 'culture learning' I mentioned at the start of my reflection.

Indonesian studies has been in the curriculum for more than 50 years now. The challenge, however, is to watch how and where the web is spun, and how far and wide the rainbow settles, in the next 50 years and beyond. Keeping our sights on where we are connected on the web, or where the rainbow begins and ends, is a responsibility for all of us.

References

Buttjes, D. & Byram, M. (Eds.). 1991. *Mediating Languages and Cultures*. Clevedon, UK: Multilingual Matters.

Harbon, L. 2007. 'On the need to mediate culture: Do college English textbooks pass the test?' In *The Exploration and Prospective of College English Textbook*, edited by D. L. Qiu & J. G. Cai. Shanghai: Fudan University Press. pp. 110–131.

Harbon, L. 1990. 'Indonesian language studies in Australia: past, present and future'. *Asian Studies Review* 13 (3), pp. 33–39.

Harbon, L. 1991. 'Learning Indonesian over distance: A case study'. Masters thesis, Armidale, NSW: University of New England.

Harbon, L., Fielding, R., Moloney, R., Kohler, M., Dashwood, A., Gearon, M. & Scrimgeour, A. 2012. 'Longtime passing: Language teacher educators' concerns in language teacher education'. In *The Next Step: Introducing the Languages and Cultures Network for Australian Universities*, edited by J. Hajek, C. Nettelbeck & A. Woods. Melbourne: Languages and Cultures Network for Australian Universities. pp. 75 – 91.

Kohler, M., & Mahnken, P. 2010. *The Current State of Indonesian Language Education in Australian Schools. Report to Department of Education, Employment and Workplace Relations*. Canberra: Curriculum Corporation.

Moran, P. R. 2001. *Teaching Culture: Perspectives in Practice*. Boston, MA: Heinle & Heinle.

Morgan, A. M., Kohler, M. & Harbon, L. 2011. 'Developing intercultural language learning textbooks: Methodological trends, engaging with the intercultural construct, and personal reflections on the process'. *International Association for Research on Textbooks and Educational Media (IARTEM) E-Journal* 4 (1), pp. 20–51.

5. INDONESIAN LITERATURE AND THE AUSTRALIAN UNIVERSITY

A Personal Journey

Keith Foulcher

University of Sydney

In the 1960s and '70s, when the teaching and learning of Indonesian began to take root in Australian universities, the study of literature was widely seen as a natural progression from the early stages of language learning. For many students of the time, the study of a literature other than English was a window on to an unknown world, an exciting first step in an ongoing engagement with a foreign country and its people. Long-established university courses in French and German literature provided a comprehensive introduction to the history of European thought and culture, equipping students who warmed to this type of study with much more broadly-based knowledge than the designation 'language and literature' might at first suggest. Literature courses were not an end in themselves, but a gateway into the wider world of history, culture and society.

Inevitably, this 'language and literature' model influenced the way Indonesian was studied and taught in the Australian universities of this era. Even when 'literature' did not figure in the designation of a university department teaching Indonesian language/s, it was always present in the undergraduate curriculum, no doubt as a reflection of its intrinsic importance in the eyes of those who devised this curriculum, but perhaps also as part of the effort to establish the legitimacy of Indonesian as a foreign language alongside the long-established departments of European (primarily French and German) and 'Oriental' (Chinese and Japanese) languages at the major Australian universities of the time. Stories abound of the widespread denigration of Indonesian as 'a language without a literature' by existing university establishments during the period when Indonesian was becoming established. Even as late as 1976, when Indonesian was introduced at Flinders University in Adelaide, it was implemented as a service course for students of the Faculty of Social Sciences, because, I was once told, the Flinders Faculty of Humanities did not regard Indonesian as an appropriate companion to its literature-based departments of French, Spanish and Italian.[1] So the study of Indonesian literature was, at least partly, designed to demonstrate, to faculty colleagues as much as to students, that Indonesian was indeed a language possessed of a literary tradition worthy of serious study.

Nevertheless, there were inherent difficulties in applying the 'language and literature' model to the study of Indonesian. The Australian National University's Department of 'Indonesian Languages and Literatures' made the problem plain: just as there was no single Indonesian 'language', so too there was no one 'literature' that could provide students with access to a knowledge of a contemporary society and a cultural and intellectual tradition along the familiar lines of French or German literature, or even the modern literature of China and Japan. The closest approximation to a literary tradition in Indonesia that fitted this model was the still very new body of writing that had come to be called 'modern Indonesian literature', written in the form of Malay that in 1928 had been designated *Bahasa Indonesia* or 'Indonesian', and which later became the national language of the independent Republic of Indonesia. At the time, this literature was seen as a new tradition that began only in the 1920s, and was made up of the work of Western-educated novelists and poets who wrote as identifiable individuals about the concerns of the modern world, so setting themselves and their work apart from what was understood as the 'traditional' literatures of the Indonesian world. Their work, it was believed, could be studied according to a universal definition of modern literature, as a counterpart to the long-established and familiar literatures that formed the core of other university language departments.

The assumption of universality inherent in the 'language and literature' model was further reinforced by an influence that came from English literature departments of the time, the practice of literary criticism that grew out of the then contemporary school of 'New Criticism'. This was an approach to the study of literature that held that the text itself, shorn of its associations with its author, reader and the social, cultural and historical circumstances

---

[1] The broader context of this decision was undoubtedly the widely-held view at this time that the study of Indonesia properly belonged within a Social Sciences context. The wheel does continue to turn, however. Indonesian at Flinders eventually evolved into a full undergraduate major from beginners to Honours level, and in 2014 it became a program offered through the Department of Languages in the School of Humanities and Creative Arts.

of its production, was the sole and proper object of study. Judgements about a text's value and meaning were to be encouraged, but only through close reading and detailed analysis of its inherent aesthetic properties. It was a way of thinking about literature that reflected the philosophical underpinnings of High Modernism in Western intellectual culture of the post-war period, as well as a revolutionary urge for reform of outmoded Anglo-American models of literary criticism dating back to the Romantic era. In its home discipline of English literature, it was one of a number of competing approaches to thinking about literature that were generating a 'paradigm shift' in literary studies that was revolutionary for its times. Whether it was an appropriate framework for the study of 'modern Indonesian literature' by non-Indonesians, however, was quite another matter. New Criticism's emphasis on close reading of texts was important, but its approach to the text as an aesthetic form complete unto itself encouraged the view that literature could be studied, and judged, according to universal aesthetic criteria, without a detailed understanding of the specific context of its production. This made it a particularly inappropriate model for the study of literature by undergraduate students of 'language and literature' departments in Australian universities. It meant that students would be expected to make aesthetic judgements about texts in a language they themselves were still struggling to master, and without a deep understanding of the influences shaping the texts' character and production.

Nonetheless, this model of literary criticism had a significant impact on early attempts to replicate the 'language and literature' model in Indonesian Studies departments. It was strengthened by influences stemming from Indonesia itself, in the form of three of the pioneering teachers of Indonesian literature in Australian universities – Achdiat Kata Mihardja at the Australian National University, Idrus at Monash University and M. Balfas at the University of Sydney – three major Indonesian writers who had originally made their way to Australia as self-imposed exiles from the cultural politics of Sukarno's Indonesia. Fleeing the ideologically-driven debates and campaigns that dominated the world of Indonesian literature and art in the late Sukarno years, these men were personally and ideologically disposed to a study of literature that emphasised the aesthetic qualities of 'good literature', as against approaches that might be seen as relativising the nature of 'literature' according to contextual and historical-political factors. For them, 'literature' was a universal human endeavour, and they encouraged their students to see in Indonesian literature an expression of that universality in an Indonesian context. Anything less was a denial both of their vocation as writers and their mission as teachers of modern Indonesian literature in Australian universities.

Indonesian Literature and the Australian University

From the perspective of the later development of Indonesian Studies in Australia, this particular application of the 'language and literature' model in the undergraduate Indonesian curriculum may appear to have been a highly inauspicious beginning. It is almost as though the study of Indonesian literature was digging itself into a hole, closing itself off from ways of learning about Indonesia that would properly engage with the story of the nation and its people. For those of us who began our involvement with Indonesia in this way, there were sometimes painful challenges and reorientations waiting to be confronted at some future date. Yet it needs to be said that at the time, students who came to Indonesian studies with an affinity for the study of language and literature often found these Indonesian literature classes to be the highlight of their undergraduate experience. For someone like myself, an undergraduate student of Indonesian, as well as European languages, in the mid to late 1960s, Indonesian held out an invitation to become involved in something completely new. In contrast to my experience of university-level French and German, where the fields were so vast and impersonal, and ways of understanding literature were fully formed and seemingly impervious to change, modern Indonesian literature was a field of study just waiting to be explored, a field where an honours student in an Australian university might write the first-ever academic study of a writer and his (or marginally also, 'her') work. For a 20 year-old with a love of literature and the study of languages, what could be a better prospect and a more exciting way to embark on an academic career? Those of us who took up the study of modern Indonesian literature at this time had the great privilege of being welcomed into a community of writers and scholars on equal terms. Both Indonesian writers and the tiny number of international scholars who had written about their work saw us as friends and colleagues, as much as foreigners and students. In retrospect, it was a humbling and undeserved honour.

However for myself, it was not long before storm clouds began to gather on the horizon of this privileged existence. Monash University in the early 1970s, where I began my teaching career at the same time as completing my PhD thesis for the University of Sydney, was one of Australia's most politically-engaged academic environments. Under the influence of people like Herbert Feith, his colleagues and students, the Monash Centre of Southeast Asian Studies fostered a lively climate of debate about the nature and direction of the early New Order regime and its relation to questions of moral and political commitment in the academic study of Indonesia. Elitism in all its forms was being condemned, and Indonesian studies was being challenged to re-orient itself to engagement with the harsh realities of life for the mass of the Indonesian population. For someone like myself, who had no properly thought-through notion of the complexity of the issues being debated, and who been taught to regard 'ideology' and 'politics' as having nothing but a highly negative influence on the writing and reading of literature, this was a disturbing and disorienting environment to find myself working in. In this climate, I found it hard to maintain my early enthusiasm for the study of literature, because enthusiasm was no substitute for the solid intellectual foundation I needed in the face of the challenges I felt I was facing. It became a struggle both to complete a PhD that had been conceived in what came to feel like more innocent times, and to teach 'modern Indonesian literature' to students who – it seemed to me – needed to be engaging with more broadly-based fields of enquiry if their study of Indonesian language was to help them develop an understanding of the Indonesian nation and its people. On both counts – my thesis and my teaching – I seemed to be on the 'wrong' side of the debate, the unwitting agent of a type of academic elitism that belonged to an earlier age. It was a time of great personal and academic upheaval, and my response was ultimately somewhat drastic: I chose to leave Monash for a more broadly-based 'Indonesian language and studies' position at a teacher training institution, the Salisbury College of Advanced Education in Adelaide, South Australia. In this environment, the teaching and learning of Indonesian had a clearly-defined pragmatic purpose. It was designed to equip students with a knowledge of Indonesian language and society that would underpin their practice as classroom teachers at the primary and secondary level. Indonesian studies was taught as an academic discipline, and it was my PhD and academic background that won me the position, but the shadow of pragmatism was always present. In my last year at the College, at the behest of my head of department, I introduced a semester of classes on Indonesian literature into the final year of the academic program. I can still recall the devastation I felt when, at the end of the first class, a student approached me with the question, 'What has this got to do with my teaching?' I was so flummoxed I had no articulate reply, but the incident did serve to confirm the misgivings I had at that time about leaving my position at Monash.

Three years after my move to Adelaide, I counted myself extremely lucky to be able to return to teaching in a university environment, in the Faculty of Social Sciences at Flinders University. Flinders became my intellectual home and a source of community for the next 17 years, the secure foundation I needed to find my way back into teaching and researching in the field of modern Indonesian literature on a new basis. I did not know it at the time, but my situation then, and my subsequent 'journey back' were not simply part of a personal biography. They were reflections of the way the 'language and literature' model itself changed during this period, and in particular, the way the teaching of Indonesian literature in Australian universities came to adapt itself to the some of the ruling intellectual paradigms of the later twentieth century.

The first stage in this process is alluded to in the title of a 1991 book by Antony Easthope, *Literary into Cultural Studies*.[2] From the mid-1960s, and especially in British academic circles, the privileged position of 'literature', as against other forms of cultural expression through language and representation, such as film, popular music and media, advertising and photography, was beginning to break down. The assumption that literature, as a form of 'high' art, was somehow beyond the commercial pressures of mass culture began to be questioned, and under the influence of theorists like Raymond Williams, Stuart Hall and the Althusserian Marxists, particularly a number of influential French intellectuals of the 1970s, a new discipline of 'Cultural Studies' began to assert itself in the universities of the English-speaking world. In Indonesian Studies, the influence of the Cultural Studies model saw an explosion of interest in the study of research and teaching on Indonesian 'popular culture', displacing 'literature' as the primary focus of learning about Indonesia through the study of texts. From the later 1970s, it seemed as though the study of popular culture offered a less elitist, more immediate, and in terms of one of the most over-used words of the time, more 'relevant' way of extending the study of language through an engagement with Indonesian language texts. It was welcomed by university teachers, however, because it appeared to respond to the growing pressure at this time to equip students with vocationally-oriented skills. It offered students an assurance that they were engaging with contemporary Indonesia through a study of texts that was both enjoyable and vocationally useful.

In this environment, and for a time, in both the undergraduate curriculum and in research agendas, a dichotomy between 'high' literature (*seni sastra*) and 'popular' literature (*sastra pop*) became the norm, often to the detriment of attention to the former. Prominent Indonesian writers and critics of the 1970s, many of whose ideological opponents in the earlier debates remained silenced and incarcerated, deplored the shift away from the study of 'serious' literature, and this often resulted in a sense of an emerging gulf between Australian researchers and teachers like myself and those who

---

2   Antony Easthope, *Literary into Cultural Studies* (London and New York Routledge, 1991).

had befriended us and welcomed our interest in their national literature in earlier times. Personal disappointments and ruptures to relationships were felt on both sides, exacerbated in many cases by the increasingly oppositionist climate that characterised Australian academic approaches to the New Order at this time.

The tensions and sometimes the breakdowns in personal relationships were intensified by a development within Indonesia that somewhat paradoxically also made a major contribution to a partial re-establishment of the place of 'high' literature in the undergraduate curriculum and research agendas during the 1980s. This was the 'return to society' of a significant number of writers and scholars of literature who had been imprisoned in the purge of leftists and leftwing thought in the years immediately following the attempted coup and victorious counter-coup of September-October 1965. For the first time, those who were vanquished in the ideological and political struggles of the years before 1965 were able to tell their own stories, often making their version of events and the bases of their own commitments known to the outside world through the work of foreign researchers and teachers such as myself. For someone like me, the effect was electrifying. It re-affirmed my original commitment to the study of literature as a field of enquiry in its own right and opened up a way of entering into engagement with Indonesia and its people on an entirely new basis. It was given a powerful impetus, and came to be reflected in the university curriculum, through two more significant influences, one coming from Indonesia itself and the other from further developments in the thinking about culture, history and society in the Western academy.

The contribution to this development coming from Indonesia was the publication in the years around 1980 of the four 'Buru novels' by Pramoedya Ananta Toer. The effect of these novels on the Indonesian literary world at that time can scarcely be overestimated, because although they re-awakened old wounds between established writers and critics in Indonesia, they also brought 'serious' Indonesian literature to the attention of a mass audience, both inside Indonesia and internationally, for the very first time. In Pramoedya's hands, the historical novel came to life and fired the imagination in a way no previous example of Indonesian literature in the New Order period had ever come close to doing on a similar scale. It was as though the 'relevance' of serious imaginative writing about Indonesian experience had once more been asserted in a way that could not be ignored. For a time, it seemed as though modern Indonesian literature was set to return to a central position in the academic agenda.

Soon after this development, the thinking and teaching about Indonesian literature in Australian universities was boosted by new and interesting ways of reading and talking about literatures of all types coming in the wake of Postmodernism and its impact on the humanities and social sciences as a whole. The excesses and obscurities promoted in the name of 'Postmodernism' are now much derided, but the relativism that postmodernist approaches encouraged, and its understanding of the contingent nature of all cultural production in the contemporary world, helped dismantle the dichotomy that had arisen in Indonesian studies between 'high' literature and 'pop' culture, and the implicit claim that popular culture was somehow a more genuine reflection of Indonesian experience. In its place came recognition that there is no direct relationship between any form of cultural production and the society from which it arises. What is important is the study of process and mediation, not essence and fixed form.

In my case, two further refinements of Postmodernist thought were highly significant contributions to re-centring the role which literature had to play in the Indonesian Studies curriculum and research agenda. The first of these was the so-called New Historicism of the 1990s, a development which highlighted the importance of historical context to cultural production and the use of literature as a means of understanding cultural and intellectual history. As an intellectual framework of understanding, new historicist approaches were like a final assault on the universalist assumptions of earlier times. They drew on the relativism of Postmodernist thought to read all written texts as historical discourse, but they also exposed the complexities and rich possibilities of understanding that could be derived from a study of a canonical literary tradition and those who had brought it into being. In the Indonesian case, this type of approach was further contextualised by the lessons of Postcolonialism. This was another 1990s intellectual outgrowth of Postmodernism, which Tony Day and I, in our edited volume of 1992, *Clearing a Space: Postcolonial Readings of Modern Indonesian Literature* defined as a concern with 'the way in which literary texts ... reveal the traces of the colonial encounter, the confrontation of races, nations and cultures under conditions of unequal power relations that has shaped a significant part of human experience since the beginning of the age of European imperialism'.[3] It had taken a long time, but finally, the sense of impasse that had grown out of New Criticism's insistence that the literary text was a world unto itself

---

3   Keith Foulcher and Tony Day (eds), *Clearing a Space: Postcolonial Readings of Modern Indonesian Literature* (Leiden: KITLV Press, 1992) p. 2.

had been replaced by a demonstration of the vital importance of literary texts as a guide to aspects of – and the implied relativism here is important – the story of modern Indonesia and its people. Postcolonialism offered an intellectual underpinning for the study of modern Indonesian literature as a unique record of Indonesian experience – unique because whether prose or poetry it is imaginative expression that grapples with the ever-changing resources of language to articulate Indonesian perspectives on life in a certain place at a certain time in human history. Conceived in this way, literature is one among many textual records, but it is one that excites the imagination as much as it challenges the intellect, and that is enough to guarantee its significance. Armed with this conviction, I found within myself the intellectual confidence to re-introduce the study of modern Indonesian literature into the senior years of the undergraduate curriculum in the years leading up to my retirement from the University of Sydney at the end of 2005. Since that time, it has sustained me in retirement through research and writing projects that seem to me to be of significance for Indonesia, Australia and the world, whether in terms of relations between nation states or in the lives of individuals. Reading literature, and talking and writing about literature, are still, I would argue, essential expressions of our humanity.

I believe that the sense of excitement and discovery that has underpinned my life's journey through Indonesian literature, both as a teacher and a student, is still available to today's students. However the tragedy is that as a presence in the Australian university curriculum, the study of modern Indonesian literature now clings on only by the merest thread. There are no longer any first year classes of nearly 300 students, such as I found myself part of at the University of Sydney in 1965. This is part of the reason why there is no longer the critical mass of students required to sustain second or third year programs of Indonesian literary studies and the ongoing production of honours theses on Indonesian writers and their work. At the postgraduate level, the expertise built up in Australia over the past half century now mainly supports Indonesian students leaving their home universities to study their own national literature in an academic environment conducive to uninterrupted research, writing and reflection. Something seems wrong somewhere. But in Indonesia itself writers and poets continue to produce those works of the imagination grounded in historical time and space we call literature. In the early 21st century, a boom in the publication of all kinds of literature has seen women writers effectively storm the bastion of what was once an almost exclusively male preserve. Islamic themes now pervade what used to be a largely secular tradition, and the voice of the regions draws attention to a wider spectrum of Indonesian experience than ever before. Meanwhile, in Australian universities, the wheel continues to turn, and imaginative, effective teaching programs continue to produce undergraduate students with an advanced knowledge of Indonesian language and a fascination with Indonesia and its people. Perhaps at some future point it will all begin again, and Australian students will one day again take up the study of Indonesian literature as an area of study in its own right in the numbers necessary to sustain a vibrant academic community, feeling as though they are treading where no-one else has trod before them. They will find it an exhilarating journey, and I wish them well.

6. TEACHING INDONESIAN LANGUAGE THROUGH DRAMA

Barbara Hatley

University of Tasmania

Staging Indonesian language plays, as I did with students at Monash in the 1980s early 1990s, was probably the most enjoyable and rewarding language 'teaching' I have ever done. And participation in such plays dramatically extended the language skills, cultural knowledge and overall Indonesia-involvement of the student actors. Yet it was not something I had planned or that was particularly encouraged within the Indonesian language program. A circular arrived announcing the availability of funding from a philanthropic fund, the Vera Moore Foundation, for projects promoting the creative arts. Almost in the same week a theatre group which worked with educational institutions visited Monash publicising their activities. Because I had a particular interest in Indonesian theatre and a store of play scripts, I put in an application for funding for this group to work with students of Indonesian language to put on a play. The application was successful and off we went to stage our first production, followed by ten more annual shows.

Although our drama initiative seemed fortuitous at the time, connections can be made with various contextual factors – the shifts in the understanding and teaching of Indonesian literature in Australian universities outlined in Keith Foulcher's contribution to this volume; and developments in modern Indonesian drama itself. I am not aware of the staging of Indonesian-language plays in Australian universities prior to the Monash activities; reading of play texts was likewise probably not widespread. Certainly drama was not part of the curriculum when I studied Indonesian literature at ANU in the 1960s. For even more so than other forms of literature, such as works of fiction which can include extensive descriptive and explanatory passages, plays require contextual discussion, explanation of the background of the speakers and the topics of their dialogue. Yet, as Keith Foulcher explains, historical and sociological concerns were marginalised due to the universalist aesthetic focus which predominated in literary studies of that time. Hence the famous

Indonesian writers who taught Indonesian literature in Australian universities in the 1960s and 1970s as an expression of this universalist vision were unlikely to choose plays as study texts. But by the 1980s 'high literature' as a domain of study had been replaced by the broad range of literary and popular culture texts constituting the new field of 'cultural studies'. Theatre texts could be included in Indonesian programs, along with pop culture forms such as films. At the same time, in Indonesia, in a post-colonial affirmation of cultural identity, playwrights were blending local theatre traditions with Western-derived modern drama to create some very interesting, socially-engaged works. Great texts to study and perform with Australian students!

On a personal note, it was the rapprochement between traditional regional performance genres and modern theatre which brought me to Indonesian drama. Disheartened by what I experienced as the dryness of studying literary texts divorced from their social context, I had turned to regional language popular theatre, attracted by its rich, colourful insights into local life.

As Indonesian playwrights in turn started drawing on regional theatre, I became very interested in the interface between local performance traditions and modern plays. In later years, this personal transition and its outcome in Australian play productions would not have worked so well. For beginning in the mid-1990s and continuing today, the predominant mode of contemporary Indonesian theatre has become group devised works, emphasising physical movement, rather than dialogue-based plays.

Other key factors were the availability of special funding for creative, out-of-the-ordinary activities (less likely in the years before or since) and the skilled guidance of young theatre professionals whom we employed to direct the plays. In the event we did not team up in the first year with the educational theatre group mentioned above; instead through a personal contact of one of the students we organised for a member of the prominent Melbourne company Anthill Theatre to direct our debut production, Rendra's *Sekda*. Some of the Anthill luminaries actually watched one of our rehearsals, and we went to see one of their splendid shows. In our other productions, too, the director's connections with the exciting, intriguing world of theatre gave an extra buzz to the play experience. As well as their invaluable professional skills, the directors contributed crucially as outside experts, wielding unquestionable authority. My familiar voice telling students that lines must be learnt by Tuesday or that this scene required more energy might have blended into the background, like that of Mum at home. But when the director spoke everyone listened. And the fact the other Indonesian language lecturers and I, like the students, were subject to the director's authority, particularly when we took on roles in the play, created new bonds spanning the teacher-pupil divide. This enhanced the camaraderie among the group established through the weeks of rehearsals and performances. A sense of common commitment to the production, to one another and broadly to involvement with Indonesia built up and lasted well beyond the duration of the show.

Figure 1: Scenes from two student plays performed on the Clayton Campus in the 1980s.
Left: Julian Millie and 'duck' in *Sindon*. Rght: Brett Hough and unnamed actor in Arfin C. Noer's *Kapai-kapai*.
Archives of the former Department of Indonesian and Malay, Monash University

How exactly did play participation strengthen language and cultural skills? A key issue is the existence of very basic similarities between acting and language learning, the way learning a language involves taking on new speech and bodily patterns, for some even a new persona. The freeing up of body and spirit, which takes place in drama training, can infuse language learning very effectively and enjoyably. Then came engagement with dramatic texts. The plays we performed were full-length dramas by leading Indonesian playwrights including Rendra, Arifin C. Noer, Putu Wijaya and Riantiarno. Interestingly, Rendra himself believed in bringing drama into the classroom and produced his book for use in workshops *Seni Drama untuk Remaja*. The dialogue was varied, demanding, using formal and informal registers, often colloquial, sometimes incorporating expressions in regional languages. Settings were often earthily realistic, sometimes surreal. So reading the plays together in preparation for the production required extending language skills, learning new expressions, discussing social interactions and cultural practices not encountered previously. And there was a strong motivation for doing so, when the scene would soon have to be played out on stage.

Next came the process of memorizing and repeatedly reproducing dialogue, using the correct pronunciation and tone, convincingly portraying character.

Speech patterns, expressions and gestures were internalised and unconsciously reproduced. In a striking example of such internalisation and reproduction, two participants in our very first production, *Sekda*, meeting years later, still greeted one another with exuberant bursts from the speeches of the governor in the play. Mastering the sounds and accents needed to portray particular characters arguably helped strengthen the students' overall pronunciation skills. Cultural awareness was also an important factor. To represent convincingly the harsh, vibrant interactions of Jakarta slum-dwellers of Riantiarno's *Bom Waktu*, the self-obsessed vanity of officials' wives in *Sekda* or the poverty-fuelled fantasies of the messenger boy protagonist in *Kapai-Kapai* (see Figure 1) required considerable understanding of the context and empathy with the characters portrayed.

This mode of acquiring language skills and cultural knowledge is, of course, enormously time-consuming. It would seem totally impracticable under the conditions of operation of Australian universities today. The compact curricula of Indonesian language and studies programs leave little space for reading whole plays, much less staging them. Students juggle part-time jobs and other commitments in order to find time to attend lectures. Fitting in many hours of play rehearsals on weeknights and weekends would be impossible. And academics have other priorities, chosen or imposed – publishing A1 journal articles, applying for research grants. Some idealistic resistance to these trends might be attempted, some requests made for extra funding and student credits for cultural activities, if student numbers in Indonesian programs were stronger. Given current budgetary considerations, however, such efforts would presumably be fruitless.

Yet in different modes and sites, the study of Indonesian drama and language has continued at Monash. In 1997-2000, students in the Indonesian program at Monash Gippsland and an associated intensive in-country course at Sanata Dharma University in Yogyakarta, staged lively, funny, self-devised short plays under the guidance of lecturers Paul and Nani Thomas and Indonesian visiting scholars. Both Paul and Nani had had theatre training – Nani in Children's Theatre in Singapore and through academic study at Monash and Flinders, Paul in theatre in education and Italian-English community theatre in Adelaide. With the skills and confidence to direct productions themselves they needed no professional assistance; at the same time, Paul reports that maintaining the reins of authority meant missing out on developing the closer relations with students, which I had experienced earlier. The productions formed part of a unit on Indonesian Drama, which included a weekly writing workshop and a theatre skills session that evolved later into play rehearsals.

Figure 2: Student designed bilingual poster for a performance of *1-800-Renungan*. The play explored the Australian government's use of media campaigns to co-opt public support in its 'fight' against terrorism. Performed on the Gippsland Campus, Monash University, 2003.

Limited to an hour in length, the performances were staged at first specifically for primary schools, but later took on wider audiences and more serious themes, in one case even the controversial issues of people smuggling and terrorism (see Figure 2).

The 1997 production *Waduh!* in Gippsland and *Kui* (Cooee!) at Sanata Dharma in 2000 focused on intercultural communication. An initially clueless, monolingual Australian student visits Indonesia and soon becomes enthusiastically acclimatised in *Waduh!*; a party of Australians undertake a walk in the Australian bush, watched by an audience of Yogyakarta school children, university students, journalists and others in a performance on Australia Day in *Kui*. Distinctive features of *Kui* include its group-devised nature (the credits on the video indicate that the whole cast participated) and the mature age of the actors, all schoolteachers of Indonesian undertaking in-country study. What the cool Indonesian teenage audience thought of the sight of an overweight forty-ish woman miming discomfiture at having to pee behind a bush watched by 'all those people', and glancing around coquettishly as she applied mosquito repellent to her ample upper thighs, is hard to tell. But hopefully along with the fun of it all they took on an idea that stereotypes can be resisted, oldies can have fun and do outrageous things too.

Sadly, these play productions ceased with the closure of Indonesian at Monash Gippsland and Paul's move to the Caulfield/Clayton campus. At the Clayton Campus, however, the integrated study of drama and language continued in a different format within a unit called Indonesian for Special Purposes: Seni Drama. Here students had access to a greater variety of examples of Indonesian drama and film, available via the unit website; their assignment choices included writing an individual academic article or creating a 15 minute short film as a group project. This range of study options and assessment tasks overcomes a problem which can arise with play preparation and performance as the common focus of activity and basis of assessment; some students relish acting while others find it confronting and out of keeping with their expectations of a language program as opposed to a drama unit. What was naturally missing from the Clayton Unit was the sense of shared group identity and commitment provided by common participation in the production of a play.

Is the excitement and fun and intense group involvement of student productions of Indonesian plays gone forever, just a memory from a more leisurely, less pressured, better funded time? Or could it be recaptured? A possible context might be the in-country intensive Indonesian language programs held annually in Indonesia by Australian universities. Here the students have no part-time jobs to rush off to after class; Australian resident directors are in relatively relaxed mode and enthusiastic young local instructors are likely to be happy to include drama activities within the assessment tasks of the program. Potential play directors abound, local performers with comparable involvement in the Indonesian theatre scene to that of our directors with Melbourne theatre back in the 1980s. Through them interested Australian students could come to learn about and get involved in that dynamic local performance world.

Perhaps some drama activities are already taking place within in-country courses. At the RUILI consortium program in Lombok in 2010, groups of third year students staged very amusing skits dramatising the local Sasak legend of Putri Nyale for their oral exam, then repeated the show at the end of program dinner. Opportunities abound for activities of this kind at individual class level. In addition, from the whole body of students studying across different levels, a group might come together interested in participating in theatre workshops and rehearsals as an extra-curricular activity, equivalent to current offerings such as martial arts, then staging a full performance for their classmates, teachers, local Indonesian students and academics and interested others. If they returned to their home universities full of enthusiasm after this experience, formed core participants in drama activities and persuaded other students to join in, we might yet see some revival of Indonesian performance on Australian campuses.

Reflections on Writing and Teaching Indonesian Grammar

The reason that colloquial Indonesian was mostly excluded from grammar (text-)books was not because the authors – myself included – were not aware of the existence of the colloquial variety and its pervasiveness in everyday casual interaction. It was rather that one was uncertain as to how to incorporate it in a grammar textbook. We knew the Jakartan variety of colloquial Indonesian had been prominent and increasingly used in areas outside of the capital. We also knew that there were other non-standard varieties used in other areas of Indonesia. But, if we chose Jakartan Indonesian as the colloquial variety to be introduced to students, we were also plagued with the question of which aspects and how much of this variety we should include in a grammar textbook. Coursebook writers too were also confronted by a similar quandary. As teachers we also had to face the reality that our students were also aware that what we had taught them was only part of the story. The increased popularity of Indonesian as a foreign language in Australian schools and universities in the late eighties and early nineties, coupled with the increased opportunity for students to visit Indonesia and practise the language they had learned, brought with it the realisation among students that the Indonesian language they had learned at school or university was not the same as the language they heard being spoken in everyday interaction in Indonesia. Many students were perplexed by their inability to understand even simple sentences uttered by native speakers. To be sure, as foreign language learners they knew that listening was not always an easy part of language learning, and but they also realised that the difference between what they had learned in class and what they heard in conversations were vastly different. Students frequently asked me why I had not introduced them to colloquial Indonesian. And here I must admit with a certain degree of embarrassment that, knowing I was not theoretically or practically equipped with the knowledge of how to incorporate colloquial Indonesian into my teaching, coupled with the realisation that teaching material on this variety was largely absent, my regular answer was: 'Oh, we teach you standard Indonesian, which is the basic and formal language, and once you have mastered the standard, you can pick up colloquial Indonesian when you visit the country'. As though like magic, they can just 'pick up' the complex workings of colloquial Indonesian!

It was a relief to learn, from talking to teachers at other universities and through reading Sneddon's (1990) article, that the problem was shared across Australia. Sneddon's article, published in the *Asian Studies Review*, offers some early thoughts on how to begin incorporating colloquial Indonesian into our teaching. The sorts of considerations he put on the table were not limited to the learning of colloquial vocabulary but more substantially to the grammar. Teachers too began reporting on strategies they had adopted for teaching colloquial Indonesian. In 1995, Barry Turner, then a teacher at Deakin University, presented a paper at the second conference of the Australian Society of Indonesian Language Educators (ASILE) held at Monash University, entitled 'Teaching formal and informal Bahasa Indonesia'.[3] In 2001, at ASILE's sixth conference, a related topic was taken up by Nyoman Riasa, then teacher at the Australia Indonesia Language Foundation (AILF), Bali, with his paper on the youth dialect of Jakartan Indonesian, entitled *Karakteristik bahasa ABG dalam cerpen dan implikasi pengajarannya bagi siswa/i sekolah menengah di Australia* (The characteristics of teen language in short stories and the implications for teaching at secondary schools in Australia). At the same conference, David Reeve, then associate professor at the University of New South Wales and leader of the TIFL project, presented a paper on 'Varieties of Informal Indonesian', reminding teachers about the fact that there was more than one non-standard variety of Indonesian. Similar papers were also given at conferences in Indonesia on languages and linguistics. All served to show that there was a greater awareness, both in Australia and in Indonesia, of the importance of colloquial Indonesian in everyday communication, and that there was a need for deeper knowledge – pedagogical and scholarly – on how to foster a more holistic conception of Indonesian as a language with multiple varieties, and how to present this conception to language learners.

Clearly, despite our keen intention to teach colloquial Indonesian, there was a lack of grammar resources on this variety. We could hardly give an adequate response when students noted with enthusiasm that colloquial Indonesian had a very simple grammar, simpler than standard Indonesian. 'You just drop the *meN-* prefix and changed the suffixes *-kan* and *-i* into *-in*, don't you?' was a statement I frequently heard. This 'myth' was dispelled by Michael Ewing's (2005) grammar description of this variety, which appeared as a chapter in a book on the grammar of Austronesian languages of Asia and Madagascar (Adelaar & Himmelmann 2005). Ewing's study, as with many linguistic studies on Indonesian, was unfortunately caught in the communication gap between language teaching and linguistics. The description is widely known by linguists working on Indonesian but little known by teachers of Indonesian. In 2006 another grammar description of colloquial Indonesian was published, this time it was a book-length study by Sneddon (2006). It is interesting to

---

3   See ASILE's website: http://wacana.usc.edu.au/2/formal_informal_90s.html.

note that, unlike previous grammars which are based on written standard Indonesian texts, the data for Ewing's and Sneddon's studies are colloquial spoken Indonesian.

Like Ewing's study, Sneddon's contains clear explanations of grammatical concepts, yet it is also relatively unknown among teachers and learners. At a time when scholarly work on colloquial Indonesian is required to provide a sound basis for teaching the grammar of colloquial Indonesian, it is a pity that there has not been a greater use of these studies. Perhaps what is needed is a textbook version of the grammar that can be used in the classroom in conjunction with other written and audio/video material showing actual language use by speakers. If or when such a book does exist, the challenge is how to present it to students in a way that makes them aware of the differences between standard and colloquial varieties but which avoids dichotomizing so that we do not end up finding ourselves moving backwards to days when only the standard variety was identified as Indonesian.

Grammar is one aspect of Indonesian language learning in which many feel they lack confidence. Even those who have relative fluency in the language often say that their knowledge of Indonesian grammar is not adequate.[4] Perhaps this insecurity is a product of the traditional conception of grammar as rules to be memorized, to be taught through constructed, sentential examples, belying the fact that even these rules change over time and that they are not independent of the speakers.

References

Anwar, K. 1979. *Indonesian: The Development and Use of a National Language*. Yogyakarta: Gadjah Mada University Press.

Chung, S. 1976. 'An object creating rule in Bahasa Indonesia'. *Linguistic Inquiry* 13, pp. 39–77.

Dardjowidjojo, S. 1978. *Sentence Patterns of Indonesian*. Honolulu: University of Hawaii Press.

Djenar, D. N. 2003. *A Student's Guide to Indonesian Grammar*. Melbourne: Oxford University Press.

Ewing, M. 2005. 'Colloquial Indonesian'. In *The Austronesian Languages of Asia and Madagascar*, edited by A. Adelaar and N. Himmelmann. New York: Routledge. p. 227–257.

---

[4] Results of student evaluation at La Trobe University where I taught for nearly 20 years, and at the University of Sydney, my current institution, show that in every cohort there are students who feel they do not know enough grammar and request more grammar exercises. Also, my experience in giving a talk at the annual Victorian Indonesian Language Teachers Association Conference on various aspects of Indonesian grammar suggests that many teachers share this sentiment.

Kay, G. & Rachmat, J. 2003. *Bersama-sama Senior Student Book*. Melbourne: Nelson Australia.
Li, C. S. 1976. *Essentials of Indonesian Grammar*. Sydney: Pustaka Malindo Publications.
MacDonald, R. & Dardjowidjojo, S. 1967. *A Student's Reference Grammar of Modern Formal Indonesian*. Washington: Georgetown University Press.
Sarumpaet, J. P. 1977. *The Structure of Bahasa Indonesia*. Box Hill, Melbourne: Sahata Publications.
Sneddon, J. N. 1990. 'Directions in Indonesian-language teaching: Formal, informal or both?' *Asian Studies Review* 11 (2), pp. 94–100.
Sneddon, J. N. 1996. *Indonesian Reference Grammar*. St Leonards, NSW: Allen & Unwin.
Sneddon, J. N. 2000. *Understanding Indonesian Grammar*. St Leonards, NSW: Allen & Unwin.
Sneddon, J. N. 2003. *The Indonesian Language: Its History and Role in Modern Society*. Sydney: UNSW Press.
Sneddon, J. N. 2006. *Colloquial Jakartan Indonesian*. Canberra: Pacific Linguistics.
Wolff, J. U., Oetomo, D. & Fietkiewicz, D. 1984. *Beginning Indonesian Through Self-Instruction*. Ithaca, New York: Cornell University Southeast Asia Program.

8. ON TEACHING THE TEACHERS OF INDONESIAN

Looking Back over 20 Years

Lindy Norris

Murdoch University

I joined the staff of Murdoch University at a time when Australia was all abuzz with Paul Keating's endeavours to build bilateral links with Australia's neighbours, particularly with Indonesia. Keating spoke frequently about there being no other country in the world more important to Australia than Indonesia. And he and Suharto were 'mates'.

These were heady days. Indonesia was important to us, and knowledge of the Indonesian language was valued. And in the midst of all this I was fortunate enough to be employed in a university where Asian Studies was supported and nurtured. It was all about being 'cutting edge', about excellence in scholarship, and it was also about being innovative.

My appointment was interesting. My position straddled two faculties – Asian Studies and Education. At the time this was a novel arrangement. More than twenty years on it could almost be considered unique.

My initial brief encompassed three areas – teaching Indonesian, designing and delivering a curriculum/methodology unit for pre-service teachers of Indonesian, and the development of curriculum materials to be used in classrooms to support what is these days is known as Asia literacy.

I was privileged to be able to work across two faculties, to be able to bridge that divide that repeatedly invokes comment every time a new report appears on the state of Languages Education in Australia. At Murdoch there was no divide. Asian Studies and Education worked together to 'grow' graduates who had deep knowledge of Indonesia and Indonesian, and from this pool of students there was a steady stream of people who saw their futures in Indonesian language classrooms – and not just secondary school classrooms

– our initial teacher education program for primary teachers also included space for language study.

For these teachers the experience of learning Indonesian at Murdoch was complimented with access to *Suara Siswa*, the National Indonesian Language Curriculum Project that produced comprehensive, contemporary learning and teaching materials for all levels of schooling in Australia. This material came out of an expansive national project that was handsomely resourced. Even today the quality of the Teachers' Handbooks is still such that they continue to be a useful reference point for teachers seeking support in programming and task design.

So, in the early 90s there was this nexus – Asian Studies and languages, schools, universities, commonwealth and state initiatives. And Mr Keating and Pak Harto were mates, and we all benefited.

But this was just the beginning. And 1994 was the landmark year. The release of the Rudd Report (*Asian Languages and Australia's Economic Future*) and the birth of ACICIS (The Australian Consortium for 'In-Country' Indonesian Studies) marked the beginning of what would be a frantic few years. Life was consumed by national projects into language teaching and learning, teacher training and retraining of language teachers, teaching Indonesian and also, curriculum and program development. All this was undertaken with the aim of significantly improving the participation and proficiency levels in Asian language learning as well as supporting the studies of Asia across the curriculum in schools.

Here in Western Australia, these initiatives emanating from the Rudd Report, through the National Asian Languages and Studies in Australian Schools (NALSAS) strategy, were strongly supported by the educational jurisdictions and Murdoch University was extensively involved. There was a frenetic energy and an overwhelmingly positive feeling that at last languages, including Indonesian, might finally become embedded in school curriculum.

I can not be exact about the number of Indonesian teachers who were trained during the NALSAS years but the numbers were certainly significant. Interestingly, the majority were already teachers who viewed NALSAS as an opportunity to develop some language competence as well as experience Indonesia for a short stint during their language program. In hindsight, too many of these people were perhaps in it because it was free, or because the vicarious pleasures presented by tourist images of Bali promised a different reality both personally and professionally.

This is not to say that NALSAS teacher retraining was unsuccessful. There are certainly teachers currently teaching Indonesian in schools who are products of this period and who continue to advocate for the cause of Indonesian. Many have, however, moved out of Indonesian teaching, and many out of teaching altogether. So was this massive investment in NALSAS worth it? For me this is a really difficult question to answer. Nationally there was a huge investment in the production of resources to support teacher development and also student learning. Many of these resources were certainly underutilised, and whilst student participation rates improved, little was achieved in terms of proficiency. The extent to which this was because of inherent weaknesses within the strategy, or because the strategy itself was terminated early, continues to be a question for debate.

Aside from NALSAS, Keating government policies and an increased, positive focus on Indonesia did seem to bring people into Asian Studies in the University. It is difficult to determine exactly why they came. For most, I really do not think it was the allure of money or high flying jobs, I think with Indonesia and Indonesian it has always been about a fascination, an intrigue, some sort of connection that is very personal that brings people into this field. Certainly, those who went on to become teachers of Indonesian, particularly those teaching in secondary schools, expressed a passion for what they were doing and a desire to 'infect' their students with the same interest in Indonesia.

The names of a number of these amazing teachers who came to the profession in the late 1990s spring to mind. They entered the profession with excellent knowledge of Indonesia and superb pedagogical skills. In-county experience through ACICIS ensured a substantial linguistic resource and they continue, even today, to return to Indonesia to maintain and contemporize their language skills. And these people, thankfully, are still in schools, and in the education system.

But times have changed and things are tough. The 'noughties' brought us 9/11, bombings and bad press in terms of Indonesia, and an increasingly conservative Howard liberal government with its contemptuous attitude to university funding and an 'English only' brand of literacy for our schools and the community more broadly.

So, unlike that very positive nexus in the 90s, the nexus of the noughties has spelt disaster for Indonesian in universities and schools. Year by year there are less people putting their hand up to teach Indonesian, and of those who do, the majority are less well prepared. Funding pressures in universities have seen unit offerings in Asian Studies diminish. My students just do not have the knowledge base that the students of the 1990s had. And my students are of a substantially different ilk. They do not seem to have that same capacity for inquiry, and in fact many just do not seem to have the same capacity. All too often there is a 'tell me what to do and I'll do it' mentality and I am finding that I expect less of them and, in general, they do it less well. This does not auger well for Indonesian in schools.

And Indonesian teaching in schools is now an extremely tough 'gig'. The hopes of the 90s for languages to be acknowledged as an intrinsic element of curriculum, right throughout the compulsory years of schooling, have been dashed. And yes, the reasons for this are numerous and well documented – perceptions about Indonesian and language learning, pitiful provision of opportunities for continuous and cumulative learning, unsupportive timetabling practices, and so the list goes on. And always included in any discussion of this dire situation is teacher quality. So, as a teacher educator, how do I respond to this?

It seems to me, as I survey Indonesian in schools, that programs are almost polarised. At one end of the spectrum there are the amazing programs of those brilliant teachers I referred to earlier. At the other end there are programs that are of little value for anyone. Often such programs reinforce negativity towards Indonesia (I am reminded of the primary school Indonesian teacher who expressed fear that one day Australia would be over run. And then there was the native speaker secondary teacher who refused to allow any mention of Islam in her classroom). Programs at this end of the spectrum are also often characterised by poor pedagogical practices – there are what I call 'aphasiac' programs where kids learn lists of content words (colours, animals, etc.) but never any grammar words. The result is that they never develop a capacity to put Indonesian together and use it meaningfully. Or there are those awful 'F word' programs about food, festivals and folktales with barely an Indonesian word ever to be seen or heard.

In fairness to some of the teachers at this end of the spectrum, they simply do not have the requisite skills – knowledge about Indonesia, language proficiency, and pedagogical competence. Or they may not have the knowledge and resilience to fight for better conditions for their program and so simply acquiesce to the circumstances that surround and subsume them.

Within the context of language teacher education countering such difficulties and shortcomings is problematic. I have already commented on the calibre of many of the students who are now choosing teaching as a profession. In addition, there are the attendant issues of the ever more crowded teacher education curriculum. There is simply not enough time to provide prospective teachers of Indonesian with all that they require – curriculum knowledge, knowledge of critical languages pedagogy, and knowledge they need to support themselves in an often hostile school environment where they work in isolation and in competition with other teachers and other curriculum areas. Add to this the need to ensure language proficiency and knowledge of Indonesia (history, cultures, politics, etc.). The task is daunting for all concerned.

And there is another dimension that now, more than ever, is complicating languages teacher education. In recent years there has been a significant increase in the number of 'native speakers' seeking to become teachers. The development of a teaching workforce that is more reflective of the cultural and linguistic diversity within the Australian community is rightly a priority but significant issues accompany it. At the beginning of each semester I now find a number of students in my classes who identify themselves as prospective teachers of Indonesian. Most of these people, however, are not Indonesian. They come from Singapore or Malaysia. The Malay/Indonesian debate is not new but the difficulties around it are now exacerbated because of a pedagogical and methodological imperative that positions interculturality centrally within language teaching. Clearly Malaysia is not Indonesia.

For native speakers many aspects of teacher education within the Australian context can also be quite confronting. Schools and classrooms are not the same as those 'back home'. Learning to manage this new environment, learning about languages curriculum, and learning to manage how to teach Indonesian adds a level of complexity that is not easily integrated into already 'squeezed' teacher education programs.

So where does this leave us on this journey of looking back over 20-plus years of Indonesian language teacher education? Are things better or worse? What is the same and what is different?

The study of Indonesia and its language, clearly still suffers from being inextricably bound to the Australia-Indonesia relationship. For someone like myself who has now been around Indonesian teaching since the 70s it is evident that the fortunes of Indonesian can be mapped against the highs and lows of the political relationship between the two nations. This then is the same as it always has been. What is different, however, is that this particular low has extended over such a long period of time, and has been accompanied by policies and practices within schools and universities that have progressively, and in some cases, aggressively, eroded the study of the Indonesian language bringing it to the brink of collapse. This clearly impacts teacher training with one of the significant consequences being a sharp decline in non-native speakers seeking to become Indonesian teachers.

With respect to the place of languages more broadly within Australian education, this can perhaps be best summed up by a colleague of mine who having recently returned from a decade overseas, remarked that there appeared to have been some sort of temporal disturbance that had transported languages back to a very distant, dark and gloomy past.

So is it possible then to end this journey on a high rather than to continue to bemoan the lows of Indonesian language teaching and learning? Yes. The classrooms of those excellent teachers of Indonesian that I keep talking about continue to excite me. The resources produced by these excellent teachers are both amazing and engaging. There is some fabulous Indonesian language learning and teaching happening 'out there' – oases in the desert. And as I work with a group of these teachers developing online Indonesian specific languages methodology and curriculum materials, I dare to dream of a new generation of Indonesian teachers, and of climate change. Perhaps a new PM and Bapak Presiden will become mates, and perhaps again there can be a fertile environment for the learning and teaching of Indonesian.